Crises
of Realism

Crises
of Realism

**Representing Experience
in the British Novel,
1816–1910**

Tom Lloyd

Lewisburg
Bucknell University Press
London: Associated University Presses

© 1997 by Associated University Presses, Inc.

Associated University Presses
440 Forsgate Drive
Cranbury, NJ 08512

Associated University Presses
16 Barter Street
London WC1A 2AH, England

Associated University Presses
P.O. Box 338, Port Credit
Mississauga, Ontario
Canada L5G 4L8

The paper used in this publication meets the requirements
of the American National Standard for Permanence of Paper
for Printed Library Materials Z39.48–1984.

Library of Congress Cataloging-in-Publication Data

Lloyd, Tom, 1952-
    Crises of realism : representing experience in the British novel, 1816–1910 / Tom Lloyd.
        p. cm.
    Includes bibliographical references (p.   ) and index.
    ISBN 0–8387–5359–0 (alk. paper)
    1. English fiction--19th century--History and criticism. 2. English fiction--20th century--History and criticism. 3. Realism in literature I. Title.
    PR868.R4L58   1997
    823'.80912--dc20   96–41683
                                                                              CIP

PRINTED IN THE UNITED STATES OF AMERICA

Contents

Crises
of Realism

Introduction

This book traces tensions in emplotment in the English novel from Jane Austen to E. M. Forster, focusing on the success with which novelists create the realistic middle space generated by what Michel de Certeau, defining history in *The Writing of History* (1988), terms the two poles of the "real," the "productive *activity* and the period *known*."[1] This middle space is fluid, its tropal structures not so confining that open-ended suggestiveness is closed off by abstract and other transfixions, or by mere escapes into idyllic univocalities. In representing life, the novel at once unsettles and reassures its readers, for the reality it replicates inevitably is domesticated in the act of retelling. Like the historian, moreover, the novelist uses memory and historical experience as the sources of "facts" to be represented, though at a further remove than the historian, who ostensibly works with data and scientific knowledge rather than with verisimilar constructions that replicate social discourses. For the historian or the novelist, the relation between fiction and reality is ambiguous, though the historian cannot afford to regard realism as merely a fiction, much as the attorney must stop short of regarding the language of law as purely a provisional play. Either activity is grounded on the assumption of an independent reality, though the practitioner may, like Conrad's Marlow, be aware that this, too, is a fiction. The novelist, in contrast, has greater freedom of play, for the work has no necessary influence on practical social activity, though it aims to represent it. Yet its subversive quality may have a greater long-term influence on society than more immediately influential emplotments, for in its tensions between affirmative and questioning voices—its self-referential fictionality— nineteenth-century realism influences the body politic, much as film does in the twentieth century.

Emplotment of the real requires more or less fluid tropal strategies, yet to impose them militates against the essence of the novel's open-endedness, which arises from otherness and conflict, accommodation and assertion. At the extreme of such emplotments is the escape into romance or transcendence, or transfixion by idealistic or literal monstrosities. I draw on Hayden White's *Metahistory: The Historical Imagination in Nineteenth-Century Europe* (1973), yet regard his tropal categorizations of historical and novelistic discourses as suspect, representing as they do the very taxonomy inimical to nineteenth-century realism. Like de Certeau, White views the historical (and by extension the novelistic) imagination in the nineteenth century as rooted in crises of representation, arising from the loss of an external meaning to which sublunary multiplicity can be related and organized. White's conception of aporia, like de Certeau's of the gap (or "caesura") between mind and object, points to the mental act that emplots the chaotic:

> *aporia* (literally "doubt"), in which the author signals in advance a real or feigned disbelief in the truth of his own statements, could be considered the favored stylistic device of Ironic language, in both fiction of the more "realistic" sort and histories that are cast in a self-consciously skeptical tone or are "relativizing" in their intention.[2]

Realism is generally metonymic and ironic, and its field increasingly narrows as the possibility of ulteriority vanishes. This presents two problems. The first is that, once acts and agents are separated, meaning rests increasingly in radically delimited explanations, finally in science alone, which acts as a limited template on experiential multiplicity. As Friedrich Nietzsche argued, however, this is inadequate, indeed, is inimical to the artistic process, for inevitably such an explanation is frozen: it is the whited sepulchre of the Medusa-stare from the abyss, and as such is monstrous. Historical and perceptual fields must remain fluid. Yet, as George Levine suggests in *The Realistic Imagination* (1981), the creative impulse behind realism necessitates the domestication of the monstrosities symbolically unleashed by the French Revolution of 1789. The desire to domesticate the monstrous ironically can redouble its power to transfix language and self, for the inverse of the monstrous, as Mary Shelley recognized, is abstraction, which subordinates experience to an idea. The Medusa-stare can come from Bertha or St. John Rivers, borderless and bordered personalities, but the effect is the same: the loss of capacity to generate meaning by working with what de Certeau calls "the rupture that constitutes a past distinct from its current enterprise," a "death" that paradoxically generates life, in contrast to the verbal transfixion that disguises extinction behind apparent univocal achievement.[3]

The second problem concerns the nature of irony itself. Artistic production requires ironic visions overarching other tropal strategies that tend towards parodic providential organization or, at the opposite extreme, mere verbal play without ulteriority. This system is locked in itself and onanistic, as the ironic perception becomes but another marmoreal univocality unable to aid in the creation of verisimilar fluidity, which adumbrates the conflict between Wilde's Basil Hallward and Sir Henry Wotton. At its most effective, ironic vision offers parodic delimitations of the absent "metaphor of metaphors" or master trope, the desire for which must not be allowed to atrophy into ironic univocalities that merely represent inverses of idyllic and romance closures. The novelists on which this study focuses desire ulteriority yet present ironic delimitations of totality that call its practicality and relevance into question, especially when, as the crisis of history increases in the nineteenth century, it becomes increasingly evident that there are no truths above events, that meaning, as Vico implies, is in the event itself, the action.[4] In this event, univocality or closure is paradoxically the enemy of broader meaning, for it closes off the activity on which meaning is predicated. Or as Tennyson puts it in "Ulysses," "all experience is an arch wherethro' / Gleams that untravell'd world whose margin fades / For ever and for ever when I move."

Emplotment *per se* is a univocality (its product is not), and hence an aspect of what realism should evade. Experience, like history, is messy, chaotic, and not easily given to organization; organization itself is the endeavor to retrieve "lost or effaced things" via, inevitably, concepts or tropes that, at best, suggest the author's mental recreation of how something was (or is).[5] This entails fascinations with limits and the Other, from which realism is generated, but also the desire to escape what this unleashes for a univocal (romantic, idyllic, providential, conceptual, or metaphorical) meaning, for engagement with chaos and flux merely impresses us with the inability of language fully to represent the real, from which the desire to escape arises, however much this is undercut within the text. Nietzsche, White notes, believed that science and religion are aesthetic "products of a human need to flee from reality into a dream, to *impose* order on experience in the absence of any substantive meaning or content."[6] This is also true of realism, however compelling its vertical and horizontal textures. Levine recognizes this in stating that realism, in its domestication of daemonic energies, arises from a "distance between desire and experience" whose byproduct may be "a retreat from experience."[7] Every unresolved tension, not least that between language and its shadowy or chaotic object, must offer respites to author and reader alike.

What I describe, then, is a radical uncertainty at the heart of realism, as it continually questions itself in the process of creating relative order out of a world in social and cultural flux. The old certainties, not the least of which is God, are in decay, for which the events surrounding the French Revolution are the symbolic cynosure. Revolution (intellectual as well as historical) has unleashed monstrosities into the world, whose bifurcation into chthonic and rational inverses suggests that the substitute for the missing master trope may be, in fact, a horror that language can only begin to approximate. Thus, Burke's demonic historical epiphany— the analogy between refinement and monstrosity—suffuses the nineteenth-century novel's development. There are overt monsters (Frankenstein's archetypal monster, Bertha, Kurtz), but likewise idealists (Angel Clare, St. John Rivers, Kurtz) whose monstrosity is evident in the aesthetic strategies they employ to flee life and responsibility. The danger of radical delimitation is far more than the creation of parodies of realism in solipsistic fields so limited that they are merely verbal plays: in life, people are victimized; in art, "aims and impulses," the field represented in realism, is yoked to an idea (an idea of realism, it may be).

Nietzsche was especially aware of the anxieties generated by the tensions between dream production and chaos, which entail movement between poles of confident assertion and pessimism, commitment and escapism. Aporias are generated by confusions of what, in *Beyond Good and Evil*, he terms the "text," or historical flux, and the "interpretation," from which arise more or less imaginative engagements with historical change. [8] Thus, the French Revolution was a "farce" that was interpreted "for so long, and so passionately, that *the text finally disappeared under the interpretation.*" [9] It is possible to apply this cunning metaphor to the novel. It is necessary, Nietzsche implies, to revalue the meanings of "text" and "interpretation." To approach life or history, we must recreate it mentally; so fluid is the event that it can be stabilized only by wrapping it under interpretation after interpretation. But this risks the transformation of image into concept as the initial impressions are lost under explanations that evolve from explanations. A similar danger (or opportunity) attaches to the relations between experience, its novelistic interpretation, and the interpretations that further accrue around them. Prior to its representation, life must be mentally organized and imaginatively recreated as the intermediate stage to its written codification. Aesthetic escapism beckons, but vital art suggests its messy origins.

Conceptualization is the enemy of realism's middle space: here, image and metaphor collapse into allegory, the crystallized enemy of art that domesticates the mysteries and transfixes the vision in a univocal reading, as White suggests in writing about the archimpressionist historian Burckhardt:

Genuine historiography, like the art of Raphael, represented a subordination of the allegorical and symbolizing impulses in the historian's consciousness to the needs of "realistic" representation.[10]

As Huizinga suggests in his discussion of late-medieval symbolism in *The Waning of the Middle Ages*, the need to foreground the allegorical, or to rest in the symbol, is to reduce the ineffable to a univocal concept, which represents failures of vision and perception.

To interpret the historical or experiential field necessitates delimiting it in words that reify visions yet evade loss in the impalpable inane. Such reification, however, in domesticating the monstrosity (idealistic or "Medusan") to which the visual is especially subject, risks leaving experience behind altogether, or becoming but the aesthetic inverse of the decaying field it flees. This is precisely Dorian Gray's experience as he desperately deploys "mists," aesthetic interpretations, to conceal the emerging horror centered in the portrait whose decay he cannot retard. Indeed, seeing is central to verisimilar belief. But visual fields are inherently unstable, as Marlow realizes in gazing at the jungle during his trip up the Congo. Thus, Jane Eyre must master others' visual strategies and the abyss whose venue is the mirror, before she can control her autobiography. Moreover, Esther Summerson needs valorization in others' eyes despite her disfiguration, and she closely regulates the first appearance of her changed face in the mirror. In the gaze or vision, the struggle for realism is won or lost, for it is at this moment, prior to the codification of experience in writing, that the monstrous is domesticated and allowed to emerge neither in Medusan nor idealistic guises.

In his epochal *Laocoön* (to which I shall return in chapter 6), Gotthold Ephraim Lessing discusses the relations between verbal and pictorial arts, associating something like Schiller's realism with the first, idealism with the second,[11] for "poetry" allows the representation of life in time and nuance, while statuary focuses on a particular moment in visual space. Translated from statuary (the frozen, idealistic moment) to language, however, Laocoön's marmoreal noblility becomes monstrosity, and the affinity between him and the snakes that consume him is manifest. Yet the ideal, like the visual, is a necessary organizing pole in realism; like chthonic monstrosity, it is the univocality—the language-transfixing parodic ulteriority—against which realism's middle space is constructed. This construction is predicated, however, on the awareness (the increasing awareness as the nineteenth century proceeds) that this middle space is threatened with disappearance, while aesthetic bulwarks (increasingly feckless, owing to their univocality) are thrown up to preserve verisimilar textures; the last redoubt, irony, is barely able to protect limited metaphorical visions, such as Margaret Schlegel's in *Howards End*.

The idyll, Schiller's as yet unrealized art form that unites the real and the ideal (and Nietzsche's exemplum of flights from experience), is a concept to which I often turn in this study, particularly in the chapters on Austen, Brontë, Dickens, and Forster. As described in *Naive and Sentimental Poetry* (1795), its function is to transcend the world of experience for some unity located in the *future*; but the novel, like history, is concerned with meaning in the real, which inevitably entails the domesticated recovery of the past, and the imposition of meaning on it.[12] Austen successfully creates what I term an "idyllic realism" that entails verisimilar delimitations that hint at circumambient realities. Thus, Lionel Trilling terms *Emma* her "closest approximation of an idyllic world that the genre of the novel will permit."[13] Most often, however, the idyllic symbolizes the difficulty of parrying the gap between brute reality and its organization, leading to poles of chaotic activity and dubious univocality. With Dickens, this unbridgeable caesura is stressed in idyllic conclusions that undercut themselves, in *Oliver Twist* and *Bleak House*. In Forster's *Howards End*, likewise, the narrative desire for an idyllic futurity is subverted by an awareness that it can exist only in avertings of the gaze, limited metaphorical perceptions that threaten to ossify into univocal allegory.

I view conflicting authorial voices as central to a genre caught between the desire for meaning and the recognition of life's multiplicity and potential incoherence. As Friedrich Schlegel and, more recently, Mikhail Bakhtin recognized, the novel at its core contains conservative-organizational and subversive-ironic voices in radical interplay; without this systole and diastole, art is unable to create meaning from aporias. This entails a penetrative vision—Burke's stripping of society's vestures, Dickens's explorations of chaos and decay—preparatory to the reconstitution of meaning in the text, any finalities appended to which are infected by the experience of the abyss. The author may still the interplay but fails if he does so too successfully, having merely imposed univocal delimitation on fields that, as Burke recognized, must be confronted with aloetic ironies before meaning can be believably affirmed. It is necessary at once to posit illusions and stress their limitations, if we are to explain experiential or historical reality through representation. The task, as Nietszche puts it in *The Birth of Tragedy*, is "to look into the terrors of the individual existence" yet not "become rigid with fear."[14] The Medusa-stares from the abyss and the ideal are merely inverses: the idyllic, like any form of the aesthetic, is monstrous if it merely functions as a substitute for transcendental unity, which, directed to experience and individuality, becomes the enemy of free verbal and visual play; thus, for Nietzsche, Christianity is "a flight into a peculiarly oppressive kind of anti-idyll," that is, but one instance of a temptation that meets the novelist or historian as he represents the unknown or inchoate.

* * *

Here I shall summarize the individual chapters. Edmund Burke's *Reflections on the Revolution in France* (1790) explores the organizing intuitive and ironic fictions imposed on historical flux. In striking metaphorical bursts that unite polemics with visual scenes, Burke contrasts traditional social organization with that of the philosophes, whose concepts create a radically limited fiction of society above the real thing; their irony, ultimately merely a new form of naiveté, paradoxically redoubles the chthonic passions of French society. Burke, himself textually infected by his parodic stripping of humanity (a parallel to the sansculottes' stripping of the social fabric) to inoculate his readers, is barely able to contain the forces he unleashes through rhetoric and daemonic (yet somewhat stabilizing) theatrical and tragic metaphors; he briefly retreats into an ideal space in his memory of Marie Antoinette. Burke adumbrates the peril of negotiating the aporia between experience and its recollection (or recreation), especially at the peripheries of social organization, a situation to which Dickens repeatedly returns.

Austen implicitly makes the same point in *Emma* (1816), in which manners and other forms of regulated social discourse (the dance, the walk) keep unregulated passion at bay, somewhere out there, beyond the bounds of provincial life—but hinted at nonetheless. Like Burke, Austen's concern is to reify and stabilize visual fields: indeed, the novel stresses the instability of the visual, above all Emma's difficulties in interpreting appearances when she becomes the object of Frank Churchill's visual manipulations. The most delimited of the novels in this study, *Emma* nevertheless traces the real from which the story distances itself in self-sustaining verbal textures that function as bulwarks against moral univocalities, which Emma must publicly accept, yet privately subordinates to aesthetic play.

Monstrosity is nearly effaced in *Emma*—even Frank Churchill is forgiven his indiscretions—but it serves as the ruling antitrope of Mary Shelley's *Frankenstein* (1818), in which rational-scientific (Victor) and chthonic (his "daemon") monstrosities are presented as inverses. Victor's penetrative scientism gives birth to an uncontrollable visual reification so horrific that it belies description or framing: thus, the horrified reactions of people who view what they cannot see, which words cannot stabilize.

Only the blind old man can establish a brief verbal intercourse: to *see* the monster is to incapacitate language. But it is Victor's scientific language—his "fairy tales" of science, Nietzsche would say—that unleashes this. The monster becomes the verbal antitrope that denies the possibility of language for many nineteenth-century novels. Mary Shelley was able to project despair and fear onto her narratives, but Victor fails because he looks directly into the horror Shelley deploys idea, story, and vision to distance.

Charlotte Brontë's Jane Eyre is confronted with literal and idealistic monstrosities in Bertha (and her own passions) and St. John Rivers. The creation of her autobiography entails mastery of visual spaces and of others' endeavors to contain her in their perceptual gazes (both Brocklehurst and Rivers are linked with Medusa). That is, *Jane Eyre* is very much a novel about the creation of realism's middle space and the subsumption of the univocal within fluid narratives that reflect, yet subvert, organizing tendencies. Like Dickens and E. M. Forster, Brontë parodically idealizes idyllic escapes from the world of experience, in her characterizations of Blanche Ingram and Rosamond Oliver. This univocality is the basis on which verisimilar multiplicity rests; but to surrender to it is to lose the capacity for image production and to exist in a future world (where Schiller situates the idyllic) removed from this one.

I devote the longest chapter in this study to Dickens, in part because he best exemplifies the radical anxiety at the heart of realism, which is less cloaked than in George Eliot's novels. Focusing on *Oliver Twist* (1837–38), *Bleak House* (1852–53), *Hard Times* (1854), and *Great Expectations* (1860–61), I trace the tension between organization and flux that continually threatens to break down, indeed, creates gaps between energy (London) and the idyllic that nearly lays bare the difficulties of emplotment. There is an incredible anxiety at work in Dickens, perhaps best seen in his problematical (or multiple) endings, where typically the natural (or idyllic) univocality is subverted by reality. Particularly in his women (Lucy Manette, Rose Maylie), Dickens desires a perfection beyond experience, but this possibility is always questioned. Indeed, like nature, it gradually dissipates as a narrative desideratum. I focus on several of Dickens's refined monsters—James Harthouse, Harold Skimpole, and, above all, Pip—and link their parodic univocalities with idyllic or anti-idyllic conclusions, particularly the conclusion to *Bleak House*. Dickens desires a "polished" ending (he is momentarily the realists' dancing master, their Turveydrop), but to provide one is to implicate himself in monstrosity. Inspector Bucket is like him in achieving closure; but, with his parodic objective reconstructions of traces, he is even more monstrous than Skimpole. This adumbrates a powerful anxiety at the heart of verisimilar production, even more so than in the unresolved gap between London and the Maylies' milieu in *Oliver Twist*.

In two fevered dreams, Esther's and Pip's, Dickens symbolically takes the breakdown of fictional capacity to its furthest point. Esther descends into a hellish dissolution of time and space and must reconstruct her identity following disfiguration. Pip, on the other hand, having confronted symbolic loss, mutilation, and imprisonment in his delirium, is unable to return to the maternal-paternal ideal the dream reflects, the unifying middle space that is Dickens's (and Pip's) buried narrative desire.

George Eliot's realism, like Austen's, distances the overtly monstrous; it domesticates the abyss to a "blankness" at the center of personality. Silas Marner represents a marmoreal *Nullpunkt* during his seizures but is unconscious of any ulteriority; meanwhile, others use him as a visual space onto which they project fictions. Here and in *Middlemarch* (1871–72), Eliot contrasts a realistic vision that stops short of literal explanation with providential organizations in which traces of monstrosity are evident (e.g., in the beliefs of the Lantern Yard Brethren, Nancy Lammeter, Casaubon, Naumann, and Bulstrode). In *Silas Marner* (1861), Eliot adumbrates her ideas about realistic delimitation in conversations at the Rainbow; in *Middlemarch,* she does so in Will Ladislaw's and Naumann's debate over how a woman, Dorothea Brooke, should be represented in art. But it is Dorothea herself who attains the deepest realistic vision, which entails a sympathetic projection that supersedes visual and verbal closures; she learns to appreciate lives according to their general aims and impulses (Schiller's definition of realism), not according to individual acts that yoke the individual to a single point in time. Lessing's discussion of the effects of visual and poetic arts in his *Laocoön* underlies Eliot's assertion of the need to contain everything sympathetically, including the abject, within a tolerant realistic vision. Naumann, like Dowlas in *Silas*, wishes to constrict experience to a single point that transfixes the visual object, while others, above all Dorothea, marshal fluid verbal representation to domesticate the ideal and other monstrosities within the real.

In *Tess of the D'Urbervilles* (1891), Hardy likewise works within the philosophical matrix of realism and idealism, which underlies the contrast between Angel Clare and Tess. But where Eliot can valorize the realistic middle space, for Hardy it seems to decay as margins fade and experience threatens to collapse into the gaps between experience and the mind's organizing capacity. In this sense, he has more in common with Wilde and Conrad, for whom the abyss and monstrosity more overtly beckon. We have arrived at the full bloom of what White and others term a crisis of Historicism, whose implications for realism in fiction are essential, since fiction, like history, is concerned with creating provisional tropal organizations of the inchoate. Thus Hardy's valorization of Tess's "purity" is connected with his desire for a palpable reality. Provisional objectivities, however, are but disguised subjectivities, that is, mental projections onto an undefinable field. Nature is a concept we bring with us in the mind. Indeed, Hardy himself replicates Angel Clare's confusion of concept and experience in his imposition of realistic philosophical categories on Tess. Angel Clare learns to appreciate Tess according to general aims and impulses, but this does her little good, and accelerates her inscription within masculine conceptions of the feminine.

Oscar Wilde's *The Picture of Dorian Gray* (1890) presents the dissipation of realism's middle space into poles of idealism (Basil Hallward) and prophylactic irony (Lord Henry Wotton), leaving Dorian unable to maintain aesthetic bulwarks against the abyss. Like Basil, Dorian seeks stability in visual fields but does not possess the ability to stabilize them; instead, he encounters over and over, as in the family portrait gallery, reflections of his moral decay and transfixion by an idea. Neither aestheticism nor scientific objectivity can save him, for he cannot forget the disintegrating portrait. Accompanying the polarization of verbal capacity into univocal ironic and idealistic poles is Dorian's and Basil's inability to eradicate the historical consciousness, which univocality demands; Wotton, in contrast, is able to live in a perpetual present constructed around his *symboliste* irony. The centrality of forgetting to univocality is recognized by Burke as well, who denounces the survival of old crimes under new rational vestures.

We arrive in Conrad's *Heart of Darkness* (1902) at an even more radical collapse of belief into horrors that resist all fictional enclosures. Any attempt to organize the flux that Africa represents dissolves before its continual change and the incapacity to generate fluid objectifications of meaning onto it. Kurtz, of course, is the idealistic monster who becomes its inverse, exchanging one univocality for another, and experiencing the collapse of meaning into "things-things," and then the "horror," and whatever lies beyond that domestication of the unspeakable, before which savagery (or idealism) is the last redoubt. Marlow's impressionistic recollections of Africa are continually threatened with dissolution: savagery and the abyss beckon. Like Dorian Gray (but with greater, though limited, success), Marlow projects dread onto the feminine and sardonically dresses it in ornamentation, much as Kurtz surrounds himself with degendered ornaments, his victims' heads. In deciding, upon closer inspection, that these are, in fact, "symbols," Marlow distances himself from the effeminate Kurtz and creates a limited redoubt of masculine meaning based on the word's ability to counter the wilderness, if he averts his gaze soon enough. His need to impose limited categories on the flux leads him to trope the dying natives at the second station with allusions to Dante's *Inferno* and to a ghastly womb-like scar; later, he projects Western tragic dignity onto Kurtz's African lover, who, as the dignified cynosure to the surrounding savagery and incoherence, becomes the momentary nexus of Marlow's need for at least limited meaning.

I conclude with a chapter on E. M. Forster's *A Room With a View* (1908) and *Howards End* (1910), since these novels illustrate the tenuous state in which realism persists in the afterglow of Victorianism. Language is able to attain only brief, metaphorical outbursts in romance and idyllic visions that just evade the allegorical closure that is inimical to realism. Like Austen, Forster finds limited hope in idyllic delimitations: however, these delimitations do not extend to the full experiential field. Rather, like Margaret Schlegel's glimpse of ulteriority at Howards End, they require that radical delimitations of time and space occur. It is as if Forster already suspects the Marabar Caves' "ou-boum," the utter nothing entailing the collapse of vision and language. Thus he retrieves language's talismanic quality in stressing, especially in *A Room With A View*, its capacity to create oases of meaning despite intentions and initial interpretations. With its idyllic ending generated by brokenness, *Howards End* positions meaning in the future, like Schiller's concept of the idyll. It also, however, reifies the past in the transgendered symbolism of *Howards End* and acknowledges the immediate victory of forces inimical to art. Both novels can be interpreted as elegies to nineteenth-century realism.

1

Edmund Burke:
Reflections on the Revolution in France

The French Revolution, Nietzsche writes in *Beyond Good and Evil*, was interpreted according to various "indignations and enthusiasms for so long, and so passionately, that *the text finally disappeared under the interpretation.*"[1] In his *Reflections on the Revolution in France* (1790), Burke, it might be said, tries to present an interpretation to counter an unstable historical "text."[2] Yet his interpretation is overwhelmed by history and marked by anxieties centering above all in dramatic passages that describe the royal family's forced removal to Paris, and in his idealized remembrance of seeing Marie Antoinette in her youth, sixteen years before the revolution.[3]

Burke was interested in the aesthetics of historical experience. His *Reflections*, written too close to the events to be a "recollection in tranquillity," presents an instructive exercise in the rhetorical presentation of historical events. It includes brief but memorable verisimilar vignettes. Underlying his denunciation of the revolution is a fear that the aesthetic and the historical have become confused, and that the best he can do for England is to construct a bulwark against this French disease. In this sense, his aesthetic is relevant to this study of the British novel, for novelists too grapple with tensions between historical flux and representation. They distance the actual events they represent through verisimilitude, and when the tensions between actual life and the desire for symbolic finality become too great, they sometimes escape into idyllic and other defenses against actualities that threaten to overwhelm them. Burke's problem is daunting: though he stresses the importance of fictions in history and politics, he also wants to affirm an objective meaning beyond the *Reflections* itself. A novelist recreates the appearance of life as it actually "is," but, paradoxically, to do so creates a mask of meaning and authority. To cite Nietzsche once more, however, the concept of "author," like that of "Providence," may be a textual "fiction."[4] Burke's very attempt to assert authority, tradition, and Providence calls their realities into question, even as his voice alternates between poles of confident assertion and pessimism, the last entailing what I term idyllic escapism. He represents, yet tries to contain, the chaos of events within his rhetorical voices. By remembering the past he hopes to resacralize the disintegrating present.

Burke's youthful Marie Antoinette inhabits an aesthetic state that ostensibly affirms politics grounded in nature and tradition. Yet hers is a feminized space at the mercy of rationality and the historical process. Burke's idealization reflects his desire to transcend analysis, recapture his distant youth, and retrieve history in a stable epiphany of meaning. Burke seeks to reify an unspoken meaning associated with the natural feelings and tradition, which contrasts with the "pert loquacity" of those who, like Rousseau and Voltaire, base action on empty rhetoric. Nature, which Burke likens to "the British oak" (181), offers "analogical" meaning associated with masculine stability and organicism. At key points he uses vivid pictorial effects to make his disgust and idealism believable. Like Carlyle in *Past and Present*, he expresses himself so that the reader can "see" the truth of his interpretation:

> Because half a dozen grasshoppers under a fern make the field ring with their importunate chink, whilst thousands of great cattle, reposed beneath the shadow of the British oak, chew the cud and are silent, pray do not imagine, that those who make the noise are the only inhabitants of the field. (181)

Burke attempts to assert authority, tradition, and Providence, but to do so he strips them and stresses the impermanence of their fictions. His indignation centers on the loss of "pleasing illusions" and their replacement by specious fictions:

> All the decent drapery of life is to be rudely torn off. All the super-added ideas, furnished from the wardrobe of a moral imagination, which the heart owns, and the understanding ratifies, as necessary to cover the defects of our naked shivering nature, and to raise it to dignity in our own estimation, are to be exploded as a ridiculous, absurd, and antiquated fashion. (171)

The philosophes and revolutionaries have carried out radical revaluations of politics, morality, and art; Burke counters with revaluations of their revaluations.

Yet the limitations of his approach are palpable, since its premise is that an audience can agree on a felt tradition that, absent such common feeling, is as empty as what he condemns in the philosophes. Moreover, Burke's polemic includes a dubious defense of prejudices: "The longer they have lasted, and the more generally they have prevailed, the more we cherish them"; better to do this "than to cast away the coat of prejudice, and to leave nothing but the naked reason" (183). Burke writes to take the reader beyond language to what can (or should) be felt, which language itself paradoxically threatens to extinguish. He is interested in the limits of autonomy, yet for all his conservatism resembles Nietzsche's "objective man" in becoming the mirror of the events he describes; he submits himself to the destructive element.

A nation must create specious or pious symbols for the marvelous; the French have done the former:

> Mr Hume told me, that he had from Rousseau himself the secret of his principles of composition. That acute, though eccentric, observer had perceived, that to strike and interest the public, the marvellous must be produced; that the marvellous of the heathen mythology had long since lost its effect ... that now nothing was left to a writer but that species of the marvellous, which might still be produced, and with as great an effect as ever, though in another way; that is, the marvellous in life, in manners, in characters, and in extraordinary situations, giving rise to new and unlooked for strokes in politics and morals. (283–84)

He is uncomfortable with Rousseau's idea that the "marvellous" must now be discovered in life, not in the transcendental, for this places ultimate meaning in humans. A secular faith should be rooted in experience and be symbolic of valid truths beyond experience. But this objective relation between tried tradition and the unspeakable assumes an oppositional unity, which collapses in Burke's unstripping of civil society. He advocates an organic conception of history in which ideas are derived from experience, not applied a priori:

> Upon that body and stock of inheritance we have taken care not to inoculate any cyon alien to the nature of the original plant. All the reformations we have hitherto made, have proceeded upon the principle of reference to antiquity; and I hope, nay I am persuaded, that all those which possibly may be made hereafter, will be carefully formed upon analogical precedent, authority, and example. (117)

Yet it may be that nature and natural analogy are fictions, as Friedrich Nietzsche and Oscar Wilde argued. This "analogical precedent, authority and example" rests on the premise that objective meaning can be approximated and that fiction facilitates, yet is not the essence of, a political art which rests on lasting principles. Burke believes that there is a text that accurate interpretation can elucidate. Yet if the premise collapses and God, so to speak, becomes just another fiction, repetitions will seem nontranscendental, and the exoteric vision of the objective narrator may lose its believability. Or, as Nietzsche puts it in *Beyond Good and Evil*, authorship (and God), like grammar and syntax, may be revealed as a fiction.[5] But how does one reconstruct belief? Verisimilar representation in the novel is one vessel in which irony and belief exist in a creative tandem. The fictional speaker presides over a world in which the reader believes, for the very reason that its illusory quality is never denied. The reader becomes godlike in constructing meaning and discovering the marvelous in manners, characters, and situations.

Burke writes that "people will not look forward to posterity, who never look backward to their ancestors" (119). A nation's "pedigree and illustrating ancestors," its "gallery of portraits; its monumental inscriptions; its records, evidences, and titles," like its "artificial institutions," "fortify the fallible and feeble contrivances of our reason" (121). Burke's argument that civil society should be based on laws and "inheritance" arises from the hope that, because it has been winnowed and sifted, the past is rooted in nature. Yet, as Schiller, another conservative critic of revolution, argues in the *Aesthetic Education of Man*, the modern (Schiller's term: "sentimental") experience entails division and specialization that threaten to make life seem a series of repetitive temporal instances, for which we substitute the simulacrum of order in rational systems. Burke's conservative reading of experience operates from the premise that knowledge is approachable, that there is a text which accurate interpretation can elucidate. Yet if the premise collapses and God seems just another fiction, repetitions become nontranscendental and vision is clouded by insecurity. Burke's "portraits," like the tradition they entail, require a generally agreed-upon public interpretive response, at least by its ruling classes. It is, Burke recognizes, a collective mythic gallery where interpretations evolve over time. But what is real? What is nature? Tradition? Burke's argument that these ideas are reified through the generations is undercut by his depiction of revolutionaries' stripping of humanity to its naked and shivering state.

The metaphorical portrait gallery represents a fairly stable artifact amidst a historical flux that can overwhelm perspective. In several of the British novels that I discuss, this metaphor is prominent. Anxiety about language's tendency to form "fictitious" strategies that collapse upon themselves, rather than nurturing "the superstition which builds" (269),

leads many, like Burke, to seek visual stabilities. This is evident in
Emma Woodhouse's endeavors to manipulate people through painting;
Brownlow's wish to affirm Oliver's innocence through analogies with
Agnes Flemings's portrait; the Dedlocks' frozen portrait gallery in *Bleak
House*; Jane Eyre's sublime paintings and visual placements; Naumann's
wish to impose an aesthetic ideal on Dorothea Brooke in *Middlemarch*;
the portraits of the "Savage Woman" and Marlow's Intended in *Heart of
Darkness*; the beautiful portrait that masks Dorian Gray's moral decay;
and Cecil Vyse's regarding Lucy Honeychurch as "Leonardesque" in *A
Room With a View*.

"The rights of men," Burke writes, "are in a sort of *middle*, incapable
of definition, but not impossible to be discerned" (153). In *Howards End*,
E. M. Forster's Margaret Schlegel realizes that the secret to discovering
"proportion" between art and "telegrams and anger" is not to start with a
rational plan. But this is more easily said than done, for the mind seeks
symbolic finalities and, if not nimble, becomes trapped in constructs it
mistakes for nature.

Burke advocates a secular faith, what he terms, when speaking about
the clergy, the "fictions of a pious imagination" (272). Society needs a
tradition that unites the individual with a social organism. However,
unlike Carlyle, who viewed gradual or, failing this, cataclysmic
revolution as inevitable, Burke was horrified at the revolutionaries'
stripping away of a fictional edifice founded on tradition, which,
whatever its shortcomings, was preferable to man in his "naked shivering
nature" (171) or to fictive confederations, spectacles, and civic feasts.
Shorn of the "rich inheritance" provided by religion and law, and of a
restorative collective memory, people "would become little better than
the flies of a summer" (193). Burke also was drawn two ways, between
his advocacy of "pious" fictions and a deep mistrust of illusion
influenced by Plato's *Republic* and an ingrown skepticism.

Behind the defender of Anglicanism and England was the Irishman
whose family included Catholics; his defense of the French Catholics,
Conor Cruise O'Brien suggests, is a sign of "the suppressed
revolutionary part of his own personality."[6] Burke's public "Whig" voice
supersedes more recondite Jacobite and furiously ironic ones. The result
is discontinuity at the core of his personality. The Marie Antoinette
exfoliation ostensibly affirms political art and regal deification. Yet its
feminized space seems less real than the "Whig" and furiously ironic
bulk of the *Reflections*.[7]

However, Burke's passion, evident in all his rhetorical modes, opened
him to Thomas Paine's charge that he was as theatrical as those he
criticized as "coxcombs" of philosophy and government. His task, then,

is daunting: he must convince the British ruling classes that they must protect their institutions from philosophes and swinish multitudes, yet to do so he must unleash, through irony, the full force of revolutionary excess so that it is "seen" on the page, not just rationally presented. Furthermore, he must organize chaos through metaphors, above all that of the mephitic theater. What, Carlyle, wondered in *Past and Present*, is the relationship between sight, words, and belief? Recreating events in more than a "Dryasdust" fashion is difficult, especially if they include rapacious mobs and absurd reinventions of history and society. Exposure of the irrational may, indeed, initiate a loss of moorings. Hence Burke's near obsession, even as he presents the revolutionaries' excesses, with grounding beneficent political myths in property and the idea of "an *entailed inheritance* derived to us from our forefathers" (119). Representation is the necessary antecedent to denunciation, and the reader must experience mentally the full force of revolutionary irony, though the *canaille*, Burke believes, must remain bound in the illusions that conceal inequality. For them especially, "following nature" requires "wisdom without reflection, and above it," if society is to be victorious over "speculations" and "inventions" (119, 121). [8]

Like Friedrich Schiller, Burke argues that, once separated from "feeling" and "nature," people reenact old crimes under new names. Schiller writes that, in France, philosophy lends "her name to a repression formerly authorized by the Church."[9] Words obfuscate events instead of approaching their realities. This becomes easy when the memory assassins have done their work and reinvented history itself. Burke writes that the French, having replaced old genealogies with a new "pedigree of crimes" (246), have failed to understand the basic nature of power:

> A certain *quantum* of power must always exist in the community, in some hands, and under some appellation. Wise men will apply their remedies to vices, not to names: to the causes of evil which are permanent, not to the occasional organs by which they act, and the transitory modes in which they appear. (248)

Whatever their limitations, the old aristocracy was tried by history. "Genealogy" was tested by tradition. But the new rulers, having abolished all titles, genealogies, and family distinctions, have created a new demonology by taking "the fiction of ancestry in a corporate succession, as a ground for punishing men who have no relation to guilty acts" (246). They have expanded "every instance of oppression and persecution" in the past to represent the whole to justify subsuming the clergy and aristocrats within their demonology. Proportion is lost, and the exception becomes the norm. Analogy becomes false. Burke writes:

> In history a great volume is unrolled for our instruction, drawing the materials
> of future wisdom from the past errors and infirmities of mankind. (247)

But whose volume? The revolutionaries have written a specious volume
to punish their enemies; better the old one, which made class distinctions
less harsh. Viewed objectively, Burke argues, history is mostly an annal
of "pride, ambition, avarice, revenge, lust, sedition, hypocrisy,
ungoverned zeal, and all the train of disorderly appetites" (247). History
stripped to its essence can help no one; embellished with pleasing
fictions, it may make life bearable. The revolutionaries merely attack
names and create demonologies: they attend to the "shell and husk of
history" (249), while the spirit of wickedness inventively "assumes a new
body" (248). The reformers are mesmerized by their "ghosts and
apparitions" (248), the fictions they have created to conceal the old
names for evil under the appearance of rational good, "whilst, under
colour of abhorring the ill principles of antiquated parties, they are
authorizing and feeding the same odious vices in different factions, and
perhaps in worse" (249).

The philosophes have used their "monstrous" fictions and "school
paradoxes" to undercut belief; their revolutionary language, to use
Nietzsche's words in *The Birth of Tragedy*, effects the "playful
construction and destruction of the individual world as the overflow of a
primordial delight."[10] Believing that language should pursue stable
meaning, Burke is aghast at "the paradoxes of eloquent writers, brought
forth purely as a sport of fancy, to try their talents, to rouze attention, and
excite surprize" (283). Thus, he likens their verbal strategies to art: their
"sport of fancy" combines two key aesthetic terms. The ironies of
Rousseau and Voltaire have corrupted taste, style, and, finally, the body
politic itself. Lesser gentlemen adopt their ironic deconstructions (the
decadence of this is evident in Wilde's Sir Harry Wotton) and spread
them throughout polite society: "These paradoxes become with them
serious grounds of action, upon which they proceed in regulating the
most important concerns of the state" (283). This "sport of fancy" is an
appropriation of ornamentation, and, as such, an invasion of the space
ascribed to the feminine, which Burke will proceed to protect. It is also
an usurpation of the godlike, for Rousseau, like other revolutionary
thinkers, produces a false sense of the "marvellous" (283) through irony
to "strike and interest the public" (284). To defend the feminine and the
godlike, Burke must reenact their ironic acrobatics, which challenge
providential stability and create a *frisson* of horror.

Also in the shadow of the French Revolution, the brothers Friedrich
and August Wilhelm Schlegel formulated their ideas about Romantic

Irony, central to which is the belief that creation and destruction must both be embraced and that life is a fragmentary and endless fluctuation between belief and disbelief.[11] "It's equally fatal for the mind to have a system and to have none," Friedrich Schlegel writes in one of his aphorisms. "It will simply have to decide to combine the two."[12] He recognizes the aporia between destructive and renovative urges. But Burke sees only the loss of meaning in fragmentariness, not its momentary reestablishment through the perpetual creation and destruction of appearances. Friedrich Schlegel writes that a new art appropriate to the age should, somewhat like memoirs, constitute "a system of aphorisms."[13] The novel, above all Goethe's *Wilhelm Meister*, one of the three "greatest tendencies of the age," is the closest thing to this art, whose dialogues, "a chain or wreath of aphorisms," explode the boundaries between subjectivity and objectivity, hierarchy and experience, reality (or its mental recreation) and abstraction.[14] Art aspires, as Schiller thinks, towards the idyllic, but, rising above both "system" and its absence,[15] the artist also must embrace the paradox, levity, and license Burke finds so ghastly. This "progressive universal poetry" mirrors the multiplicity of modern life:

> Romantic poetry alone can, like the epic, become a mirror of the entire surrounding world, a picture of its age. And yet, it too can soar, free from all real and ideal interests, on the wings of poetic reflection, midway between the work and the artist. It can even exponentiate the reflection and multiply it as in an endless series of mirrors.[16]

But Burke cannot accept this creative tension between the world and intellectual reformulations of it.

In fact, Burke suggests, to dissect events too closely can only cause harm. The Glorious Revolution arose from respect for tradition, not a Socratic irony translated to the historical stage, what Friedrich Schlegel terms the essential "continuous alternation of self-creation and self-destruction."[17] "The Revolution," Burke insists, "was made to preserve our *antient* indisputable laws and liberties, and that *antient* constitution of government which is our only security for law and liberty" (117). Like religion, this instance of the "Justa bella quibus *necessaria*" (116) arose mysteriously from within the body politic, beyond the reach of untrustworthy exoteric formulations:

> As it was not made for common abuses, so it is not to be agitated by common minds. The speculative line of demarcation, where obedience ought to end, and resistance must begin, is faint, obscure, and not easily definable. It is not a single act, or a single event, which determines it. (116)

The 1688 revolution arose "upon analogical precedent, authority, example" (117). However, since commonwealths are "moral essences," such events should not be explored too rationally. The state is complex and mysterious; hence, like God, it must be approached with awe and circumspection.

The "analogy" between 1688 and 1789 that Dr. Price insists on is false. He and his allies would imitate some of their predecessors, who "dragged the bodies of our antient sovereigns out of the quiet of their tombs" and "attaint and disable backwards all the kings that have reigned before the Revolution, and consequently to stain the throne of England with the blot of a continual usurpation" (107). They will reinvent hierarchy itself despite their protestations of democracy. But the 1688 revolutionaries based their actions on the 1215 Magna Charta (107), itself "connected with another positive charter from Henry I" (118): they sought traditional "analogy." "With infinite reluctance," they charged James II

> with nothing less than a design, confirmed by a multitude of illegal overt acts, to *subvert the Protestant church and state*, and their *fundamental*, unquestionable laws and liberties: they charged him with having broken the *original contract* between king and people. (113)

To create a bulwark against future revolutions, they composed a "Declaration of Right" and were careful to replace James II, "a bad king with a good title, and not an usurper" (108), with a legitimate ruler.

Because history is often brutal, it is necessary to posit "inheritance" as an aesthetic, not a rational, idea. The most difficult act to incorporate within the English myth was Henry VIII's seizure of church properties (217). But even here, Burke argues, shame, virtue, and moderation were not completely expelled: "Harry" paid dubious homage to law and tradition by establishing "a commission to examine into crimes and abuses which prevailed in those communities" (217–18). He did not, like the French, seek to extirpate religion. Moreover, he hesitated to confiscate Church lands outright, but rather

> procured the formal surrender of these estates. All these operose proceedings were adopted by one of the most decided tyrants in the rolls of history, as necessary preliminaries, before he could venture, by bribing the members of his two servile houses with a share of the spoil, and holding out to them an eternal immunity from taxation, to demand a confirmation of his iniquitous proceedings by an act of parliament. (218)

Had he lived today, Burke states, "four technical terms would have done his business, and saved him all this trouble; he needed nothing more than one short form of incantation—'*Philosophy, Light, Liberality, the Rights of Men*'" (218).

In 1688, Parliament, recognizing the gravity of replacing one monarch with another,

> threw a politic, well-wrought veil over every circumstance tending to weaken the rights, which in the meliorated order of succession they meant to perpetuate; or which might furnish a precedent for any future departure from what they had then settled forever. (103)

They wanted to prevent their action from being easily repeatable:

> They knew that a doubtful title of succession would but too much resemble an election; and that an election would be utterly destructive of the "unity, peace, and tranquillity of this nation," which they thought to be considerations of some moment. (103)

Burke links the refusal of the "coxcombs of philosophy" (141) to acknowledge tradition to the "monstrous fiction" that people are equal. The new French leaders, the lawyers and "stock-jobbers," reinterpret the past to justify a society in which *assignats* have the power of "philosopher's stones." They "commit waste on the inheritance, by destroying at their pleasure the whole original fabric of their society" (192), and they invent a rational replacement for the "marvellous." They substitute for that "original fabric" pure concepts which cannot revivify "that aged parent" hacked "into pieces" (194). In alluding to Medea's ruse to convince Pelias's daughters to hack him up and boil the pieces to restore the old man's youth, Burke at once feminizes and demonizes the philosophes, whose cunning, like Medea's, is the vengeance of buried demons. The civic religion which restrained passions has been rejected, but its fictive replacement cannot withstand the rage that finally impels revolution to consume its children: "If the present project of a republic should fail, all securities to a moderated freedom fail along with it; all the indirect restraints which mitigate despotism are removed" (301).

By transforming people into "counters," the Paris government detaches appearances from nature and invents origins. This is illustrated by the political process itself. Membership in the National Assembly is twice removed from the voters in the cantons, who, through a "qualification" of three days of labor paid to the public (288), elect deputies to the Commune, who in turn choose delegates to the Department. Yet the "qualification" contradicts the pure "basis of population"

(286) based on abstract "rights of men" (289), while contribution, the third tripod of the state (the other two are territory and population) rests entirely on property. All of this contradicts the state's supposed demo-cratic basis. The distance of the governed from their governors parodies the mystifying distance between governors and populace in the old monarchy. Absent an idea of God, however, the French will not be able to bind their interpretation, so it must be held together through property confiscation, the army, and the parodic-deified "supreme power of the city of Paris" (306).

In this new state, power is disguised as "toleration," the simulacrum of liberality that replaces commitment and sympathy. Like the layers of government between the people and their government, toleration represents a specious "marvellous": "that those persons should tolerate all opinions, who think none to be of estimation, is a matter of small merit" (259). At the same time, they denounce the real "marvellous" and its priests as socially constructed lies:

> They say that ecclesiastics are fictitious persons, creatures of the state; whom at pleasure they may destroy, and of course limit and modify in every particular; that the goods they possess are not properly theirs, but belong to the state which created the fiction. (206)

Even their pensions are "fictitious," for "their services had not been rendered to the country that now exists" (208).

The French revolutionaries are like "their ornamental gardeners" in "forming every thing into an exact level" (285): they confuse the political and ethical with the aesthetic. This is disastrous:

> The subject of our demolition and construction is not brick and timber, but sentient beings, by the sudden alteration of whose state, condition, and habits, multitudes may be rendered miserable. (280–81)

Their political "artistry" transforms what should be a "well-wrought veil" (103) into a mutilating rationalist myth. We might turn to Jane Austen's Burkean *Pride and Prejudice* to illustrate the stability that is lost. At Pemberley House, art and nature are rooted in tradition; Darcy is more himself here than elsewhere. Here, "natural beauty" is "little counteracted by an awkward taste," and "nature" is in pleasing artful ascendance. Yet importunate historicity is held at distance: the novel form parries its flux. Even Wickham and Lydia are rescued from the practical consequences of their flight from order into that distant arena of Napoleonic war and uncontrolled passion.

Burke argues that the ancients knew better than the moderns the importance of organic political complexity: today, the "airy metaphysicians" reduce "men to loose counters merely for the sake of simple telling, and not to figures whose power is to arise from their place in the table" (300). "Simple telling" suggests fiction, though the literal meaning here is "counting." Art, Burke suggests, has been reduced to monetary equation and as such is inhuman. Now that the French have dismissed social hierarchies as "fictions of superstition," anything is possible, for the new civic religion has created fungible characters who are merely objects of the state. Yet politics always operates according to oppositions, whatever it claims to do. Having erased the "pleasing illusions" that make bearable the inequalities grounded in human nature, the politicians will be unable to find what Nietzsche terms "a new transfiguring illusion" to "cover dissonance with a veil of beauty."[18] Art at first parodies, then cancels itself, and society foreshadows Mr. Kurtz's progress from idealism to the hollowness that collapses into savagery. Anarchy underlies the overthrow of a monarch from rationalist assumptions: it and unaided reason are inverses.

Central to Burke's insistence on mystery is his anxiety about its reality vis-à-vis its Manichaean opposite, the "antagonist" violence that overwhelms the royal family. Burke's rhetoric strains towards belief, but what occurs is what Kristeva calls the "desubstantification of linguistic ideals."[19] Burke uses his rhetorical voices to explain the real and suggest an unspeakable "marvellous." Jane Austen, in contrast, creates a more stable representation of life in which the marvelous is abandoned to the circumambient flux, while the agents of the unnameable, like Collins and Elton, are thoroughly placed socially and are comically unable to interpret signs. But even if the narrator's world is a series of subjective mirrors, it comprises a little universe in which God, if absent, is present in symbolic delimitations.

Though leery of that Carlyle terms "sansculottic" ironies, Burke can ironically strip history as easily as the revolutionaries to see brute nature and inequality. This is perilous. England's constitutional monarchy asserts liberties:

> This policy appears to me to be the result of profound reflection; or rather the happy effect of following nature, which is wisdom without reflection, and above it. A spirit of innovation is generally the result of a selfish temper and confined views. (119)

But only a select few are capable of "profound reflection." Mirroring the revolutionaries he condemns, Burke explodes limited readings and enters

the sansculottes' space. He is also drawn to a renovative "*a power out of*"
himself (151) that bridles and subdues passions. Yet he is aware that, in
naming this "power" and dissecting its decay, he participates in the
process he deplores. Yet try to explain, to visualize, he must.

The most emotional sections of the *Reflections* embrace the royal
family's removal to Paris, the National Assembly's spectacle, and
meditations on Marie Antoinette's tragedy, about twenty pages in all.

The mob's "unhallowed transports," intensifications of Dr. Price's
epicene "enthusiasm," characterize the confusions of order and gender
that call meaning into question. They are accompanied by a ferocious
sexuality endemic in a society in which stage and audience are inverted
like the masculine and the feminine. This is especially evident in the
National Assembly:

> There a majority, sometimes real, sometimes pretended, captive itself,
> compels a captive king to issue as royal edicts, at third hand, the polluted
> nonsense of their most licentious and giddy coffee-houses. It is notorious, that
> all their measures are decided before they are debated. (160)

The coffeehouses are effeminate, "giddy," and sexually perverse, or so
the term "licentious" implies. Louis XVI's being forced to "issue" edicts
suggests a gender-birthing reversal over which he has no control. Burke's
analogy between bad law and infernal birthing is also evident in his
statement that in the clubs and academies "publick measures are
deformed into monsters" (160). Like Mary Shelley and John Milton, he
associates monstrosity with the collapse of procreative order.

The role reversals in the National Assembly are appropriate in a
theater where lawmakers and audience shift positions:

> They act like the comedians of a fair before a riotous audience; they act
> amidst the tumultuous cries of a mixed mob of ferocious men, and of women
> lost to shame, who, according to their insolent fancies, direct, control,
> applaud, explode them; and sometimes mix and take their seats amongst
> them; domineering over them with a strange mixture of servile petulance and
> proud presumptuous authority. (161)

In this "inverted order in all things," "the gallery is in place of the house"
(161). This fearful inversion dissolves social hierarchies. The use of the
term "gallery" underscores the revolutionaries' perversions of art and
theater; Dickens develops the same analogy in the mob's pursuit of Sikes
and in Fagin's trial in *Oliver Twist*.[20]

The queen's near-capture by the mob who storm the Tuileries is
dominated by rape imagery, starting with her guards' "promiscuous

slaughter."[21] The mob is sexually ambiguous in its frenzy; Burke associates it with the Bacchanale and with the "furies of hell" (165):

> From this sleep the queen was first startled by the voice of the centinel at her door, who cried out to her, to save herself by flight—that this was the last proof of fidelity he could give—that they were upon him, and he was dead. Instantly he was cut down. A band of cruel ruffians and assassins, reeking with his blood, rushed into the chamber of the queen, and pierced with an hundred strokes of bayonets and poniards the bed, from whence this persecuted woman had but just time to fly almost naked. (164)

Burke links the the "polluted" and "licentious" coffeehouses, where ideas are generated, with the Assembly's parodic feminization of the king, and finally with this rape imagery. The queen, in her "almost naked flight" from a sanctuary "swimming in blood, polluted by massacre" (164), is protected only by her tragic dignity and its inscriber, Burke himself.[22]

These "furies of hell" have brought unbridled sexual energy onto the political stage and subordinated the masculine to the menadic feminine (165). The Reverend Dr. Price's epicene "enthusiastik ejaculation," and his "fit of unguarded transport" (165), are connected, Burke implies, with "Theban and Thracian orgies" that cancel his manhood and transform the awful and the sublime—masculine effects, Burke suggests in his *Philosophical Enquiry*—into an effeminate "*beautiful day*" and other "holy ejaculations" (166). An analogy between idiotic rhetoric and onanism seems evident in Burke's words. The epicene male is subordinated to the menadic feminine, and both have greater force than traditional gender constructions. Society cross-dresses. All that is wanting to the realization of Dr. Price's rhetoric is the "actual murder of the king and queen," which will translate a "*beautiful day*" unanchored in nature into a "history-piece of the massacre of innocents" (166). Perverse art will become life.

In contrast to this, Burke describes a "great drama" presided over by a "Supreme Director" and based in "natural feelings" and passions that "instruct our reason":

> We are so made as to be affected at such spectacles with melancholy sentiments upon the unstable condition of mortal prosperity, and the tremendous uncertainty of human greatness ... because when kings are hurl'd from their thrones by the Supreme Director of this great drama, and become the objects of insult to the base, and of pity to the good, we behold such disasters in the moral, as we should behold a miracle in the physical order of things. We are alarmed into reflexion; our minds (as it has long since been observed) are purified by terror and pity; our weak unthinking pride is humbled, under the dispensations of a mysterious wisdom. (175)

But natural feelings that "instruct our reason" are threatened when the specious and the authentic cannot be distinguished. Natural feelings depend for their force on the very hierarchy Burke sees threatened. Aristotelian tragedy presupposes heroic rank; so does society. If this is lost, so is everything else. The capacity to retain aesthetic distance and displace the emotions of pity and terror are threatened, as the political theater merely "outrages" the feelings instead of refining them. In recounting how the mysterious gives way to the merely confused, and the capacity to retain aesthetic distance—itself the sign of hierarchy— disappears, Burke underscores the possibility of that disappearance elsewhere.

The French "theater" is determined by criminal events that erase the Aristotelian rank on which tragedy is based; in England, where Dr. Price's church is infected by infernal theatricality, the theater may be "a better school of moral sentiments than churches":

> I should be truly ashamed of finding in myself that superficial, theatric sense of painted distress, whilst I could exult over it in real life. With such a perverted mind, I could never venture to shew my face at a tragedy. People would think the tears that Garrick formerly, or that Siddons not long since, have extorted from me, were the tears of hypocrisy; I should know them to be the tears of folly. (175–76)

The purification "by terror and pity" threatens to lose itself in a bad theater under which it, like everything else, is subsumed. As de Bruyn argues, Burke experiences a loss of tragic distancing as the logic of the Aristotelian theater breaks down:[23]

> No theatric audience in Athens would bear what has been borne, in the midst of the real tragedy of this triumphal day. ... They would not bear to see the crimes of new democracy posted as in a ledger against the crimes of old despotism, and the bookkeepers of politics finding democracy still in debt, but by no means unable or unwilling to pay the balance. (176)

The dispensations of "mysterious wisdom" give way to a horrified recognition of loss; hence the need to protect Albion from Gallic infection by enacting the loss of theatrical reserve in his own narrative voice. Burke's text is his own *via dolorosa*, his momentary sacrifice intended as a textual inoculation for the English ruling classes against revolution.

The tragically serene Marie Antoinette carries concealed in her bosom a "sharp antidote against disgrace" (169) proper to the heroine of a Restoration heroic tragedy. But there is also her younger self, with whom Burke momentarily seeks refuge:

It is now sixteen or seventeen years since I saw the queen of France, then the dauphiness, at Versailles; and surely never lighted on this orb, which she hardly seemed to touch, a more delightful vision. I saw her just above the horizon, decorating and cheering the elevated sphere she just began to move in,—glittering like the morning-star, full of life, and splendour, and joy. Oh! What a revolution! and what an heart must I have, to contemplate without emotion that elevation and that fall! (169)

He proceeds to lament the loss of "proud submission" to authority in which the masculine obeys and is cheered by feminine grace:

All the pleasing illusions, which made power gentle, and obedience liberal, which harmonized the different shades of life, and which, by a bland assimilation, incorporated into politics the sentiments which beautify and soften private society, are to be dissolved by this new conquering empire of light and reason. (171)

Now gender is but a social construct:

On this scheme of things, a king is but a man; a queen is but a woman; a woman is but an animal; and an animal not of the highest order. All homage paid to the sex in general as such, and without distinct views, is to be regarded as romance and folly. Regicide, and parricide, and sacrilege, are but fictions of superstition, corrupting jurisprudence by destroying its simplicity. (171)

Manners are the basis of civilized society: "To make us love our country, our country ought to be lovely" (172).

But the "ten thousand swords" that should have "leaped from their scabbards" to avenge "even a look" have metaphorically become the pens that have reinvented her; hence, the "sharp antidote" she wears around her neck is the sign of the conclusion to be wriiten to her drama, the one thing "wanted."

Marie Antoinette, the youthful symbol of "the spirit of an exalted freedom" (170), could be admired and worshipped from afar. But now her role will be sublime as she enacts "serene patience" and the "dignity of a Roman matron" (169). Burke inscribes her within tragic aesthetic categories, much as, years later, Wordsworth, Carlyle, and Dickens would do with Madame Roland. Seventeen years after his first sighting, he translates her to the last redoubt of a tragic realm where "if she must fall, she will fall by no ignoble hand" (169)—her own. Like Schiller's Maria Stuart, she is a feminine renunciant whose valorization requires her death.

Over the youthful Marie, Burke has greater narrative control. His
memory counters the fear that the "politics of revolution" will harden the
heart and enables him to recall her sympathetically, while the mob
transforms her into the embodiment of their frustration at not having
bread. His fiction humanizes; theirs dehumanizes. Burke is aware of the
fictional nature of his Marie Antoinette; nevertheless, he spends himself
in a "vision," which asks the reader to recreate and mythologize Marie
Antoinette as a "morning star"—Venus, but likewise (Burke seems
unaware) Lucifer—the locus of hopes and dreams projected backwards
to escape an actuality that threatens his own autonomy vis-à-vis "all the
unutterable abominations of the furies of hell" and their epicene inverses,
the philosophes.[24]

Like the novelists we will discuss, Edmund Burke mediates reality and
maintains a precarious distance from a "chaos of actuality" (Carlyle's
term) in which sovereigns are overthrown and counterfeited. He uses
language, in what J. Hillis Miller terms an action of "sovereign power,"
to keep historical flux at bay even as he represents the revolutionary
frenzies he condemns. In *Thomas Hardy: Distance and Desire*, Miller
writes that, for the novelist,

> to change the world as he has experienced it into a fictional world is to nullify
> it, to hold it at a distance, to make it over into a linguistic form which renders
> it less dangerous. The real world is a glare and garish rattling, mysteriously
> threatening. A novel is only words. The act of writing a novel is the covert
> exercise of a sovereign power over the world. It neutralizes it.[25]

Burke seeks to engage history, but he is bounced back and forth
between the poles of rhetorical infection and indignant response as he
does battle with revolution's monsters. He defends tradition but is unable
to reconcile it with what Schlegel terms "new insanities"; he denies a link
between ugly fact and aesthetic pleasure. His concept of political art is
organized, like Kant's, along hierarchical-objectivist lines. This ensures
his discomfort not only with historical change but with the cunning
strategies needed to stabilize it. He sets against the revolutionaries' infernal activities his own beautiful portrait and sublime tragedy to create a
space for an "exalted freedom." This is vital to breaking the iron causality central to the rationalists' reduction of history to what Nietzsche
terms the fairy tales of science.[26] Burke does not posit an Apollonian
illusion impelled by the "terror and horror of existence" but one much
closer to Kant's moral idea. Nor does he embrace realism, which, George
Eliot's narrator in *Adam Bede* suggests, finds the marvelous in "old
women scraping carrots" and "heavy clowns taking holiday." Eliot's

metaphorical god is in the common, whose representations stand contrary to aesthetic angels and what Nietzsche calls the "pseudo-idealism" of Goethe and Schiller. As different as he is from Eliot, Nietzsche discerns "a higher pleasure" in "that which is ugly and disharmonic."[27] Burke can do no such thing.

Burke's mistrust of fictions that reduce humans to "counters" is also characteristic of the nineteenth-century British novel. F. R. Leavis thinks that the English novel relates the "individual talent" to a tradition, and that its great authors are concerned with an "awareness of the possibilities of life."[28] It is from the profoundly ironic tension between life and flights from history that verisimilitude is derived. With its Lockean emphasis on the development of consciousness in time, the novel developed a realism that tolerates diversity yet resists the separation of consciousness from tradition. These novelists, whatever their political beliefs, are mistrustful of fictive approaches to the human condition and solicitous towards the subjective human. As God is replaced by an oppressive social determinism, the revivification of feeling through memory and sympathy requires that the historical flux be included, not excluded.

2

Jane Austen's *Emma*: Realism and Delimitation

In his *Metahistory,* Hayden White suggests that there are as many modes of realism as there are modalities for construing the world in "figurative discourse."[1] The realism of the first novel I have chosen, Jane Austen's *Emma*, contrasts radically with that of the next one, *Frankenstein*, in which the systole-diastole of monstrosity (indicative of revolutionary disorder) and aesthetic bulwarks constructed against it is ever apparent. Realism, as Levine suggests, posits "mixed" conditions.[2] It seeks a middle space between formless reality and formulation, where interplay creates coherence while acknowledging life's untidiness, danger, and flux. George Eliot best exemplifies this ever precarious middle space in a world where God and providential order are all but absent, represented at best by metonymic and parodic authorial structures. Shelley's novel may be a paradigm of realism, as Levine suggests, but where does this leave *Emma*, which engages the world least and displays fewer of its fissures than any other work in this study? That Austen is aware of a historical field (two of her brothers were admirals) is indubitable; but, despite French revolution and war, she demarcates her aesthetic territory both vertically and horizontally, detaching her mythopoetic world from historical events and psychological dissolutions, while hinting at both in peripheral events and characters, the stream-of-consciousness speech of Miss Bates, or the gracefully disguised phallicism of Knightley's estate. Austen's narrative asserts an illusion of order and esteem for patriarchal structures while nearly effacing the origins of its verisimilar reality. The historicity at which it hints in Miss Bates's associative speech, as well as in the origins of Jane Fairfax, Harriet Smith, and the Coles family, plays with historical flux, whose metaphors, like the gypsies and the robbed henhouse, it purports to efface with a happy ending. The novel's idyllic form creates a subversive space that modifies the ideas of perfection and closure it offers. Yet, though hinting at circumambient events, Austen's narrative insists on likeness and inclusion within its mythopoetic space, and the exclusion of those who, like Harriet, resist inclusion. She is aware of what lies beyond but chooses to create an idyllic universe in which aesthetic strategies and bulwarks are directed, less against overt monstrosity (as in Shelley, Dickens, or Conrad) than against bad manners or unreflective passions, like those of Lydia and Wickham in *Pride and Prejudice*. If Burke strips away manners and the fictions of a pious imagination to reveal something horrible beneath, Austen, whose social attitudes really parallel Burke's, chooses rather to affirm her self-contained, idyllic field without directing a penetrating gaze into the ultimate sources of those unregulated actions and manners. In this sense, Emma's growing ability to manipulate her aesthetic space adumbrates the delimited realism Austen self-consciously stakes out for herself.[3]

Vargish argues that Austen assumes a "fundamental cosmic order and design that contains a perceptible moral, perhaps even spiritual decorum," but this makes her voice seem more univocal than it really is within the terms of the limited representative field she chooses.[4] We have seen that Burke uses lingual subversion to uphold his essentially conservative vision; so, too, does Austen, though in a more limited sense. Even Miss Bates's stream of consciousness is a delimitation (so, too, are terms like "abyss" or "horror" in other novels), a mere suggestion of the disorganization that lies beyond organized perception. From the other end of the spectrum, however, Austen's clergymen, those representatives of providential vision like Elton and Collins, are parodically anal in their endeavors to script their own proposals. There is, instead, an ironic, self-sufficient verbal representation that gazes neither into chaos nor into infinitude, but modulates its gaze and rhetoric to suggest a world absent of ultimate judgments and conclusions. Perhaps Lionel Trilling had the best take on Austen's method years ago, when he described *Emma* as Austen's "closest approximation of an idyllic world."[5] The idyll, Schiller argues, would reconcile reason and the imagination, objectivity and feeling, the real and the ideal. As he states, the form is as yet unrealized and, perhaps, foreign to human nature. As Nietzsche argues, this dialectical conception is much too limited, given the more radical and irreconcilable oppositions that comprise human existence. Austen makes her choice, but, as we will see, the other novelists in this study more fully incorporate the aporias and fissures evident in the historical field into the structures of their works. Thus, in Dickens, for instance, the idyllic is overtly valorized (e.g., in Rose Maylie) yet at odds with the infernal realities of London and the diseased psyche. In the nineteenth century, an awareness of the disjunction between the aesthetic and existence becomes more pronounced, though Eliot and Forster try to close the gap, "connect" as it were, in a middle space between aesthetic or idyllic constructions and fragmentation.

Within the scope of her realism, however, Austen creates a density and texture that reify visual and verbal control over her materials. Indeed, to a significant degree the novel is *about* visual control and creation and Emma's education in conserving an ironic, creative space for herself based on manipulations of appearance. She is a prototypical, if flawed, artist who exemplifies the possibilities and limitations of verisimilar activity in a limited sphere. Others in the novel are much less adept than Emma at manipulating aesthetic spaces. If she is limited artistically, others are more so, even Frank Churchill. Her father, for instance, constructs a miniworld around his library, gruel, the avoidance of drafts, and an obsession with locks.[6] The last is suggestive of the self-enclosed nature of the country-house milieu Austen represents, but taken to a comically obsessive extent. Mr. Woodhouse represents the danger in Austen's realism project, and it is interesting that she situates this danger in the father, an inadequate patriarch whose withdrawal adumbrates (though less so than Mr. Bennet's cynical withdrawal in *Pride and Prejudice*) the absence of guaranteed traditional or patriarchal order, and therefore the artist's need (Emma's or Austen's) to discover, appreciate, and parry with it wherever it is found, finally, in Knightley and his Donwell Abbey. Emma's danger, parodied in her father's hypochondria, is solipsism, the hesitation to parry (or recognize) the aporias between the "real" and one's emplotments of the real, for the idyllic is essentially a univocal world where fissures and dialogical voices are relatively muted. The danger is that, absent the ongoing awareness of such fissures, the capacity to step back, to generate images from the awareness of difference between experience and its literary reenactment, will produce a too stable—and limited—art form. In *The Writing of History,* Michel de Certeau suggests that an ongoing, productive interplay exists in valid historical reconstruction between the productive activity and the period known, the two poles of the "real."[7] This interplay also characterizes realism in the novel: the disappearance of the gap between these poles leads to an aesthetic uniformity that implicates one in merely repetitive activity, like Mr. Woodhouse's.

Yet, as I suggested, in Austen the hesitation to negotiate the caesura between fiction and experience opens up neither an abyss nor monstrous aesthetic strategies of control; though Frank Churchill comes closest to the last, his is not the marmoreal aestheticism of Angel Clare, St. John

Rivers, Mr. Skimpole, or James Harthouse. Aesthetic monstrosity, merely the inverse of overt monstrosity, as effectively freezes realistic fluidity, the interplay of field and representation, as the Medusa-stare from the abyss, experienced by Jane Eyre, Esther Summerson, and Marlow. It is, I suggest, the whited sepulchre of monstrosity, an insight Marlow repeats as he recalls the Intended. The possibility of verbal fragmentation undermining visual verisimilar representation is also evident (Miss Bates's rhetoric is remarkably unvisual, unlike other narratives) in the letters and fragments Emma must turn into meaning, or discard altogether. Mr. Woodhouse, indeed, can be amused with fragments, as Knightley proves with his displays of "books of engravings, drawers of medals, cameos, corals, shells" at Donwell Abbey (247). But so solipsistic is his world that fragments don't seem fragments to him, for everything outside that limited space is simply appended to it in a nonreflective way. Mr. Woodhouse, in other words, lives in a perpetual present, unlike the novelist (or the historian) who must continually play with remembrance and representation in their respective fields.

With Emma, it is otherwise. Her protégé, Harriet Smith, collects mementos of her infatuation with Mr. Elton. When this infatuation proves illusory, the pencil and court plaster change in significance, and she wants to destroy them. In insisting that the plaster—a sort of eighteenth-century bandage—be put to practical use, Emma in effect acknowledges the collapse of her matchmaker fiction into fragmented ruins that cannot be reconstructed (232). But the plaster is a sign of her ineptitude in covering the gaps between her organizing fictions and the real. That she wants to put it to practical use suggests that she is on the edge between suspecting her ineptitude and improvising to transform the sign of her fictive strategy to a merely practical use.

Visual control precedes verbal production; this characterizes realism. Emma's saving grace is a paradoxical love for "every thing that is decided and open" (318), that is, not bound by visual or verbal linearization. Emma, like Austen, discovers (however ineptly in Emma's case) the caesura between the visual and the verbal from which verisimilitude is constructed; thus, even in her aesthetic infancy, she refutes Knightley's assessment about her having not influenced Mrs. Weston's marriage by looking for truth somewhere in the interstices between competing absolutes. Moreover, she translates his lingual control into the visual field she feels she is much better at controlling, even if she is as unlikely to complete her paintings as her books: "You have drawn two pretty pictures—but I think there may be a third—a something between the do-nothing and the do-all" (7). She gets into trouble when she is bound by her own or others' verbal or visual strategies, above all Churchill's. Indeed, she learns to play with emplotments in ways that don't impinge on their feelings or autonomy: it is when her strategies are too direct or univocal that they fail, or that, as at Box Hill, she hurts others. So Emma adumbrates Austen's task of learning to produce a world free of direct impingement on the "real" world out there, while acknowledging it (in effect, working with it) in the very delimitations she chooses. Austen explicitly links words with visual images in developing this theme, especially when Frank visualizes and articulates Jane's beauty in a semisecretive aesthetic field unbeknownst to the fiancée he has harmed so often through visual manipulations and verbal prevarications. Towards the end of the novel, Emma banters with Mr. Knightley about whether Robert Martin was talking about the "dimensions of some famous ox" (327) when he asked for Harriet Smith's hand in marriage. Here the visual ("dimensions"), the hand, and language converge in a play that hinges on their confusion: in effect, Emma parodies her earlier ineptitude.

Emma's verbal and visual ineptitude is evident in the game of charades and in her interpretations of the effects of her painting of Harriet Smith.[8] In either case, she fails to detect Elton's more inept strategy.[9] Harriet is a convenient person to manipulate, for, without a detectable genealogy, Emma can invent her visually and verbally. The desire to invent a genealogy, to "detach her from her bad acquaintance, and introduce her into good society" (14), erases in her mind any dialectic or gap between the fictive construction and the real girl, who, being merely "blank," cannot exist outside Emma's mythopoetic field, or so she thinks. Disagreeing with Barthes, de Certeau insists that history does not obliterate reference to the real, that the real is not *just* a fiction of the real. But every representation begins with a *catachresis,* which transforms experience or memory into a verbal, hence fictional, matrix prior to its further stabilization in the written word. In Emma's endeavors to reduce others to a purely aesthetic field of play, Austen suggests that the problem of realism in fiction is not entirely unlike this. All the characters *are* fictional; moreover, they are represented in a limited idyllic field; yet implicitly they are defined, like Miss Bates's language, against a circumambient impression of history and society, character and action. Thus, those characters cannot merely be created in a void, as Emma thinks she can do in inventing Harriet Smith. Austen points to the dangers of transfixion in a too delimited writing in Knightley's suggestion that, if she turns down Martin, Harriet Smith may be "glad to catch at the old writing master's son" (43), that is, be symbolically stuck in verbal repetitions that allow no egress.

Though she is aware of her exaggerations of her protégé, Emma's painting is a nexus of inappropriate readings:

> There was no want of likeness, she had been fortunate in the attitude, and as she meant to throw in a little improvement to the figure, to give a little more height, and considerably more elegance, she had great confidence of its being in every way a pretty drawing at last, and of its filling its destined place with credit to them both. (30)

Elton, of course, praises Emma's "hand," but her assumption that he praises the hand's creation reveals an inability to imagine any interpretation at variance with her own. If Mr. Woodhouse likes gruel, everyone must; if Emma paints to stimulate Elton, he must be stimulated the way she wants him to be, and everyone must concur.

At the same time, Emma's failure to finish likenesses (or reading lists) suggests both laziness, as Knightley suggests, and a hesitation to accept closures. This, too, is a problem at the heart of Austen's idyllic realism: as Dickens, too, suggests, "polishing" a text is inimical to realistic representation, a theme especially evident in *Bleak House*. The idyll especially lends itself to false, romance closures (Emma, after all, seeks romance endings in her matchmakings), even more so than those texts in which the gaps between life and its poetic representations are more evident. It is in artistic incompletion that Emma conserves her environment. In describing the portraits she has left unfinished and largely hidden away, Emma creates a tension between repetitions of "likeness"—their similarity to the subjects represented—and incompletion, which adumbrates the tension between the real and its emplotment in *Emma* itself. As with repetitions of the word "amiable" throughout the novel, we are aware of a gap between sign and character, a holding back from closure that the novel's ending, with its pilfered chicken houses, confirms.[10] Her portrait of John Knightley was especially problematical:

> This did not want much of being finished, when I put it away in a pet, and vowed I would never take another likeness. I could not help being provoked; for after all my pains, and when I had really made a very good likeness of it—(Mrs. Weston and I were quite agreed in thinking it *very* like)—only too handsome—too flattering—but that was a fault on the right side—after all this, came poor dear Isabella's cold approbation of—"Yes, it was a little like—but to be sure it did not do him justice." (29)

In its repetitions of "likeness" in this chapter, Emma's language becomes a kind of lingual bulwark against the *frisson* of incompletion. Resisting its display in public, she doesn't wish to have to apologize for this "unfavorable likeness" (29). Visual representation leaves her open to disclosure and embarrassment; in the end, Emma, like Jane Austen, sees in ironic evasiveness the best means to conserve herself. She would rather not display the painting than be subject to public realization that her portrait is other than discernibly "like"; implicitly, she rejects mimesis itself as a masculine construct. The difficulty, of course, is that human nature makes any likeness problematical and every artistic intention open to question. The repetitions of "likeness" suggest Emma's insecurity about the shifting relations between surface and self that constitute identity. To control artistry and decipher likeness requires a "strong hand," about which, for all her bravado, Emma is insecure.

If visual or verbal self-disclosure has its perils, so too does secrecy: in either case, one can be at the mercy of misreadings, willful or otherwise. Moreover, the perceptual field itself is unstable, absent publicly valorized signs ("understanding," "reason," etc., as traces of an order decaying outside the field), or the master-trope that might give meaning to paradox. Austen's replacement for it is her idyllic realism; within *Emma*, the disappearance of God in all but parodic delimitations necessitates other, though questionable, traces of providential order: objectivist aesthetics, perhaps, or the post office that gives Jane Fairfax so much trouble. [11] As Burke feared, the "objective" government institution replaces God once his "pious" fictions have been broken: power needs investiture. Here, then, is another indication of Austen's indirect presentation of what is breaking down in the historical field, beyond even the verbal delimitations that all but exclude "real" history. The post office's parodic objectivity is evident in Jane's bitterness over what we (but not Austen's characters) surmise is an absence of correspondence from her secret fiancé:

"The post office is a wonderful establishment!" said she—"The regularity and dispatch of it! If one thinks of all that it has to do, and all that it does so well, it is really astonishing!"

"It is certainly very well regulated."

"So seldom that any negligence or blunder appears! So seldom that a letter, among the thousands that are constantly passing about the kingdom, is even carried wrong—and not one in a million, I suppose, actually lost! And when one considers the variety of hands, and of bad hands too, that are to be deciphered, it increases the wonder!" (201)

The post office suggests the limitations of objectivity; as with Emma's misinterpreted "hand" in her painting of Harriet, fallible hands commit blunders that are all the more open to misinterpretation owing to secrecy. Trapped in her secret, Jane can only display ambiguous signs, "a blush, a quivering lip, a tear in the eye" (200), which suggest loss of control over visual and verbal capacities. Moreover, it is over absent but assumed correspondence (with a lover, Emma thinks) that misunderstanding is amplified. Absent any stable text, or Jane's willingness to explain her reticence, guesswork over the meaning of writing ensues, for the assumption is strong that a stable handwriting-sign must exist out there, despite hints, as in the gypsies' trickery, that society is much less stable outside the idyll than inside. The infallible post office is able to regulate all those subjective hands, prone though they are to error, yet closer delimitations of objectivity seem dubious. Nonetheless, the Knightley brothers insist on finding stable interpretations of writing based on family or gender, last redoubts of the loss of larger providential orders. John Knightley asserts that, while the same handwriting style often prevails in a family,

> the likeness must be chiefly confined to the females, for boys have very little teaching after an early age, and scramble into any hand they can get. Isabella and Emma, I think, do write very much alike. I have not always known their writing apart. (201–2)

Boys are allowed to develop distinct personalities and handwritings—within acceptable bounds, of course. They are *taught* to write this way. Girls, on the other hand, are taught to write alike: as with aesthetic expectations, an objective form of handwriting is conceptualized. The aesthetic, the visual, and the lingual are thus reduced to parodic objectivities to which women are expected to adhere. Their secrecy—like Jane's or Emma's—endangers them with misreading or exclusion; yet secrecy also is necessary to their private individuality, which men are allotted in public spheres, as represented by Donwell Abbey, where Knightley is able to disappear behind the artifact or emerge from it, as he sees fit, without danger of misreading. Emma's failure to finish her paintings, like her failure to complete her reading lists, is her instinctive defense against being subsumed into women's discourse; yet she must adopt the appearance of likeness while remaining ironically independent. Emma's hand, like Isabella's, is fine, though, as George notes, "Emma's hand is the strongest" (202). Still, this strength is in relation to women's discourse. Mr. Knightley intuits Emma's need for dominance over others' hands. Emma, too, is prone to discriminate between men's and women's "hands," as when she rationalizes that Robert Martin could not have written his letter of proposal to Harriet because "it is too strong and concise; not diffuse enough for a woman" (33). Yet, unlike Knightley, she sees that the essence of women's discourse is diffusion, not concentration, which I associate with univocal likeness.

Thus, near the end of *Emma*, Knightley insists on a private "woman's language" (326) in which he need not participate; his disdain for Churchill's "aimable" qualities and his "woman's writing" (202) is aroused by Churchill's secretive activities, which contrast with the moral discourse on which Knightley insists in his manly sphere. The possibility of noncommunication between public-masculine and private-feminine discourses is a tension at the heart of *Emma* that underscores the relation between verisimilar and general representations of human nature: somehow the two must be combined to replicate the particular in the universal (and the universal in the particular) now lost in the circumambient flux. This problem is indicated by Emma's gradual acceptance of Knightley while she retains an ironic aesthetic space that saves her from being effaced by the patriarchal word, above all its reason. Interestingly, Mr. Knightley in effect repudiates the particular for the universal in telling Emma that "woman's language" can make Harriet's engagement "interesting" to her (326) (but presumably less so to him):

> Your friend Harriet will make you a much longer history when you see her.— She will give you all the minute particulars, which only women's language can make interesting.—In our communications we deal only in the great. (326)

In this contrast between masculine and feminine discourses is the intersection between universal and novelistic languages, the first offering broad precepts, the second the depths and textures that comprise realism. Women's discourse is the novel itself, in which public experience, with all its perils, is rendered relatively stable in a private discourse made public. In *Rasselas,* Imlac stakes out something like Knightley's neoclassical position:

> The business of a poet ... is to examine, not the individual, but the species; to remark general properties and large appearances he does not number the streaks of the tulip, or describe the different shades in the verdure of the forest.[12]

The novelist presents details and organizes fragments yet accommodates the masculine discourse of "the great." This, however, entails ironic plays of form and content, verisimilar detail and ambiguity. Knightley relegates the personal and intimate to a silent realm of discourse, now that he has used his public power to facilitate the match. Robert Martin, Knightley insists, is "open, straight forward, and very well judging" (39), yet we catch only glimpses of him and directly encounter neither his words nor his writing, trusting instead that "women's language" can make him interesting, as he is to Harriet. But how does discourse become "interesting" if, like Harriet and Robert, it is banished to the novel's margins?

Donwell Abbey impresses Emma with its moorings in familial tradition and nature; it appears to be "just what it ought to be" and "what it was" (245):

> She felt all the honest pride and complacency which her alliance with the present and future proprietor could fairly warrant, as she viewed the respectable size and style of the building, its suitable, becoming, characteristic situation, low and sheltered—its ample gardens stretching down to meadows washed by a stream, of which the Abbey, with all the old neglect of prospect, had scarcely a sight—and its abundance of timber in rows and avenues, which neither fashion nor extravagance had rooted up. (244–45)

Yet the confluence of "is" and "ought," tradition and change, nature and art, is as distant as it is ideal. The unity between likeness and difference is too unproblematical to elude narrative subversion. Sure enough, the idyllic is modified by tensions centering around the odd behavior of Frank and Jane, whose respective "agitation" and ill-humor arise from her unwillingness to walk with him through those serene grounds, thereby risking disclosure (247–48). Rosmarin writes that "even individual sentences manifest devious design."[13] Emma discovers in Donwell Abbey the symbol of Mr. Knightley's repeated lessons that she must connect her fancies to reality and nature, not construct them out of thin air. Her "respect" for "the residence of a family of such true gentility, untainted in blood and understanding" (245) is ideal yet enclosed. Its "well-clothed" serenity is at odds with the "sort of gipsy party" (242) with which Mrs. Elton would usurp it, which, like Harriet's encounter with the gipsy party (226) and the poultry house theft, hints at circumambient realities and passions less subject to regulation.

Knightley seems the extension of his estate, with its "English verdure, English culture, English comfort, seen under a sun bright, without being oppressive" (246). Yet there is in fact an oppressive sun, which does not cancel yet modifies the original unifying impression: "it was hot" (246) enough that the party, scattered and insensible, must escape into "the delicious shade of a broad short avenue of limes," while, later, Frank complains of excessive heat ("he had never suffered any thing like it"

[249]), though his motives for doing so are suspect. Thus, nature is not the *locus amoenus* Emma at first perceives; Mr. Knightley suggests as much when he says he will eat indoors. The grounds suggest closure and phallicism, though of a graceful, almost hidden kind, the product of the generations-long constructed artifice of aristocracy, which affords Knightley the leisure and power to be self-assured in his morality. Though skeptical about art, Knightley is lord of a demesne in which closure and domination are rendered attractive, subtilized under an appearance of gracious order that still hints at what it is intended to render gracious. This is evident in the description of the avenue of limes:

> It led to nothing; nothing but a view at the end over a low stone wall with high pillars, which seemed intended, in their erection, to give the appearance of an approach to the house, which never had been there. (246)

The charming walk is over grounds that lead to "nothing" but a *trompe l'oeil* "erection" that is still nothing, yet clearly something which modifies the original impression that appearances and expectations are one. Emma's aesthetic framing of the estate, the symbol of her growing desire, is questionable and modified by the contrasts between stated serenity and the descriptions, sights, and characters that subvert it. Then again, the English garden, as described by Francis Bacon, is neither stable nor predictable, displaying instead a tension between nature and artifice.

Emma is struck by the hierarchical unity suggested by the contiguity of Donwell Abbey and Robert Martin's Abbey-Mill Farm, which is "favourably placed and sheltered" (246). Though she sees order in their contiguity, she is unaware of Harriet's infatuation with Knightley, which will complicate this metaphorical arrangement. Her need to exclude the unlike will cause her gradually to write Harriet out of her life after she marries Martin, which follows the collapse of the fiction that Harriet must be a gentleman's natural daughter. Though her blood "was likely to be as untainted, perhaps, as the blood of many a gentleman" (333), a risk of taint remains, the "stain indeed" that might threaten Emma's subversive idyll. There are limits to Emma's (and Austen's) willingness to include "taints" of unlikeness within their texts. This is the ironic counter to Austen's conclusion (and to Emma's dilemmas about finishing her paintings), which incorporates only those "tainted" elements that can be stabilized or kept ineffectually one-dimensional.[14]

According to Nietzsche, the problem of art is to impose order on the dream yet retain its fluidity in the representation. Austen, of course, radically delimits the primal chaos, yet in connecting the dream with the unregulated or incompetently produced aesthetic strategy, underscores the problematics of emplotting the real or its mental recreation in novelistic fiction. In *Emma,* the word "blunder" signals the breakdown between experience and emplotment; for Conrad, this fissure might open a horror, for Hardy an aesthetic monstrosity, but Austen largely cloaks the instability engendered by aesthetic and moral failures, refusing finally to open her fissure into the unspeakable. Emma's insult of Miss Bates is a "blunder" that causes her finally to link aesthetic and ethical discourses (283); she learns to see the word in ethical, not just aesthetic, terms, unlike Churchill, for whom it remains in the aesthetic sphere, whether in his word game, or in his self-exculpatory letter to Mrs. Weston. In the former, he has blundered by mistaking information about a carriage he received in Jane's letter for something Mrs. Weston told him. The post office's objectivity can't help him here, so he translates the information to a "dream," that is to say, an artistic sphere detached from the real and, hence, ethically inviolate. Knightley, in contrast, judges "blunder" in ethical terms, regarding its apparent consequences with indignation, alarm, and disgust.

At the climactic Box Hill outing, Emma finally realizes the harm that mere words can create. Jane was hurt by Frank's word game; now Emma insults Miss Bates by limiting her in yet another game to three dull things. Miss Bates's associative stream of consciousness contrasts with Emma's aesthetic sphere, and it is uncomfortably close to the unshaped reality, the bric-a-brac of life that Emma feels impelled to escape if she cannot organize it. If Jane Fairfax upsets Emma because of her secrecy, Miss Bates evokes Emma's impatience owing to her absolute openness. Emma's desideratum is clever "prose or verse" (253), which effects escape from tedium. Miss Bates indeed *is* tedious, but her inability to subtilize language into stable metaphor reminds Emma of her own difficulties. Emma's delusion is that autonomous perfection can exist in the public sphere. Only by taking feelings into account, Knightley implies, is a social discourse possible. This entails a recognition that we are all partially imperfect and fragmentary. Knightley's rebuke at Box Hill, like his earlier criticisms, is based on his belief in "amiable," not "aimable," conduct:

> She is poor; she has sunk from the comforts she was born to; and, if she live to old age, must probably sink more. Her situation should secure your compassion. It was badly done indeed! (257)

It is necessary, he suggests, to leave this artlessness unstated, and look instead to the goodness he values above appearances.

But Emma's initial response to her *faux pas* is aesthetic, not moral, for she sees the "good" as cooperating in an infection of the whole "ridiculous" appearance the woman projects: "What is good and what is ridiculous are most unfortunately blended in her" (257). She is uncomfortable with the moral—Mr. Knightley functions as her heretofore resisted superego—for this suggests closure, now parodied in its strange intercourse with another univocality, the aesthetic. Miss Bates seems the embodiment of verisimilar failure, her inchoate language confused with aesthetics and ethics. Any sense of distanced emplotment is absent, for in Miss Bates the caesura between the real and form have broken down, at least for Emma, whose proneness to think that words have a harmless autonomy leads her to ignore the need, in the public sphere, to deploy them carefully. Returning again to the symbolism of Donwell Abbey, Emma must combine artifice with nature in such a way that nature is shaped yet not made to seem artificially grotesque; life should neither be dismissed nor oppressed. For all its cloaked phallicism, Donwell Abbey is evidence that power can be made gentle and discourse mild, that Edmund Burke's ideal, in other words, is operative. Both the ethical and the aesthetic are importunate; but combining them, especially in the context of narrative realism, is a difficult problem to which there is no easy answer. Dickens suggests in *Oliver Twist* the decay that underlies univocal assertions of the good and the beautiful; Austen seems hopeful that there can be a creative interplay between public morality and private aesthetic display, so that the inchoate is uplifted into playful form, or at least not disclosed in its ridiculousness or disorganization.

Knightley, of course, sees a neoclassical *discordia concors* as possible, but I'm not sure that Austen is as hopeful, at least if robbed henhouses are any indication. In telling Emma that "fine dancing, I believe, like virtue, must be its own reward" (174), he suggests that the social *activity* itself creates an autonomous art that has no meaning beyond itself. Only the outsiders, those who do not participate in this union of act, manner, and art, have an end, because they wish to participate, being outside the dancing discourse altogether. Yet Knightley contradicts himself, at least in one instance, when he dances with Harriet after Elton's refusal to do so (223). Significantly, Austen's narrator sees dancing in less serious terms, preceding Knightley's reading with classic Austen irony:

> It may be possible to do without dancing entirely. Instances have been known of young people passing many, many months successively, without being at any ball of any description, and no material injury accrue either to body or mind;—but when a beginning is made—when the felicities of rapid motion

have once been, though slightly, felt—it must be a very heavy set that does not ask for more. (167)

The utility of dancing is questioned; yet, when plans are made and feelings are engaged, it is difficult to disengage oneself. This is a wonderfully arch suggestion of the difficulties of the artistic process, for Knightley's assumption that anyone who can *choose* to dance will want to enter this autonomous locus, is juxtaposed with the suggestion that dance per se is unimportant yet irresistible in its capacity to subsume individuality into its "rapid motion." Knightley, I suggest, assumes a masculinist-objectivist autonomy to dance, which he is free to contravene, while the narrator maintains an ironic distance from the event. Mr. Knightley controls this discourse; in advocating, like Kant might, an autonomy, he represents (like Donwell Abbey) the masculine aesthetic in its most compelling form. But he can afford to insist that dance, like virtue, is its own reward, since he has the power that affords the illusion of self-sufficiency. Emma, on the other hand, must retain a private space to avoid being subsumed in others' discourses. Her ironic spaces, in other words, adumbrate Austen's, which are necessary to a realism based as much on secrecy as disclosure. Thus I question Ralph Rader's statement that Emma and George make "cognitive music together through the moral and aesthetic harmonies of the work composed by one and tuned into by the other," for this suggests a nearly univocal *discordia concors*, and Austen leaves us with rougher edges than this.[15] Finally, we are unable to forget that Emma must maintain aesthetic univocality to define a realistic particularity of self, while Knightley's moralism, at its best a sympathy for others, is constructed upon a language that defines the moral, owns the property, and fundamentally relegates feeling to a marginalized "women's language." Knightley's cooperation is based on avoidance of women's discourse, while the compassion he demands, like the esteem he earns, is expressed through a moral discourse that Emma can manipulate but never control. In asking for her compassion, Knightley puts a feminine emotion at the service of social harmony, just as, at Donwell Abbey, feminine ornamentation makes pleasing a landscape of class divisions, dead ends, and phallic signs.

Emma Woodhouse is drawn to Frank Churchill because he replicates her inclination to control her environment through aesthetic manipulations. Problems occur when aesthetic strategies impinge on real people; in the course of the novel, she learns to relegate purely aesthetic play to a private, visual sphere. Here again, Austen suggests a dilemma of her novel form, which must not merely manipulate imaginative forms but represent experience and suggest both engagement with and momentary escapes from it. The aesthetic escape, be it idyllic or otherwise univocal, has an essential place in realism, for it is the necessary pole against which the experiential flux is organized, the other side of the fissure necessary to the creation of verisimilar meaning. However, if detached aesthetic play or unregulated experience becomes paramount, the form falters, the fissure closes, and what remains is inadequate. Austen, like Forster, pushes self-containment to its limit, but Emma's collaborations with Frank demonstrate an even greater detachment whose aesthetic play may exist within the overall structure but must not be allowed to efface realism's multiplicities completely.

In inventing Frank before his arrival, and without, unlike Knightley's estimation, any grounding in empirical fact, Emma superficially engages in the novelist's art. Knightley does not know Churchill, but he suspects him because of his behavior to others, above all his excuses for not visiting his biological father. Emma, however, ignores such evidence, creating out of the whole cloth a male reflection of her desire for imaginative recreation and control. Above all, she is drawn to his name, another blank space on which she can create an alternate reality:

> There was something in the name, in the idea of Mr. Frank Churchill, which always interested her. She had frequently thought—especially since his father's marriage with Miss Taylor—that if she *were* to marry, he was the very person to suit her in age, character and condition. He seemed by this connection between the families quite to belong to her. (80–81)

But Frank's name is not merely an objective canvas she can fill as she pleases: here, too, her artistry is subject to misreading and manipulation from outside. Emma identifies with him. Or, to be more exact, her affinity is aesthetic, unlike her moral and rational sympathy for Knightley. The first is relegated to the private, while the second is the acknowledged public position. Only in this private sphere, detached from emotion and disclosure, can appearances be manipulated without peril of hurt or social absurdity. The uniformly aesthetic stands outside, yet is deployed to create, verisimilar reality, which must engage the loss of providential order, even if this is only hinted at in comically fragmentary delimitations.

Frank Churchill proves to be a comparatively inept aesthetic strategist, but it takes Emma some time to decipher him. She is troubled by his promiscuity about inviting guests of different classes to the Crown Inn Ball: "His indifference to a confusion of rank, bordered too much on inelegance of mind" (133). The people he suggests inviting, like the

Coles family, remind her of a world out there—of grimy industrialism, work, and conflict. That she is wrong, that these country gentry have lost their rough edges and become subsumed in the mannered and idyllic, hardly matters, for they represent the real, from which layers of delimitation have protected her and, indeed, us. Like Emma, Frank needs to conceal his hand to retain control of his fictions. This is suggested during the scene in which he evades an answer to Emma about Jane Fairfax by saying he must inspect the gloves in a shop (134). The glove is the visual emblem of Churchill's need to conserve words carefully to buttress the fictions he has generated through manipulations of *visual* appearances, for example, of Jane's physical ineptitude. When he finally responds to Emma's question about whether he met Jane at Weymouth, it is to evade a direct response: "It is always the lady's right to decide on the degree of acquaintance." But when Emma criticizes Jane's reserve, he discloses that, indeed, he met her often (135). He is only direct, in other words, when he is sure of Emma's misinterpretation of a reserve based on Jane's nondisclosure of information, which confirms her status as a blank onto which he can project meaning. He incompetently discloses himself when, later, Emma catches him staring at Jane, but he regains control through an aesthetic judgment on bad hair:

> But really Miss Fairfax has done her hair in so odd a way—so very odd a way—that I cannot keep my eyes from her. I never saw any thing so outrée!—Those curls!—This must be a fancy of her own. I see nobody else looking like her!—I must go and ask her whether it is an Irish fashion. Shall I?—Yes, I will—I declare I will—and you shall see how she takes it;—whether she colours. (150)

In a parody of realism, Frank combines visual with verbal control of the misrepresented object. The "Irish fashion" confirms Emma's illusion of a failed romance between Jane Fairfax and Mr. Dixon; Churchill manipulates the piano, his secretive gift, to the same effect. His reality is merely a question of word manipulation and verisimilar misrepresentation. Moreover, the glove, so to speak, reappears, for Frank literally places himself between the two women to keep Emma from reading Jane's facial expressions. When, later, in his letter to Mrs. Weston, Churchill insists on his "likeness" with Emma, it is already apparent that Emma has learned to recognize the difference between private aesthetic play and visual or verbal strategies that impinge directly on life. Such aesthetic play is sterile if amusing, for it entoils one in self-enclosed repetitions of the sort he accuses Mrs. Elton of, the "vulgarity of needless repetition" that is the product of any univocality, whether mannered or monstrous.

Yet Emma cooperates with Churchill's aesthetic play with Jane Fairfax once more, following her engagement to Knightley.[16] In volume 3, chapter 18, Emma thinks that Knightley is superior to Churchill and, hence, a more appropriate husband; yet, just as he has distanced her "woman's speech" from himself, she maintains a verbal space, despite her thought that the time for "disguise, equivocation, mystery" is nearly over (328). Whether or not her private, ironic conversation with Frank in a drawing room is her last such collaboration, the way she engages in it points to her need for an autonomous space, whose tension with Knightley's morality is key to social harmony and personal narrative. At the center of this gap is a degree of noncommunication, partly allowed, indeed, by Knightley (Harriet's particulars), but partly and privately created by Emma as a redoubt for the aesthetic autonomy of which Knightley is suspicious. The withholding of language is as important to meaning as its generation: to tell Knightley about Harriet's infatuation for him might lower his estimation of her. Moreover, the Mr. Elton-like celerity with which the girl shifts from this infatuation to matrimonial "love" for Robert Martin calls into question Knightley's own matchmaking competency.[17] "Disguise, equivocation, mystery" have been central to Emma's practice, and there is no reason to believe that she abandons it entirely. Thus, she collaborates with Churchill in raising Jane to an idealized aesthetic field, parodying the objective language of masculine aesthetics, much as Donwell Abbey's masculine artifice appropriates the feminine to cover (without fully concealing) the power that underlies it. In Churchill's encomium, aesthetic discourse is distanced in a nearly private irony not unlike Jane Eyre's towards the "Grecian" attributes of Blanche Ingram and Rosamond Oliver:

> Did you ever see such a skin?—such smoothness! such delicacy!—and yet without being actually fair. One cannot call her fair. It is a most uncommon complexion, with her dark eye-lashes and hair—a most distinguishing complexion!—So peculiarly the lady in it.—Just colour enough for beauty. (330)

Civilization, it is said, is built on lies; and fiction, Carlyle notes, is lies. Emma's statement that she has "always admired" Jane's complexion is contradicted by an earlier statement that it wanted color, and she "found fault with her for being so pale." The object raised in the aesthetic field, in other words, is a congeries of lies. In Frank's aesthetic distancing the central problem of realism is evident and merely amplified by the simplistic, univocal neo-Kantean aesthetics that passes for one variety of aesthetic meaning. The neoclassical poet, as Imlac suggests, seeks to discover the universal, that is, the likeness among all (or at least some) humans. The realist, on the other hand, seeks representation through particulars, through which we possibly may be able to draw universal meanings—or perhaps not. So connected is the universal with masculine power and discourse that it is necessary to subvert it to conserve oneself, as here; it must be acknowledged yet distanced. Thus, Emma's hesitations to finish likenesses is connected with both realistic discourse and the problem of feminine autonomy in a masculine world. She and Frank create a likeness between Jane and an angel; Emma also discerns some likeness between her and Frank, though this is not a likeness that threatens her, for he, too, will now be distanced:

> I am sure it was a source of high entertainment to you, to feel that you were taking us all in.—Perhaps I am the readier to suspect, because, to tell you the truth, I think it might have been some amusement to myself in the same situation. I think there is a little likeness between us. (330)

If feeling and sympathy are necessary to social intercourse, so too are the tensions between secrecy and disclosure that render language supple and life interesting. Necessary to Emma and to the novel is the play of likenesses and unlikenesses that shift appearance and reality, the masculine and the feminine, in ways that neither obscure nor render completely palpable the nuances of language or the system of communication on which society and the novel subsist.

Like Burke, Austen was aware of the fictive strategies people deploy to organize life. But she more successfully distances the real through an idyllic form whose self-sufficiency is radically questioned by Brontë and Dickens. Emma Woodhouse perpetuates fictional strategies that enable her privately to evade the moral and aesthetic closure, but the private-public dichotomy that Austen presents, and almost closes seamlessly by the novel's end, points to a gap between experience and its recreation essential to realism, through which meaning is posited through the matrix of language. Through the tension between the moral and the aesthetic as they engage the visual, the spoken, and the acted, a possibility of social representation exists, but in Austen's case, on a limited canvas in which both chaos and providential orders are radically delimited in ways not open to writers like Brontë, Dickens, and Conrad.

3

Frankenstein and Aesthetic Decay

When Robert Walton first sees the monster in Mary Shelley's *Franken-stein*, he cannot "find words" to communicate the "something so scaring and unearthly in his ugliness."[1] But he stops short of Frankenstein's pet-rifying revulsion towards the horrible that silences speech (257). Behind the nightmare visitation of the "demoniacal corpse" (102) is the center, the source of animation, where speech and art break down. A daemonic Medusa (a "feminine" monster given the appearance of masculinity), constructed of parts whose individual "beauty" and "proportion" create a ghastly whole (101), the monster symbolizes the disintegration of beauty into a horror that dream and vision are unable to evade. The descriptive and narrative lacunae of *Frankenstein* are essential to its meaning: Vic-tor's search, like those of Walton and the monster, is to know and control origins, which are precariously generated at aporias that bring either progress or Medusa-petrifaction. This drive leads Victor to the uncreation of self in a series of repetitions, as "ardent" ambition gives way to pas-sive mania and rage, and the capacity to read signs breaks down in the Arctic north. Wishing to stabilize identity and control the past, he ani-mates a fleshly sign at odds with his intention, which leaves him with "breathless horror and disgust" (101). The monster's form was supposed to be beautiful, yet it is a "filthy type" of Victor's own humanity (172), at once mortal and "not even of the same nature as man" (162). It symbol-izes his inability to create beneficent illusions from the paradoxes of existence. Victor's science is but a mask to cover death.[2]

Shelley's anxiety towards art, signaled repeatedly in her 1831 "Author's Introduction" (e.g., "I bid my hideous progeny go forth and prosper" [56]), centers on the fear of the blankness that cancels the capacity for metaphorical and visual invention. At first, when she began *"to think of a story"* (53) she felt a "blank incapability of invention" (54).

However, unlike the monster, who, in tracing his origins, sees only "a blot, a blind vacancy in which I distinguished nothing" (163), Mary Shelley recalls being able to translate a waking dream-*frisson* into vision. The "yellow, watery, but speculative eyes" (55), projected onto plot and text, freed her imagination from social and gender constraints:

> My imagination, unbidden, possessed and guided me, gifting the successive images that arose in my mind with a vividness far beyond the usual bounds of reverie. I saw—with shut eyes, but acute mental vision—I saw the pale student of unhallowed arts kneeling beside the thing he had put together. I saw the hideous phantasm of a man stretched out, and then, on the working of some powerful engine, show signs of life, and stir with an uneasy, half-vital motion. (54–55)

The emphasis on seeing is insistent. She stabilizes the horror by using "invention" to create meaning out of a "chaos" that at least contains inchoate materials. She uses the story of Columbus and his egg to suggest the "stable" path that she, too, creates:

> We are continually reminded of the story of Columbus and his egg. Invention consists in the capacity of seizing on the capabilities of a subject; and in the power of moulding and fashioning ideas suggested to it. (54)

The thrill of fear, of discovery, of story, at once evokes and distances chaos; it arises not from "blank incapacity" but from "dark, shapeless substances" (54). Chaos is the palpable, if unorganized, material over which control is possible, while the "blank" void generates only a freezing horror. Victor, the projected masculine ego, explores beyond substance and subject to death and vacancy, pursuing the "type" of himself, the sign of the unspeakable whose creation stops art and generates rage. Mary Shelley projects this horror beyond herself in multiple narratives that, like the allegorical hand with which Virgil covers Dante's eyes in the *Inferno*, enable her to survive the telling. The monster's narrative is enclosed in Victor's, and Victor's in Robert Walton's letters. Further distancing is effected by her "Author's Introduction" and "Preface" and by the 1831 revised edition itself.

Frankenstein penetrates nature's secrets to find reassurance and to soothe his anxiety about change; he paradoxically seeks to create life in order to end the need for progress. Yet his creation of a daemonic double merely redoubles his sense of life's instability. His Faustian quest to attain absolute knowledge fails because, by denying the feminine, he alienates himself from life and attaches himself to a fictional nature whose secrets, he believes, can be rationally known.

While Elizabeth Lavenza finds "admiration and delight" in the "magnificent appearances of things" (81), Victor is driven to seek the "things" themselves, pursue the secret of life to its origin, and reenact the Creation of God the Father. Yet the price of his pursuit is an abyss, beyond even the fairy tales of science, which renders impossible what Nietzsche terms a "middle world" of art that creates joy out of dejection.[3] The vital tensions between Edenic unity and division, meaning and nonmeaning, art and science, break down. Stripped of metaphor, life becomes a silence that "ends the disparity between word and life,"[4] prior to which rage represents a final bulwark. Unlike Conrad's Marlow in *Heart of Darkness*, Frankenstein finally glimpses the heart of silence that cancels meaning, while his human-inhuman type of the decaying logos, having told his story of alienation and origins in a pocket full of laboratory notes (171), systematically destroys his creator's world.

Henry Clerval, Frankenstein tells Walton, was drawn to "books of chivalry and romance" and "the moral relations of things" (82). That is, his friend approached life through art and the imagination. As a student at Ingolstadt, Clerval symbolically pursues origins in studying Oriental languages. Elizabeth, too, sister, "cousin," and sacrificial bride, was there to "subdue me to a semblance of her own gentleness" (83). Victor's "enthusiasm" contrasts with their grounding of the beautiful in moral sympathy. But "ardour" repudiates limited fictions for goals that obviate the possibility of incorporating the like-unlike tension, or what the monster calls finding himself "similar yet at the same time strangely unlike to the beings concerning whom I read and to whose conversation I was a listener" (170). For ambition, the pursuit of mastery and univocal appropriation, draws Frankenstein to the decaying sign behind which lurks death and nonmeaning, against which he desperately constructs fictions of escape and pursuit, story and silence. In the end, Victor can only warn Walton to "seek happiness in tranquillity and avoid ambition" (256). Between nature and "the author at once of my existence and of its unspeakable torments" (258) are the empty spaces that cannot generate fictional reassurances that progress is not merely the repetition of collapsing meanings that reach in the dream state beyond the beloved's body, beyond "the horrors of my secret toil" (98), towards the horror itself, the Medusa "grave worms" that reduce language to silence and vision to blankness.

Significantly, Frankenstein is better able to describe his readings of Cornelius Agrippa, Paracelsus, and Albertus Magnus than his experiments (beyond books and the ken of his mentors Krempe and Waldman) to "examine the causes of life" that entail "recourse to death" (95). As a youth, his pursuit of the imaginative alchemists to "the threshold of real knowledge" (86) kept his monomania within analogical bounds. Though imbued with a "fervent longing to penetrate the secrets of nature" (84), he has not yet experienced the father's criticism that strips his ambitions of all aesthetic restraint. When Alphonse dismisses Cornelius Agrippa as "sad trash" (83) without providing anything with which to replace him, the cycle of disillusionment with increasingly unstable fictions commences. The three alchemists were, Frankenstein recalls, "the lords of my imagination" (85). The "dreams of forgotten alchemists" explored nature yet hid its "mysteries" behind imaginative veils. The "untaught peasant" and the "most learned philosopher" were alike in their childlike wonder. Newton, for instance, "is said to have avowed that he felt like a child picking up shells beside the great and unexplored ocean of truth" (84). Even Newton approached truth through analogy:

> The untaught peasant beheld the elements around him and was acquainted with their practical uses. The most learned philosopher knew little more. He had partially unveiled the face of Nature, but her immortal lineaments were still a wonder and a mystery. He might dissect, anatomize, and give names; but, not to speak of a final cause, causes in their secondary and tertiary grades were utterly unknown to him. (84)

However, following his father's dismissal, "electricity and galvanism" seem more real as the oak disappears in "the dazzling light" with nothing remaining but "a blasted stump" (85). Disillusionment with fiction turns into a fascination with violence. Yet, instead of turning immediately to modern science, Frankenstein, "by some fatality," leaves off his studies, rejecting "natural history and all its progeny as a deformed and abortive creation" (86). He seeks to distance himself from "accustomed" and modern science alike, disdaining the latter as incapable of stepping "within the threshhold of real knowledge" (86). This, Victor tells Walton, was "the last effort made by the spirit of preservation to avert the storm that was even then hanging in the stars and ready to envelope me" (86).

Victor's contrasting attitudes towards Krempe and Waldman, his university professors, illustrate his need for a father figure who can provide the fictions Alphonse would not. While Krempe gruffly dismisses the alchemists, Waldman reassures him by placing Cornelius Agrippa and Paracelsus within an organic process of which modern science is the beneficiary: "The labours of men of genius, however erroneously directed, scarcely ever fail in ultimately turning to the solid advantage of mankind" (93). Victor's reactions to his teachers are essentially aesthetic. He focuses on Krempe's "uncouth" appearance (90), while the more supportive Waldman, who praises "the astonishing progress I had made in the sciences" (111), seems benevolent, his voice "the sweetest I had ever heard" (91).

Nature, however, soon collapses into a "conception" just short of vacancy, for the monster that he creates mocks scientific optimism as just another glittering fiction, thus destroying Frankenstein's belief that he can find objective meaning and substitute his authorship for the absent father's. His desire to know nature leads him beyond the signs that cover death. Just as nature gives way to the conception, the unspeakable that freezes language and volition (119), so the desire to penetrate mystery leads to the projection of horror onto life.

The "demoniacal corpse" seems to be "a thing such as even Dante could not have conceived" (102). But in the *Inferno*, which Frankenstein has in mind, Dante-the-pilgrim's eyes are covered by the veil of art, Virgil's hands, as the soul (and pen) transfixing Medusa passes: here the "veil of the strange verses that hides the doctrine" is the final metaphorical defense against the thing that cancels language.[5] Indeed, the monster becomes a parodic Virgil protecting Victor from the unspeakable when, just prior to telling his story, he covers his creator's eyes: "'Thus I relieve thee, my creator,' he said, and placed his hated hands before my eyes, which I flung from me with violence" (143). Unlike Dante the pilgrim, Victor is driven to view the horror which he also wishes to escape and destroy.

In chapter 5, Victor recalls how he wanted to infuse life "into an inanimate body" to create a sort of human artwork. But the monster's beautiful features, once animated, merely accentuate the pollution they were intended to cover:

> His limbs were in proportion, and I had selected his features as beautiful. Beautiful! Great God! His yellow skin scarcely covered the work of muscles and arteries beneath; his hair was of a lustrous black, and flowing; his teeth of pearly whiteness; but these luxuriances only formed a more horrid contrast with his watery eyes, that seemed almost of the same colour as the dun-white sockets in which they were set, his shrivelled complexion and straight black lips. (101)

This illustrates Victor's inability to create beauty out of particulars. Verisimilitude is impossible; stability is mocked by decaying forms and an incapacity to connect words to things. The masculine body onto whom Victor tries to project feminine proportion horrifically displays the mutilation the beauty was meant to conceal. Victor's subsequent refusal to complete the assembly of parts for a female mate points to his frustration at being unable to control his creation, above all the reproduction he would unleash in the female freed from all constraint.

"In creating the monster," George Levine writes, "Frankenstein tries to name nature and thus control it."[6] But his enthusiasm to discover the principle of life takes him out of nature and into an isolation that affords his life a perverse stability. Edenic unity with its perpetual springtime is parodied in his abandonment of nature for a solipsistic construct. He has fled "passion and transitory desire" (99), friendship, family, and the love of woman:

> Winter, spring, and summer passed away during my labours; but I did not watch the blossom or the expanding leaves—sights which before always yielded me supreme delight—so deeply was I engrossed in my occupation. The leaves of that year had withered before my work drew to a close, and now every day showed me more plainly how well I had succeeded. (99–100)

Victor's scientific pursuit apparently is free of the dross of shadow, the chimerical, and the metaphorical. He seeks the real knowledge beyond naming that replaces what Krempe terms "exploded systems and useless names" (90). The scientific Dark Night of the Soul spent in "vaults and charnel houses" (95), reconstructing inanimate matter, will bestow animation and create joy for the creator. But Frankenstein's Apollonian project is a failure; he discards myth and mystery for a knowledge that brings not control but its opposite, and releases the monster whose violence is the last instinctive defense before blankness. Sherwin calls Frankenstein "an overreacting, moralizing misreader, rather like the self-blinded ego that travesties the id."[7] Central to his personality is the fear that if he interprets existence correctly its hieroglyphs will mean nothing.

Robert Walton stops short of viewing the polluted secrets of the monster, whom he first sees up close with "his vast hand ... extended, in colour and apparent texture like that of a mummy" (257). His inability to find words to describe the monster illustrates his saving inability to pursue mystery to collapse of language. Like Tulkinghorn's allegorical Roman in *Bleak House*, the pointing hand mocks meaning. The monster points at his father's corpse, the logos and word canceling each other in death. Walton's voyage of discovery parallels Frankenstein's scientific monomania, but he stops short of the absolute. The "country of eternal light" (59) he seeks, he writes his sister, originated in Uncle Thomas's library, where travel literature whetted his appetite. So, like Victor (and Lydgate in Eliot's *Middlemarch*), he comes to life via fiction and is tempted to move beyond literature to more direct engagements with knowledge. His scientific quest, like Victor's, is influenced perversely by the father's forbidding word, the "dying injunction" that "had forbidden my uncle to allow me to embark in a seafaring life" (60). Literature offered a vision of paradise that might be recreated through the poetic imagination. Worldly ambitions faded when, reading poetry, he experienced "effusions" that "entranced" his soul and "lifted it to heaven" (60). But his desire for physical exploration returned all the more strongly with his failure as a poet. He writes his sister:

> I also became a poet and for one year lived in a Paradise of my own creation; I imagined that I also might obtain a niche in the temple where the names of Homer and Shakespeare are consecrated. You are well acquainted with my failure and how heavily I bore the disappointment. (60)

The impulse to conquer nature arises from a disillusionment with art. Having failed to find his idyllic paradise in poetry, he seeks instead a physical region of "beauty and delight" (59). Loss and failure motivate him to regain the Edenic unity he momentarily glimpsed in literature but failed to create for himself. His quest to the polar regions is doomed to failure, for he seeks what only can be found within. The physical "land surpassing in wonders and in beauty every region hitherto discovered on the habitable globe" (59) is, like the paradise he pursued as a poet, a fictional construct, whose reality is interminable water and the ice that nearly crushes the ship and helps unleash his sailors' mutinous rage (252). Ironically, by accepting failure and limitation, he succeeds in dashing "the cup" from his lips and avoiding the "furies" that possess Frankenstein. Walton returns home with the narrative, amended by Frankenstein, who "would not that a mutilated one should go down to posterity" (249).

Not having thought through his usurpation of God and woman in creating a sentient being, Victor finds that reality dissolves as the "wildest dreams" devour the beneficent illusions that create, in Walton's words, "a love for the marvellous, a belief in the marvellous" (66), and hence make life bearable. As Burke and George Eliot suggest in different ways, the "marvellous" must remain mysterious. Victor's desire for (as Walton puts it) "penetration into the causes of things" (74), is a destructive assault on appearance whose issues are things that reveal the unbearable nonreality of the marvelous. The danger in dissecting the "marvellous," Burke suggests, is a devastating loss of order and progress, which are grounded in pious fictions. Mysterious spaces must be maintained and respected. But if God becomes His inverse, a void, this is impossible. Mary Shelley is even closer to the abyss than Burke is in the *Reflections*.

In his enthusiasm for scientific process, Frankenstein is sure that intention and product, sign and signifier, will be one and the same.

However, once he has "finished, the beauty of the dream vanished" (101). He constructs an animated human sign at odds with itself (at once Adam, Eve, and Satan, "the same nature as man" yet Victor's "filthy type" [162,172]). Frankenstein's beautiful illusion of finality gives way to the horror that underlies a scientific process that, up to now, has upheld illusion rather than radically questioned it. He creates life, but is mistaken in thinking he can achieve certitude by supplanting God. In his nightmare in chapter 5, Frankenstein experiences "wildest dreams" that coalesce into the hellish sight of the monster, whose ugliness reminds him of the instability he sought to regulate:

> I thought I saw Elizabeth, in the bloom of health, walking in the streets of Ingolstadt. Delighted and surprized, I embraced her, but as I imprinted the first kiss on her lips, they became livid with the hue of death; her features appeared to change, and I thought that I held the corpse of my dead mother in my arms; a shroud enveloped her form, and I saw the grave-worms crawling in the folds of the flannel. I started from my sleep with horror; a cold dew covered my forehead, my teeth chattered, and every limb became convulsed; when, by the dim and yellow light of the moon, as it forced its way through the window shutters, I beheld the wretch—the miserable monster whom I had created. He held up the curtain of the bed; and his eyes, if eyes they may be called, were fixed on me. His jaws opened, and he muttered some inarticulate sounds, while a grin wrinkled his cheeks. (102)

Victor's transfixed horror is counterpointed by the "mummy's" "inarticulate sounds" and pointing hand, a parody of symbolic artistic expression that now is broken as language is overwhelmed by hellish dreams (102). In his dream, Victor witnesses something resembling the birthing process he has tried to appropriate. The moon, traditionally associated with the imagination, mental instability, and the feminine, lights the way to his vision of the monster, whose appearance, like the transformation of the beautiful woman, Elizabeth, into the mother and then the "grave-worms," points to his association of woman with instability, ugliness, and death. Having sought stability through the exclusion of the feminine, whose ornamentation he scavenges to prettify his creation, he must confront a mocking *Doppelgänger* that reifies the feminine as decay and death, the inverse of the beautiful that Frankenstein desperately seeks to retrieve by marrying Elizabeth. The monster's jaws open, as if to devour his creator in a primordial womb, but "inarticulate words" emerge, the parodic embodiments of his failed pursuit of a new epistemology: instead of beauty and Elysium, he has found a venue into devouring passion, the chthonic realm associated, in *The Aeneid*, with serpents, passions, and the feminine, where Dido will journey to "Call up the spirits of deep Night" and "annihilate all vestige of the man, / Vile as he is." [8]

Yet, during the illness that follows this, Victor seems to reenter nature's flow. Nursed by Henry Clerval, he reestablishes human connections. Springtime has arrived and everything seems reborn (114), so that he is "undisturbed by thoughts" (114) that previously abstracted him from life to the degree that he was "insensible to the charms of nature" (98) and forgetful of his friends (99):

> A serene sky and verdant fields filled me with ecstasy. The present season was indeed divine: the flowers of spring bloomed in the hedges, while those of summer were already in bud. I was undisturbed by thoughts which during the preceding year had pressed upon me, notwithstanding my endeavors to throw them off, with an invincible burden. (114)

However, this is all a delusion. Henceforth his existence is a series of desperate maneuvers to counter deathly terror with pleasing illusions of an organic, regenerative, and divine nature, which inexorably turn into terror, the consequence (to cite Jean Paul on "poetic nihilism") of creating a "bond" by tearing off the "bandage" of one's wounds. [9]

Victor's joy evaporates upon the news from Alphonse that William has been murdered. Now he turns from his construct of nature as beauty to a wish to find meaning—and lose himself—in Alpine sublimity. He tried to control the principle of life; now, like Dorian Gray, he seeks to escape memory and responsibility for his acts. But he merely discovers the mirror image of his suppressed rage as the monster emerges from the natural hieroglyph through which he hoped to celebrate Williams's departed soul and discover meaning in his death:

> While I watched the tempest, so beautiful yet terrific, I wandered on with a hasty step. This noble war in the sky elevated my spirits; I clasped my hands and exclaimed aloud, 'William, dear angel! This is thy funeral, this thy dirge!' As I said these words, I perceived in the gloom a figure which stole from behind a clump of trees near me; I stood fixed, gazing intently; I could not be mistaken. A flash of lightning illuminated the object and discovered its shape plainly to me; its gigantic stature, and the deformity of its aspect, more hideous than belongs to humanity, instantly informed me that it was the wretch, the filthy daemon to whom I had given life. What did he there? Could he be (I shuddered at the conception) the murderer of my brother? (119)

His guilt arises from a terrible but unacknowledged identification with his progeny. Behind nature's apparent beauty and sublimity there is rage, then emptiness. Victor tries to organize his surroundings, much as

Marlow does in his more flexible impressions of the jungle in *Heart of Darkness*. But this is to no avail, for these are little more than mental flailings against the collapse of external order, which he has dressed up as meaning. What emerges from the tempest is the decaying symbol of life's instability, the "filthy daemon to whom I had given life," whose reduction to imprecatory terms like "wretch" reflects the scientist's growing imaginative failure. Mont Blanc, the Jura, and the Mole offer neither univocal nor ambiguous reassurances like those in Percy Shelley's "Mont Blanc," which celebrates the mind's capacity to organize creatively "The everlasting universe of things" (ll. 1–2), while nature retains a mysterious space where faith and doubt are both possible.

At home for William's funeral, Frankenstein is drawn to his mother's picture, below which is his brother's miniature:

> I gazed on the picture of my mother which stood over the mantelpiece. It was a historical subject, painted at my father's desire, and represented Caroline Beaufort in an agony of despair, kneeling by the coffin of her dead father. Her garb was rustic and her cheek pale, but there was an air of dignity and beauty that hardly permitted the sentiment of pity. (121)

But William's miniature makes him weep. By weeping, Frankenstein evades his complicity in William's death through sentimentality. Meanwhile, the monster frames Justine Moritz, planting the mother's portrait on her; this confirms Frankenstein's growing suspicion that all appearances merely conceal horror.

The horrific deformities Frankenstein releases cannot be organized through art or language. They extend everywhere, articulated into spectral appearance whenever he thinks he has gained some control over experience. After a time, however, the monster is also his substitute for empirical meaning. Hence his conclusion that the monster's presence verifies that he is William's murderer: "I could not doubt it. The mere presence of the idea was an irresistible proof of the fact" (119). He subordinates fact to idea now that he no longer can control the former. The monster's creation is essentially the projection of an idea onto parts assembled for that purpose. Alone they have no purpose. Their nature is merely to rot further, reentering the impersonal natural process.

Yet Frankenstein clings to the idea that life can be organized aesthetically. He sees Henry as "the image of my former self" (199). His friend prepares to apply his knowledge to organize a fragmentary subcontinent, India, where he will "materially" assist "the progress of European colonization and trade" (199). Like Conrad and, in a radically different way, Kipling, Mary Shelley connects scientific ambition with the impulse to impose aesthetic and material control over the foreign unknown. But to accomplish this, one must organize the past to give the present the appearance of purpose; similarly, the history of the colonized country must be reinvented, in this instance with an orientalism defined according to German academic Romantic criteria, for the past is also a disorganized Other that threatens to overpower the psyche. To redeem us, history must be recreated and made palatable. The past is the last redoubt of redemptive capacity, as William Wordsworth recognized, for in a universe where God is absent and all are orphans, it becomes the variable space on which one can create protean myths of control over, and transcendence of, the self.

In chapter 18, Frankenstein quotes Wordsworth's "Tintern Abbey" to afford the dead Clerval an inviolability through memory:

> And where does he now exist? Is this gentle and lovely being lost forever? Has this mind, so replete with ideas, imaginations fanciful and magnificent, which formed a world, whose existence depended on the life of its creator— has this mind perished? Does it now only exist in my memory? No, it is not thus; your form so divinely wrought, and beaming with beauty, has decayed, but your spirit still visits and consoles your unhappy friend. (197)

Or so he hopes. Clerval represents Victor's feeling "That had no need of a remoter charm, / By thought supplied, or any interest / Unborrowed from the eye" (197). His memory of Clerval rests upon an idealized nature that does not endanger him with the collapse of his identity into the circumambient flux. Frankenstein hopes that Clerval's mind exists not only as a biochemical memory but as a spiritual presence. He hopes that the spirit that visits his memory is independent of Henry's mind *in* his memory, which must decay with the brain cells that contain it. He hopes there is a reality to the spiritual—that it is not, like memory, an evanescent thing as mortal as its human vessels. Yet Victor immediately tells Walton that his "gush of sorrow" is merely "ineffectual words" (197), a pathetic attempt to substantiate a past that is "a frightful dream" (223) whose remembrance evokes "mad enthusiasm" and "a thousand objects" that scare him (223). Laudanum, the agent of forgetfulness, succeeds his Romantic enthusiasm, much as opium offers Dorian Gray a specious cover for memories he can neither prettify nor bury.

During his trip through England, Victor seeks aesthetic stability in an Oxford where "the spirit of elder days found a dwelling." Amidst the violent struggles of the Civil War of the 1640s, as Charles I fought Oliver Cromwell, the city represented loyalty and connection:

This city had remained faithful to him, after the whole nation had forsaken his cause to join the standard of Parliament and liberty. The memory of that unfortunate king and his companions, the amiable Falkland, the insolent Goring, his queen, and son, gave a peculiar interest to every part of the city which they might be supposed to have inhabited. (200–201)

He is attracted to Oxford's association with Hampden and Charles I, whose defeat offers analogical hope that his own life may have purpose in some broader historical context of which he is unaware. From suffering comes transcendence, after all, and amidst apparent failure may be the seeds of some great future success. Yet this offers little sustenance; it is but another fiction whose purpose is to enable him to "shake off" his chains before inevitably he sinks again, "trembling and hopeless, into my miserable self" (201). Victor is impelled to contrast this "miserable self" with the "divine ideas of liberty and self-sacrifice of which these sights were but the monuments and remembrancers" (201). In these monuments are the stable metaphors of struggle and defeat that time cannot erase; they affirm the efforts of men who may have felt as miserable as he. He cannot find stable beauty and proportion in his creation or in nature, but in Oxford's artifacts that memorialize the "fair and fatal king" whose death made life grow "sublime," to cite Lionel Johnson's poem, he seeks the victory of art over death. He wants his history somehow to be aesthetic and autonomous, so that his soul, like the Isis, which reflects the "majestic assemblage of towers, and spires, and domes, embosomed among aged trees," can attain a simulacrum of the unity between art, time, and nature that his scientific endeavor has not accomplished, something like the unity Coleridge evokes in "the shadow of the dome of pleasure" that "floated midway on the waves" in "Kubla Khan." Only he remains a stranger and cannot forget the horror for which he is responsible. His enjoyment is "embittered both by the memory of the past and the anticipation of the future." Once again he is reminded of the illusoriness of process and organicism.

Clerval's murder is the monster's revenge for Frankenstein's destruction of the partially completed female who "might become ten thousand times more malignant than her mate and delight, for its own sake, in murder and wretchedness" (206). He is near the end of his hope that he can stabilize his existence. Still, to deny this, he tries to hide his work:

The remains of the half-finished creature, whom I had destroyed, lay scattered on the floor, and I almost felt as if I had mangled the living flesh of a human being. I paused to collect myself and then entered the chamber. With trembling hand I conveyed the instruments out of the room, but I reflected

that I ought not to leave the relics of my work to excite the horror and
suspicion of the peasants. (211)

He buries the parts at sea, but to no avail.

In marrying Elizabeth, he seeks not so much mental repose as a
meaning derived from projecting the "airy dreams of futurity" onto
another. This is egoism masquerading as sympathy. Victor tries to create
the illusion of stability in the idealized female, who must be protected
from the horrific knowledge symbolized by the discarded body parts of
the daemonic Eve:

> Sweet and beloved Elizabeth! I read and reread her letter, and some softened
> feelings stole into my heart and dared to whisper paradisiacal dreams of love
> and joy; but the apple was already eaten, and the angel's arm bared to drive
> me from all hope. Yet I would die to make her happy. (228)

He recalls the monster's promise to "be with you on your wedding-night"
(209) but illogically concludes that the danger is to him, not to Elizabeth.
His complicity in Elizabeth's murder is evident in his leaving her alone
as if to await the "shrill and dreadful scream" that signals her
strangulation.

Like his creator, the monster is unable to discover a consistent fiction
that renders life bearable. His first view of himself in a "transparent
pool" (155), unlike Eve's view of herself in the scene in *Paradise Lost* 4
on which it is based, sets up a contrast with the "perfect forms of my
cottagers—their grace, beauty, and delicate complexions" (155), for he
does not possess the "writing" that enables him imaginatively to distance
himself from the monster reflected there; and when he learns to read, his
books merely confirm the alienated "bitterest sensations of despondence
and alienation." He learns spoken language from the De Laceys before he
experiences emotional connections:

> This was indeed a godlike science, and I ardently desired to become
> acquainted with it. But I was baffled in every attempt I made for this purpose.
> Their pronunciation was quick, and the words they uttered, not having any
> apparent connection with visible objects, I was unable to discover any clue by
> which I could unravel the mystery of their reference. By great application,
> however, and after having remained during the space of several revolutions of
> the moon in my hovel, I discovered the names that were given to some of the
> most familiar objects of discourse. (154)

The monster is almost immediately aware of the contrast between words
and things, and consequently finds it all the more difficult to lose himself

in pleasing fictions. In *Bleak House,* Dickens's Esther Summerson succeeds in turning the experience of seeing her disease-scarred and
"strange" face into a renewed happiness among those she loves. However, Mary Shelley's monster has no such egress. Failing to find human
companionship or transcendental affirmation, he must define himself
through his reading and observation. Yet the "godlike science" (154),
language, comes to him separated from nature, for he learns it through a
voyeuristic observation that merely engages him in a pleasing manipulation of appearances that finally cannot conceal his hideousness from him.

The works that most influence him are Plutarch's *Lives,* Goethe's
Sorrows of Young Werther, and Milton's *Paradise Lost*. He misinterprets
Goethe's Werther as "a more divine being than I had ever beheld or
imagined." He is "inclined towards the opinions of the hero," whose
suicide he did not "precisely" understand (170). A naive reader unable to
separate himself from the work, he is unable to regard the novel (as
Goethe did) as a means of purging, not defining, obsessive character
traits. Literature seems to offer an alternative to the disconnections
between spoken words and things. Yet this is to mistake art for life. The
most influential work he reads, *Paradise Lost*, merely reinforces his
inability to integrate the parts from which Victor created him. His
likeness with Adam, for instance, is overshadowed by his awareness of
how different they are:

> He had come forth from the hands of God a perfect creature, happy and
> prosperous, guarded by the especial care of his Creator; he was allowed to
> converse with and acquire knowledge from beings of a superior nature, but I
> was wretched, helpless, and alone. (171)

Speaking with God and the angels, Adam before his Fall felt no
divergence between language and nature. Hence, the monster sees Satan
as "the fitter emblem" of his condition. Yet Frankenstein's scientific
papers, like the monster's terrible reflection in the pool, point to the
ungiven name that best characterizes his divided personality: Eve. His
"accursed origin" is in body parts taken from others, a fact he learns yet
cannot directly state, choosing instead to term his creation a "series of
disgusting circumstances" (171): in Victor's journal the hope that the
written text can generate identity dies, for the scientist's language renders
his creation's horrors "indelible" (171).

In transforming Safie and the De Lacey family into a romance with a
happy ending, the monster also confuses life with art. Agatha's music
produces "sounds sweeter than the thrush or the nightingale. It was a
lovely sight" (149). Projecting himself as a providential artist, he

provides them with food and wood, as if to reassure himself that there must be an invisible hand shaping his destiny as well. But his happy ending collapses when he tries to introduce himself as a character, initially with success with the blind De Lacey, but with disaster when Felix, Safie, and Agatha see him and flee.

He cannot conceal the death and decay that comprise his entire being in others' eyes.[10] He never can avoid the dissolution of identity over which humans build pleasing and limiting (but also renovative) fictions; a walking parody of the aesthetic, he reminds people of the meaninglessness of the fictional escapes they pursue. He reminds them that what Nietzsche calls the "intense longing for illusion"[11] offers no sustenance because, like the gods of ancient Greece, its meaning is broken. Beauty and proportion no longer conceal the discrete particularities, the "muscles and arteries beneath" (101). Unlike George Eliot, Shelley doubts that particulars can be combined to create a believable illusion. This is evident in the monster's rage at his reduction to a hideousness constructed of particulars that comprise decay rather than beauty. His misreadings of Goethe and Milton are pathetic attempts to create a stable selfhood: he pursues representations that confirm his misery and alienation. In fluctuating among literary and historical characters, he reveals the instability at the core of his desperately grasped fictional appropriations.

In his fateful encounter with William in chapter 16, the monster attempts once more to discover certitude through a pleasing illusion, the idea of the child united with nature and ignorant of socially conditioned prejudices:

> At this time a slight sleep relieved me from the pain of reflection, which was disturbed by the approach of a beautiful child, who came running into the recess I had chosen, with all the sportiveness of infancy. Suddenly, as I gazed on him, an idea seized me that this little creature was unprejudiced and had lived too short a time to have imbibed a horror of deformity. If, therefore, I could seize him and educate him as my companion and friend, I should not be so desolate in this peopled earth. (183)

Yet the "beautiful child" can appreciate only his form, and (recalling the monster's attempt to cover Victor's eyes) places his hands before his eyes to avoid the horror, having immediately recognized a "monster" and an "ugly wretch" who wishes to eat and tear him to pieces (183). Once William identifies himself, the monster grasps his throat "to silence him" (183), beginning a series of murders aimed at avenging his condition by destroying Victor's every self-valorizing fiction.

Walton only believes the monster is "real," not merely the "supernatural" emotion generated by an aesthetic stimulus, when the deadly, mummy-wrapped polluted sign appears. Prior to this, his credence is only partial, reified by the letters of Felix and Safie, but alternating wildly between assertions of "real existence" and the protoaesthetic "yet I am lost in surprize and admiration" (248–49). He has seen the monster's "apparition" at a distance, but the apparition (like the mummy wrappings) remains a perilous bulwark of meaning. Walton finds meaning in the "brother," Victor, whose benevolence "fills me with sympathy and compassion" (72). Belief, it seems, is created through sympathy, while solipsistic pursuit and flight destroy meaning. Victor cannot accept that the spirits who leave food for him are really the monster, who provides sustenance for Victor's homicidal-suicidal pursuit.

Yet the monster is more human than his monomaniacal creator. Just before he flees to seek death (or so he says), he declares:

> I shall no longer see the sun or stars or feel the winds play on my cheeks. Light, feeling, and sense will pass away; and in this condition must I find my happiness.

In the synaesthetic state from which he emerged into language, division, and alienation, he seeks rest and unity:

> Some years ago, when the images which this world affords first opened upon me, when I felt the cheering warmth of summer and heard the rustling of the leaves and the warbling of the birds, and these were all to me, I should have wept to die; now it is my only consolation. (260)

Frankenstein is incapable of such lyricism. Now his creation seeks the end of all illusions. Death no longer transfixes his mind or renders it incapable of metaphorical assurances. Frankenstein penetrated nature to control life's secret and grasp symbolic finality; he was the scientist as Medusa. He transfixed himself, but the monster, embracing death rather than fleeing it, is able for a brief moment to experience lyrical union with a remembered nature. Now he accepts the incoherence inherent in human identity, with its "transcendent visions" and rage (259).

4

Jane Eyre: Vision and Aesthetic Control

In Charlotte Brontë's *Jane Eyre,* we find the close proximity of the monstrous and its inverse in St. John Rivers, with his flight from history and experience into rigid forms of conduct. The human need, in Hayden White's words about Nietzsche, to "flee from reality into a dream,"[1] arises from the inability to maintain a middle space in which emplotment and the experiential field are in creative, fluid interchange.[2] Michel de Certeau suggests that "writing is born of and treats of admitted doubt. ... It articulates the constantly initial fact that the subject is *never authorized* by a place."[3] Rosemary Bodenheimer suggests that Jane Eyre is imperiled by enclosure within others' narratives (e.g., Abbot's and Bessie's in chapter 3, Rochester's in chapter 19, and the innkeeper's in chapter 36), but is also the autobiographer whose story finally supplants theirs.[4] In trying to control her text and evade others' visual placements, Jane Eyre is constantly aware of her peril and of the fact that Christianity's oppressive anti-idyll, embodied in St. John Rivers, threatens her with "Medusan" transfixion no less than its more evident chthonic horrors like Bertha. Brontë stresses, like Shelley, the monstrosity of the ideal, whose whited sepulchre merely masks the thing from which escape is necessary in lingual activity that effaces, yet confirms through traces, the unspeakable from which fictions of identity and stability are created. Caught between renouncing and belonging, Jane must create meaning by arresting and effacing death, which is the purpose of history and fiction alike. She must create herself amidst emanations of the absent father and aesthetic-patriarchal discourses whose law, to cite Freud's interpretation of Michelangelo's *Moses,* extinguishes passion in favor of a "marmoreal monument."[5]

"Realism," George Levine writes, "was in part a denial that the excesses of the past could survive, except in occasional barbarous bursts of irrationality."[6] *Jane Eyre* is about the struggle to control such bursts (like Jane's "deep ire and desperate revolt" [59]) in the process of living life and representing it in autobiography. The author, like the historian, creates from the gap between present and past an interplay between truth and emplotment, experience and form. For Jane, as for Frankenstein and Marlow, what lies at the origin of experience, over which fictive origins are constructed, is something so terrible that even words like "thing" and "abyss" do not suffice but are merely domestications. It is necessary to create lingual fictions, which to some extent are escapes from reality. Similarly, the nineteenth-century realists create forms of meaning yet evade fixation in lingual structures. Nietzsche speaks of the need to recognize that all truths are "perversions of the original aesthetic impulse."[7] The author or autobiographer must create a matrix of words that at once offers venue to the horror yet continually recreates form and meaning, defeating the influences that would freeze truth into a form.

At the peripheries of society at the outset of her life, Jane Eyre perceives herself as a "thing" thwarted in its desire to create meaning at what John S. Nelson, discussing tropal structures, terms "the intersection among conception, perception, and imagination":[8]

I was a discord in Gateshead Hall; I was like nobody there; I had nothing in harmony with Mrs. Reed or her children, or her chosen vassalage. If they did not love me, in fact, as little did I love them. They were not bound to regard with affection a thing that could not sympathize with one amongst them; a heterogeneous thing, opposed to them in temperament, in capacity, in propensities; a useless thing, incapable of serving their interest, or adding to their pleasure; a noxious thing, cherishing the germs of indignation at their treatment, of contempt of their judgement.[9]

The repetition of "thing" in this passage points to a retrospective field over which, in the course of the autobiography, Jane constructs an identity despite the pressures of the abyss in one direction, univocal idealisms and moral injunctions on the other. The "thing" stands at the peripheries of differentiation, like Shelley's monster momentarily does at the intersection between synaesthetic unity and perception. But the perception of "thingness" is itself an act of historical retrieval, at the limits of language's metaphorical capacity. The way the Reeds treated her elicits not so much simultaneous self-definition as indignation and rage, passions related to the transfixing monster that must be domesticated in the production of identity.

Bertha represents the collapse of all fictions; she is a transfixing horror that cancels language and the imaginative. Collapsing the aporia from which meaning is created, she is stripped of all beautiful visual ornamentation; hence Rochester's impulsive need to dress Jane up when he pursues her. She reminds Jane of the "foul German spectre—the vampire" (311), which generates endlessly reenacted, but insatiable, desires.[10] The vampire's hypnotic gaze entrances one in a kind of stopped time in which all illusion of progress is lost: gaze, language, and action parody fluid realistic engagement with experience, while the creative interplay between image and its breaking and forgetting is replaced by a transfixed remembrance. Thus, Bertha functions much the same way the monster does in *Frankenstein*; moreover, her effects are akin to what we discover in Lord Dedlock or Miss Havisham, who are transfixed by pasts whose fictive emanations barely conceal death. Bertha's vampire-like "virile force" is really anterior to gender, unlike the parrying of gender barriers that enable Jane Eyre and Rochester to communicate, and Jane to subsume others' discourses within her own. Grace is the parodic emanation of Bertha, with whom Jane instinctively associates the latter's laughter and violence, for, as Virginia Woolf suggests, Jane Eyre, as she gazes at the landscape from the roof of Thornfield, is distracted by a laughter whose source she studiously ignores, in the attic and in herself. It is as if she cannot look until she can control the framing of her visual discourse, whose physical symbol is the door through which Bertha escapes to wreak havoc on Thornfield. When Jane, somewhere between sleep and waking, sees Bertha's bedimmed figure trying on her wedding apparel in the mirror, she indirectly gazes at monstrosity, as indeed she must prior to regulating her own discourse. As Woolf suggests, Bertha's laughter is linked with the rage that, underlying even the stripped "thing," is the absolute antitype to personal and literary production.[11] By reducing language to laughter, the madwoman creates an aural incoherence that adumbrates the visual horror and incoherence she displays. But how can Jane resist society's insistence on appearance and adornment without likewise become a hysteric? In *Beyond Good and Evil*, Nietzsche associates hysteria and degeneration with women who eschew cunning humility, adornment, and beauty.[12] Jane rejects the first and does not possess the second or third. Thus, she is in a dilemma: submission to society's rules suppresses the unspeakable yet, beyond a point, guarantees its eruption. The blurring of gender boundaries produces the sort of degeneration the bizarre Max Nordau later denounced, yet for Jane a controlled transgression is necessary. She must control her autobiography as she translates sight and experience into writing. Cast outside the beautiful, she must subvert it through ironic visual placement.

Later, as he courts her, Rochester wishes to ornament her with jewels, dress her up "like a doll," and mythologize her as "a second Danae." Jane

Eyre rejects such visual signs of his control; resisting his constricting "infinite series of waistcoats" (297), she would "rather be a *thing* than an angel" (291). Thus, she recalls the object to which she thinks she was reduced in the Reeds' eyes; moreover, she rejects his visual placement in favor of a plainer dress linked with her own "volume," the autobiographical realism towards which she works: "I'll wear nothing but my old Lowood frocks to the end of the chapter" (297).

Writing is born, de Certeau says, of death and "the invisible bloodstain whence the text is generated,"[13] so perhaps it is telling that Jane Eyre's defining moment as a child occurs in a red-room, a place of violent exclusion associated with the misunderstood father and the desired mother. Here the capacity to generate changeable aesthetic space momentarily collapses into a transfixing horror that combines the psychological effects of the color red and the spectral, absent uncle-father who seems to emanate everywhere around his death room. Prior to her swoon, however, a kind of psychic shorting-out as consciousness approaches an ultimate rage beyond language, Jane prefigures her later endeavors to control her identity through autobiography:

> Returning, I had to cross before the looking-glass; my fascinated glance involuntarily explored the depth it revealed. All looked colder and darker in that visionary hollow than in reality: and the strange little figure there gazing at me with a white face and arms specking the gloom, and glittering eyes of fear moving where all else was still, had the effect of a real spirit: I thought it like one of the tiny phantoms, half fairy, half imp, Bessie's evening stories represented as coming out of lone, ferny dells in moors, and appearing before the eyes of belated travellers. I returned to my stool. (46)

The Reeds are frozen parodies of fairy-tale characters; Jane sees herself as a kind of minimalist fairy or imp, created under the influence of Bessie's fluid, melancholy tales of dells and moors. Like the Ancient Mariner, her eyes glitter and express fear, for she experiences terrible alienation. Yet the very act of seeing herself as strange, as the Other, elicits a possibility of meaning more stable than the spectral fears welling up from within. This mirror reflection reveals a nascent ability to read herself and, in so doing, to structure the inchoate. This, in turn, is further stabilized—and, inevitably, distorted, as all productive activities to know an earlier period must be—in its retrospective placement in a continuum of development that remains, nevertheless, open-ended, despite the "reader, I married him" closure. Jane both distances and transforms the Other in the mirror, rendering it "colder and darker" than in reality (46), much as she seeks out and transforms what she reads in Swift and

Bewick. Already the distorting and saving imagination is at work, reworking what is actually there with a desired image. Moreover, the frame that delimits this distanced Other adumbrates Jane's endeavors to create boundaries around her discourses, initially in the scenes she mentally regulates (like her vantage points in the window seat and at a distance during Rochester's fancy party), in her paintings and drawings, and in the autobiography itself, where realistic language becomes at once a bulwark-frame and a means of fluid revelation.

Such framing allows for imaginative (re)creation within the experiential field, whose interplay between boundary and boundlessness evades transfixion by either alone. Bertha is physically shapeless and mentally boundless; her usurpation of Jane's mirror and veil during her appearance before the failed wedding parodies Jane's self-enactment, yet it also reifies the danger entailed in losing this disciplined subversion of affirmed boundaries that exemplifies realism. Jane's reading of Bewick illustrates this. She seeks out illustrations of her inner desolation, as she does later with the three paintings Rochester chooses:

> Of these death-white realms I formed an idea of my own: shadowy, like all the half-comprehended notions that float dim through children's brains, but strangely impressive. The words in these introductory pages connected themselves with the succeeding vignettes, and gave significance to the rock standing up alone in a sea of billow and spray; to the broken boat stranded on a desolate coast; to the cold and ghastly moon glancing through bars of cloud at a wreck just sinking. (40)

The "death-white realms," reminiscent of the territory through which Coleridge's mariner travels, are domesticated in the words that confirm them. They "gave significance": this foreshadows Jane's efforts in negotiating life in order to frame, then stabilize, the boundless through language. Her autobiography is a means of conservation. Like Mary Shelley, she explores worlds of dream and terror yet conserves herself through the written word. She captures visual language so that, having achieved relative stability, it is less threatening. Jane moves from original fear to painting to language.

Yet she is drawn to, and her life changed at strategic moments by, words that transcend experience altogether. Hers is a world essentially bereft of God, but the desire persists for a univocal voice that gives meaning to life and art. The novel ends with a fallen Eden stripped of God and patriarchal authority, Rochester having been nearly blinded, maimed, and changed mentally. But at certain points, caesuras in Jane's experience are filled by voices that enact change yet cannot be proved to have existed in reality. Temporality, like inscription, is canceled in the apocalyptic moment that brings voices that aren't voices, like the mother's, who tells Jane to flee Thornfield from the red-room to which she later is transported in dream, and Rochester's, whose disembodied "Jane! Jane! Jane!" (444) enables her to "penetrate very near a Mighty Spirit" (445). These words, unlike Brockehurst's and St. John's, are detached from the transfixing gaze. The mother's voice exhorts and Rochester's implores, thus reversing the expected gender roles. They are, it may be said, Jane's words—she appropriates them for herself, to flee the sexual predator and return to his chastened replacement—for they represent the fulfillments of desire arising from fear and love. As a child, of course, she is drawn to the Bible's most apocalyptic books, "Revelations, and the Book of Daniel, and Genesis, and Samuel, and a little bit of Exodus, and some parts of Kings and Chronicles, and Job and Jonah" (65). She searches for a transition between "thingness" and identity, what Wolfgang Iser terms an "aevum" that connects her with a stable, independent identity in a just world.[14] Paradoxically, however, this engagement requires a confrontation with, and domestication of, the ineffable. In reversing the relation between commanding and imploring, Jane retains freedom of movement and creativity. Near the novel's end, her success in subverting the patriarchal Word in the service of realism is evident in the gender reversal evident in imagining herself a male lover, Rochester's house the dead woman to whom he returns. Here is represented the complex relations among gazing, fixation, fear, and control of her fluid text that characterize Jane's desire, and the finished autobiography itself:

> How hurried was their first glance! But how they fix! How he starts! How he suddenly and vehemently clasps in both arms the form he dared not, a moment since, touch with his finger! How he calls aloud a name, and drops his burden, and gazes on it wildly! He thus grasps, and cries, and gazes, because he no longer fears to waken by any sound he can utter—by any movement he can make. He thought his love slept sweetly: he finds she is stone dead. (449)

But such fluidity, even in the face of loss, is arrived at only after much struggle to subsume others' narratives and fixating aesthetic strategies.

At Lowood, where the advent of gorgeous springtime masks an epidemic, Jane encounters aesthetic masks and escapes that reflect variants of the Kantean autonomy ideology. Helen Burns escapes through literature, while Miss Temple, after some protest, wears a marmoreal mask of obedience. In both cases, aesthetic systems contrary to realism

underlie behavior. But their imperative essentially is the same as
Brocklehurst's and patriarchy's in general: renunciation, the parody of
realistic delimitation. The power relations behind the aesthetic are much
more evident than at, say, Knightley's or Darcy's estates, for there is less
certainty in Brontë that univocality can be concealed, even partially.
Helen Burns's masochistic Christian stoicism, derived partly from a
misreading of Johnson's *Rasselas*, leads her to define herself according
to an external imperative "word" over which she has little control, unlike
the case with Jane's appropriation of the transcendental "Word." The
escapist impetus behind her attraction to death is evident in how Helen,
like Frankenstein, is drawn to the aesthetic Charles I and the Cavaliers,
last redoubts of what Eagleton terms a "Romantic conservatism": [15]

> If he had but been able to look to a distance, and see how what they call the
> spirit of the age was tending! Still, I like Charles—I respect him—I pity him,
> poor murdered king! Yes, his enemies were the worst: they shed blood they
> had no right to shed. How dared they kill him! (89)

By hiding the ethical and political behind the aesthetic, Helen is able to
make his failure seem insignificant, her equivalent of the Southern Lost
Cause myth in the United States. But this merely repeats other cloakings
of power and outrage under aesthetic formulations aimed (even if
unconsciously) at making power gentle, to refer to Burke's conception.

Helen's unwillingness to "resent" (103), like her aversion to the flesh
and attraction to an "invisible world and a kingdom of spirits" (101), is a
dependent fiction that masquerades as autonomy. Her sublimity, based
on a life-denying "separation of spirit from flesh" (101), is the logical
culmination of Brocklehurst's lesson that the girls should be "hardy,
patient, self-denying" (95). She illustrates how constructions of the
beautiful and sublime devolve from religious and moral categories that
organize and control women. Yet Jane realizes she is "no Helen Burns"
(98) when, as public punishment for lying, she has to mount "aloft" on a
"pedestal," like some Schillerian dramatic-marmoreal renunciant, a
living statue frozen in an idealistic moment. Helen's smile, her
"effluence of fine intellect, of true courage" (99), helps Jane suppress a
rising hysteria, like the one she felt in the red-room. Forced to assume a
pose, reduced to an object of public shame, she experiences a
confinement in others' discourse, which prevents her from controlling
her identity. At the same time, she learns from Helen and Miss Temple
the need to regulate her passions. The difficulty is to discover how to
nurture a realistic field between "formless reality" and the "frozen life" [16]
evident in Brocklehurt's hypocritical injunction that "my mission is to

mortify in these girls the lusts of the flesh, to teach them to clothe themselves with shamefacedness and sobriety, not with braided hair and costly apparel"(96). His statement, "I wish these girls to be the children of Grace," is ostensibly evangelical, but given the matrix of aesthetic associations (and the name of the madwoman's keeper) in *Jane Eyre*, Brontë clearly suggests a direct relation between aesthetic repression ("grace") and unbounded hysteria and madness.

The same omnipresent imposition of an aesthetic structure is evident in Miss Temple, who has internalized patriarchal univocality with few apparent fissures. She wears the mask of proper womanhood yet maintains a degree of sanity through mostly private ironic expressions. When she is direct, she knows her limits, only self-effacedly defending serving bread and cheese when the porridge is burned, and "still more quietly" pointing out that Julia's hair "curls naturally." When Brocklehurst speaks, she cloaks her "involuntary" smile behind her handkerchief (96). Women are forced into a disjunction between masks and "vile bodies" that traces the inverse relation between pure philosophy and monstrosity. They are continually reminded, however, of the monstrosity, the filth, which underlies what men evade in themselves, unless, like Victor Frankenstein or Dorian Gray, they are forced to confront their own uncovered spectacle. Women's vile flesh is made omnipresent, even if it is hidden away in the attic, for the doors and perceptions that cover it merely reveal its being, upon which the stabilizing and enacting word insists. Brocklehurst's demand that the girls' "vile bodies" be mortified in favor of their "immortal souls" (95) projects onto woman the chaos at the center of existence: hence a woman becomes the aesthetic object, potentially "white" and Grecian, but also potentially polluted. Domesticated, she must transform impurity into quintessence. A single failure, however, renders her permanently obscene, for the idealist insists that every act, every statement, be pure, unlike the realist, who judges life according to aims and impulses. This seems to be the suggestion behind Brontë's interest in the intersections between aesthetic strategies and women's vile bodies. Brontë further signals this relation between Medusa's gaze (the ideal or its horrible inverse) and the loss of humanity when Brocklehurst, himself like "black marble" (98), seems to turn Miss Temple into the same material with his gaze and admonition:

Miss Temple had looked down when he first began to speak to her; but she now gazed straight before her, and her face, naturally pale as marble, appeared to be assuming also the coldness and fixity of that material; especially her mouth, closed as if it would have required a sculptor's chisel to open it, and her brow settled gradually into petrified severity. (95)

Jane Eyre is concerned with the problem of turning seeing into believing and of representing this process in words. However, seeing, like that of St. John Rivers (or his inverse prototype, Lovelace), is also the means of transfixing the Other through visual control. Visual control precedes verbal production; this is the way Jane Eyre achieves control over her text and in so doing provides a paradigm for realism's endeavor to represent both the chaotic and the ordered without being transfixed by either. Unlike Jane Austen, Brontë eschews the production of a limited, if creative, visual-verbal space but aims for the sentient target and beyond. This fledgling visual control is evident in Jane Eyre's portraits of Blanche Ingram and, later, Rosamond Oliver, in which ironic distancing of the ornamented feminine artifact helps her articulate and valorize a realism whose embodiment is her own life, looks, and autobiography. Jane is real, Blanche is ideal. Using Mrs. Fairfax's description, she imagines how she will portray Blanche, both to dismiss her and to punish herself for thinking that Rochester could be interested in her:

> Tall, fine bust, sloping shoulders; long, graceful neck; olive complexion, dark and clear; noble features; eyes rather like Mr. Rochester's, large and black, and as brilliant as her jewels. And then she had such a fine head of hair, raven-black, and so becomingly arranged; a crown of thick plaits behind, and in front the longest, glossiest curls I ever saw. She was dressed in pure white; an amber-coloured scarf was passed over her shoulder and across her breast, tied at the side, and descending in long, fringed ends below her knee. She wore an amber-coloured flower, too, in her hair: it contrasted well with the jetty mass of her curls. (189)

Altering Mrs. Fairfax's description, Jane foregrounds Blanche's "Grecian" attributes yet subverts this ideal from the margins, into which she introduces Mr. Rochester as a comical interloper, somewhat like Browning's Fra Lippo Lippi among the celestial "bowery flowery angel brood," the profane realist who explodes the univocal aesthetic artifact.[17] Jane Eyre's marginal subversion is only public once the autobiography appears, for as a governess and a woman, she must create in a semiprivate space always subject to appropriation. Yet she really desires to include Rochester within her own visual-verbal space:

> Afterwards take a piece of smooth ivory—you have one prepared in your drawing box: take your palette; mix your freshest, finest, clearest tints; choose your most delicate camel-hair pencils; delineate carefully the loveliest face you can imagine; paint it in your softest shades and sweetest hues, according to the description given by Mrs. Fairfax of Blanche Ingram: remember the raven ringlets, the oriental eye;—What! you revert to Mr. Rochester

as a model! Order! No snivel!—no sentiment!—no regret! I will endure only sense and resolution. Recall the august yet harmonious lineaments, the Grecian neck and bust; let the round and dazzling arm be visible, and the delicate hand. (191)

Thus Blanche is imaginatively transgressed by disorder, much as, we will see, Rose Maylie's idyll is transgressed by London's chaotic energies and disease. In effect, Jane valorizes her own plainness and rebukes herself for having deviated momentarily from it. Blanche is contrasted with Jane's (and Rochester's) homely antiaesthetic: hence the formerly "dark" woman of Mrs. Fairfax's description is to be painted with the "softest shades and sweetest hues." Jane runs down a virtual register of "Grecian" attributes, which include "order," "august yet harmonious lineaments," "Grecian neck and bust,""the round and dazzling arm," and the "delicate hand." Yet the "raven ringlets, the oriental eye" do not really fall within this register; they are more characteristic of Mrs. Fairfax's description of Blanche's complexion as "olive" and "dark and clear," in which only her "pure white" clothing, her drapery so to speak, suggests Greek form and harmony. By introducing Rochester as a dissonant element amidst Blanche's beauty, Jane mocks grace every bit as much as Brontë does in naming Grace for the same aesthetic quality, for as Conrad intimates in *Heart of Darkness*, horror underlies the sort of self-referential beauty Blanche exemplifies, whose absurdity is evident in her mocking of men's usurpation of feminine ornamentation (the focus on dress and makeup), and her desire ("were I a man") to order men to "hunt, shoot, fight, and avoid mirrors":

Creatures so absorbed in care about their pretty faces, and their white hands, and their small feet; as if a man had anything to do with beauty! As if loveliness were not the special prerogative of woman—her legitimate appanage and heritage!" (208)

This foreshadows St. John Rivers's appropriations of feminine ornamentation. A metonymic dispersion (faces, hands, feet) associated with ornamentation is evident. What Blanche suggests is a connection between mirrors, ornaments, and identity: living, as her name suggests, in the superficial, she advocates a rigid gender apartheid in which she is nevertheless the man who gives orders. Maintaining such univocal rigidity means removing mirrors from men, who then will kill elsewhere, and leaving the mirrors for women, who can affirm their beauty in purely visual ways, not based on men's discourse (they are off hunting) or on any deeper awareness of transfixion by the image. Disruption and dismembering are removed, and the purely aesthetic is valorized.

Jane pursues fluid metaphorical and visual approaches that suspend her among variable interpretations, at the same time providing the mature author her conclusion. Her visual placements prepare her for the written autobiography, which contains a series of palinodic transcendences of others' narratives. Blanche, in contrast, is a bad author. Her self-conscious "genius" (202) (Schiller links genius with naiveté) is a too-transparent pursuit of money and a manipulation of the social rules she so easily embodies: her ineptitude (Jane and Rochester can read her too easily) contrasts with Jane's subversive, if still private, aesthetic readings.

Brontë emphasizes the importance of controlling the visual field in recovering one's own past in Jane Eyre's battle with St. John Rivers over the aesthetic spaces that dominate the Marsh End section of the novel. This repressed Christian embodies anti-idyllic pain and *Sehnsucht nach dem Tode*, while Rosamond Oliver is, like Rose Maylie, a parodic idyllic creature. It is over her portrait of Rosamond that Jane and St. John effectively struggle for visual control. Indeed, in discovering her name on the easel (401), St. John tries to appropriate the intersection between the visual and the written that Jane must conserve. Thus, it is not her sense of rightness alone that causes her to share her inheritance with the Rivers family. St. John himself has a formidable gaze, and indeed, like Brocklehurst, displays a trace of monstrosity in a stare that transfixes its object. This is evident when he reveals that he has discovered her identity:

> "You unbend your forehead at last," said Mr. Rivers. "I thought Medusa had looked at you, and that you were turning to stone. Perhaps now you will ask how much you are worth?" (408)

Described, like Brocklehurst, as a "pillar," Rivers is both Medusa and the statue. His flesh is like marble, his tongue "a speaking instrument—nothing more" (436). The possibility looms that all meaning derived from the original aesthetic impulse may be frozen. Rivers's "austere and despotic nature" requires iron silences (434), and his flesh seems to rigidify into "marble" (436). In other words, verbal and visual production are as linked for him as they are for Jane, but at the service of a life-denying aesthetic that is the antitype of the life and realism Jane Eyre seeks. He wishes to subsume her under his ideal and extinguish his own "insignificant private individual" (431). Jane's approach to life is realistic, his idealistic; she asserts the individual and community, he the idea. Rivers exemplifies the danger when the gaze, rather than producing fluid images, merely produces concepts. Jane places him within this matrix, often recalling his marmoreal features (he is like "a statue") and the Grecian qualities that link him with Rosamond and Blanche, who likewise exemplify the denatured word, art, and gaze. He is "harmonious" (371) (Jane herself has irregular features), but this is only on the surface, for he wants to "control the workings of inclination and turn the bent of nature" (387). As Helene Moglen points out, he is a "masculine version of Helen Burns"; like her, he espouses "classical" virtues.[18] St. John replaces flexible visual production with a hard gaze; his idealism precludes the need to glimpse the abyss yet merely reinforces its power. The missionary seems pure, yet his repression barely conceals something terrible; if it seems he will die in a more transfigured state of grace than Mr. Kurtz, it is also evident that his gaze is monstrous, like that of the Medusa in Dante's *Inferno*, whose gaze similarly destroys speech by usurping the visual through marmoreal transformation. For St. John, as for Dante, absolute despair underlies idealistic assertiveness: idealism is the ultimate aesthetic escape that merely leads back to its beginning, the horrific, whether the pilgrim is fully aware of this or not.

Like Conrad and Dickens, Brontë focuses on the scientism associated with the Medusa-gaze, whose ostensible object is the control of a limited visual field and whose apparent ulteriority is, it is evident, the whited sepulchre that conceals the boundless unspeakable. By studying the face, the phrenologist, which St. John momentarily becomes, reduces human complexity to an easily readable, but dead, symbol. The organism is reduced to a simplistic allegorical statement, the trope most accessible to scientific systemization. Thus, Rivers tries to read Jane Eyre before he knows her, reducing her to a sign (as later to a name appropriated from her easel):

Rather an unusual physiognomy; certainly, not indicative of vulgarity or degradation. ... I trace lines of force in her face which make me skeptical of her tractability. ... She looks sensible, but not at all handsome. (366)

Upon arrival at Moor House, Jane Eyre must negotiate two languages, Greek and German, which she does not understand:

And in a low voice she read something, of which not one word was intelligible to me; for it was in an unknown tongue—neither French nor Latin. Whether it were Greek or German I could not tell. (358)

Both languages are associated with the masculinist aesthetic objectivity that is the counterpart of Rivers's deadly gaze. Jane exists outside their signs. Indeed, she resists inclusion into them. To the extent that she recognizes their signs, she turns them against their (be)holders in verbal plays evident in her visual placements of Blanche Ingram. Her control over this (from Brontë's perspective) reductive aesthetic discourse is evident in its ironic placement and enclosure within the realist autobiographical document, *Jane Eyre*, where unilateral visual control (e.g., Rochester's) is subordinate to the creative interchange of word and image that blurs boundaries, including those of gender.

Rivers, ironically, is the temporary sojourner at a house Brontë names for Schiller's Storm-And-Stress Moor family in *The Robbers*. When Jane arrives, Mary is reading in German Franz von Moor's apocalyptic account of a nightmare, which adumbrates the very abyss Rivers has plastered over with an aesthetic control with which Schiller—the "classicist" Schiller—became associated. Jane hears the first sentence and part of the last ("Ich wäge die Gedanken") of this long speech that, verbally cloaked in an unknown tongue and mostly absent, underscores the muffling and bulwark-making that protects us from the ultimate terror beyond words:

> Someone stepped forth who looked like the starry night. Between ascent and descent he held in his hands an iron signet-ring, and said: "Eternal, holy, just, incorruptible! There is only *one* truth, there is only *one* virtue! Woe, woe, woe to the doubting worm!" There stepped forth a second, who had a blinding mirror in his hand, which he held between ascent and descent and said: "This mirror is truth; hypocrisy and masks can not endure." Then I and everyone else screamed, for we saw snake and tiger and leopard faces reflected from the terrifying mirror. Then a third stepped forth, who had eternal scales in his hands, which he held between ascent and descent. He said: "Step here, you child of Adam—I'll weigh your thoughts in the husk of my anger, and works with the weight of my rage!"[19]

In a language only retrospectively understood, Jane Eyre returns to the gaze, the mirror, and the apocalyptic text to which she has been drawn since girlhood. Here once more is the nether world reopened by repression as madness or its inverse, rational scientism, either of which can destroy the soul. This is the power Rivers hoped can be controlled through visual and moral control. The mirror reveals something anterior even to the strange fairy-imp Jane saw in the red-room mirror, itself the product of books and Bessie's storytelling that protected Jane from something worse. But even here the ultimate reality is hidden behind signs—the snake, tiger, and leopard faces—that are further obfuscated in the language as yet unknown, and when known, wrapped in protective remembrance.

Jane Eyre's attempt to get Rivers to relate emotionally to her portrait of Rosamond Oliver reveals his grotesquely repressed personality:

> He continued to gaze at the picture: the longer he looked, the firmer he held
> it, the more he seemed to covet it. "It is like!" he murmured; "the eye is well
> managed: the colour, light, expression, are perfect. It smiles!'" (397)

His insistence on controlling both the space and the time of his aesthetic
appreciation (he times his appreciation) of the woman he desires yet
resists reveals a parodic objectivity that contemplates its own melting
before a poisonous femininity:

> Fancy me yielding and melting, as I am doing: human love rising like a
> freshly opened fountain in my mind and overflowing with sweet inundation
> all the field I have so carefully and with such labour prepared—so
> assiduously sown with the seeds of good intentions, of self-denying plans.
> And now it is deluged with a nectarous flood—the young germs swamped—
> delicious poison cankering them: now I see myself stretched on an ottoman in
> the drawing room at Vale Hall at my bride Rosamond Oliver's feet. (399)

Passion, like any contemplation of the profane, is a loss of control:

> When I colour, and when I shake before Miss Oliver, I do not pity myself, I
> scorn the weakness. I know it is ignoble: a mere fever of the flesh: not, I
> declare, the convulsion of the soul. *That* is just as fixed as a rock, firm set in
> the depths of a restless sea. Know me to be what I am—a cold, hard man.
> (400) [20]

St. John's masturbatory fear of loss of control is self-evident. At the
center of his being is, he insists, a rudimentary "rock." The phallicism
becomes virtually parodic the more we contemplate what Brontë is about
here. The "hard" rock has nearly comic implications, though to Rivers it
is a metaphor for his rejection of sexual surrender. Brontë has in mind
Winckelmann's description of self-control despite agony in his
archetypal description of Laocoön in the *Nachaumung*, the *Urtext* behind
the debate about the relations between visual and verbal arts in Lessing's
Laocoön. Laocoön and his sons are bitten to death for the father's
transgression of warning the Trojans that the horse is a lethal ruse.
Laocoön marshals rhetoric to warn his people that the horse (visually) in
front of them is a lie. Yet the visual appearance is more convincing to the
Trojans than his rhetoric; hence, they believe Sinon's lies. St. John makes
a spectacle of desire even as he denies its validity: this is confirmed by
the care with which he controls the painting's effects. The conflict
between fevers of the flesh and hardness is unresolved and violent, while
his need to show Jane the struggle with which he suppresses his love is
strangely exhibitionistic. He wishes to reduce life to an endlessly
repeated ideal moment rather than accept identity as a more complex

process of general aims and impulses. [21] He curbs passion "as a resolute rider would curb a rearing steed" (391). But he only displays his enslavement to the same passion he repudiates; his religion, like Alec D'Urberville's in his evangelistic phase, is merely sublimated passion. When Jane offers to make him a copy of her "Rose of the World" (401), he declines: with its "touch of carmine," "ripe lips," "soft curl," and "azured eyelid" (396), this miniature, like the living flesh, is merely an enticing threat, which he must prove he can resist.

As Gezari suggests, Jane Eyre is an especially visual artist; [22] thus, she visualizes Rivers's repression to ward him off. By focusing on him as "pictorial-looking" (371), she counters his manipulations of her guilt and sense of duty with a parodic distancing that entails enclosure in aesthetic categories of the beautiful and sublime more typically projected onto women. If Rochester momentarily fooled Jane Eyre with his cross-dressing as a gypsy, she has the last laugh in several gender reversals, including this one. St. John looks "nearly as beautiful for a man" as Rosamond does "for a woman" (390). Just as Bertha pays back her social erasure with a virile violence, St. John displays the rage behind the passivity forced on women, insisting on his self-control even as this teeters on collapse.

Rosamond Oliver's self-containment in idyllic beauty is as problematical as Rose Maylie's in *Oliver Twist*, and it has similar narrative implications. Brontë was uncomfortable with the passionless surfaces of Jane Austen's novels and resisted univocal conclusions. Rosamond's life is similarly questionable in its superficiality and autonomy. The register of idyllic and elysian terms is insistent. Jane mentions "the elysium" (394) of Rosamond's love as well as her "childlike" activity (394) and "grace" (390); it is not coincidental that the wealthy manufacturer's daughter fingers a volume of Schiller at the schoolhouse one evening, as if to emphasize her association with Schiller's Elysium. If St. John's classicism is tortured and unnatural, hers is instinctive and happy. Self-sufficient, she has no need to create fictions of identity to domesticate a strange mirror reflection. But her disparagement of the local gentry compared with the "agreeable" officers is one of several parallels between her and Blanche Ingram (390). Again Jane places her rival ironically. In failing to visit Jane's classes as she promises she will, Rosamond reveals a lack of personal reliability. And Jane undercuts her aesthetic perfection in the way she presents a catalogue of paradoxes that, say, in Schiller's description of the *Juno Ludovici* in his *Aesthetic Education*, would not jar:

> She was coquettish, but not heartless; exacting, but not worthlessly selfish. She had been indulged from her birth, but was not absolutely spoilt. She was

hasty, but good humoured; vain (she could not help it, when every glance in the glass showed her such a flush of loveliness), but not affected; liberal-handed; innocent of the pride of wealth; ingenuous; sufficiently intelligent; gay, lively, and unthinking. She was very charming, in short, even to a cool observer of her own sex like me; but she was not profoundly interesting or thoroughly impressive. (394)

Jane Eyre, in conclusion, is focused on grounding visual and narrative instabilities in a text over which the autobiographer has the final word. Her control entails subsuming univocal, language-transfixing voices within a fluid realism whose conclusion, at Ferndean, entails a creative transgression of gender barriers and a place at the peripheries of all social and mythic (Edenic) organization. If Austen, like Forster, includes the idyllic within a comic ending, Brontë, like Dickens, refuses to collapse the fissure that stands between idyllic-univocal and realistic–open-ended meanings; this fissure permits the generation of verisimilar meaning that is based on the creative interplay between multiplicity and its organiza- tion. To connect, finally, is to misrepresent, as Forster finally recognized, but the desire to connect persists. Rosamond Oliver, as an embodied aesthetic conception, belongs in the world of romance; she is inadequate the moment she impinges on society.

5

Aesthetic Escapes
in Four Novels by Charles Dickens

In Charles Dickens's novels *Oliver Twist*, *Bleak House*, *Hard Times*, and *Great Expectations*, the need to construct fictions of identity is combined with a growing skepticism that this is possible. In a previous chapter, I suggested that monstrosity represents a horrific paroxysm before the onset of an abyss, whose nomenclature cloaks the unspeakable. As George Levine notes in *The Realistic Imagination*, realism's strategies to contain the monstrous become precarious as the nineteenth century proceeds, until, with Conrad, the horrors Mary Shelley distanced through fiction can neither be forgotten nor fully domesticated. At La Force prison in *A Tale of Two Cities*, Charles Darnay's identity starts to disintegrate as he paces his cell; such distintegrations imperil many other characters in Dickens, including the poor woman whom Oliver Twist visits with Sowerberry as well as Louisa Gradgrind, Esther Summerson, and Pip. The fictions of romanticism, utilitarianism, theatricality, and gentility are inadequate bulwarks against the dissolution of identity, against which only the heart's affections offer a limited defense. In this chapter, I shall explore the aesthetic bulwarks with which characters organize their worlds and suggest that Dickens, especially in his conclusions, desires univocal meanings yet undercuts them with dialogical voices that affirm a realism that rests on the awareness that disillusionment and incoherence may underlie stated meanings. Dickens's novels contain many characters who deny the complexities of experience with interpretive strategies that "polish" (Mr. Turveydrop's expression) via manners, philosophy, phony sentiment, or the sort of historical appropriation (Lord Dedlock's, Miss Havisham's, and Pip's) that seeks to stabilize time and process. The aesthetic impulse is necessary to organize reality, of course, but, as Hayden White observes in summarizing Nietzsche's beliefs, the propensity "to freeze life in the form provided by the dream" has disastrous consequences, for this merely guarantees the reemergence of chaos.[1] Thus, Lady Dedlock's carefully constructed facade disintegrates at the grave of Nemo.

Theatricality and Other Abstractions

In *Oliver Twist,* unstable theatricality and the idyll are the major aesthetic formulations employed to represent London and the Maylies' world. Dickens applies the "theatricality" metaphor to London much as Edmund Burke applies it to the Paris of the 1789 revolution: in both cases, mob violence and public assemblies (the National Assembly in Burke, Fagin's trial in Dickens) are depicted as infernal theaters. Those closest to the edge can only tenuously distance themselves aesthetically, as we discover early on when Oliver accompanies Sowerberry to an impoverished family to prepare a woman for burial. Her "play" is pathetic, not infernal, her daughter's death a rudimentary enactment from which she must distance herself, just as Burke must distance himself from the collapse of political meaning:

> Well, it *is* strange that I who gave birth to her, and was a woman then, should be alive and merry now; and she lying there: so cold and stiff! Lord, Lord!— to think of it;—it's as good as a play—as good as a play![2]

For the poor, the abyss beckons awfully near and can be, at best, only tenuously hidden. Eventually, however, it catches up to nearly everyone not protected by some form of inviolability, like Sissy Jupe's or Rose Maylie's childlike power. Society likewise creates simulacra of order through public spectacles, above all in judicial scapegoating and frenzied pursuit and punishment. Beneath its veneers, society is chaotic and instinctual; individuals are capable of enabling and transcendent activity, but people in the mass are like hounds on the hunt. Dickens suggests a close affinity between propriety and criminality.[3] The first legal "theatricality," Oliver's summary trial in chapter 10, nearly turns into a prosecution of Brownlow, who wonders if the boy's apparently innocent face reflects reality: "*Can* he be innocent?" (*OT,* 63). Fang, in contrast, assumes that Oliver is "shamming" (*OT,* 66); he associates acting with essence, as Fagin (his anagram namesake) does. When Oliver is cleared, Fang accuses Brownlow: as Foucault might argue, society needs both the criminal and avenging justice to maintain the oppositional structures that create apparent meaning. If need be, the law will impose a fiction of criminality on an innocent person, which Oliver essentially is, though technically an accessory to the robbery.[4] But when the testimony proves Oliver innocent, Fang transforms him into an innocent preyed upon by the blackguard Brownlow.

It is at Jack Dawkins's trial, however, that the theatrical nature of crime and punishment becomes most obvious. The courtroom reflects the essential rot at the center of society: "The room smelt close and unwholesome; the walls were dirt-discoloured; and the ceiling blackened" (*OT,* 280). In this social cloaca, whose ceremony ends with transportation or execution, the Artful Dodger mocks the august pretensions of the court, claiming his "priwileges" as an Englishman but threatening the court with the "Secretary of State for the Home Affairs." His grandiose, swaggering lies parody the lie on which the court itself is based:

> "Wot is this here business? I shall thank the madg'strates to dispose of this here little affair, and not to keep me while they read the paper, for I've got an appintment with a genelman in the city." (*OT,* 281)

As Claypole and Bates indicate, Dawkins succeeds in creating the romantic "glorious reputation" (*OT,* 283) so perversely valued by their society. Whether playing the romanticized proto-Macheath or the depraved animal, the criminal is expected to follow a script. Dawkins, however, at once plays the role and subverts it. He creates a romantic identity yet angrily rejects the court's right to write his script. He tells the court, "This ain't the shop for justice" (*OT,* 282). Behind its professed objectivity, it is a "shop" that sells a commodity, justice, in which class makes a difference. Playing one's allotted role buttresses a social system based on the opposition between criminal and society in which people so believe the roles they play that they are unaware of the stage on which they act. Dawkins, the parodic echo of the hegemonic legal institution, grandiloquently claims its prerogatives as his own volition. He is the thief as neo-Kantean. Hence, when the clerk commits him, his response is to parrot him and the jailer:

> I wouldn't go free, now, if you was to fall on your knees and ask me. Here, carry me off to prison! Take me away! (*OT,* 282)

The Artful Dodger knows a scam when he sees one.

Sikes fulfills society's need for a monster that is the correlative of the "ugly things" it wishes to bury but cannot, leading it to produce theatricalities that codify the exclusion or execution of the criminal, whose depravities systematize the anarchic in ways that "make the blood run cold" yet provide a perverse play-book for criminals. The middle class will experience horror at a distance, as they might in reading Gothic novels, while the criminal classes will understand how to employ the language of confession to exorcise the haunting bodies they have hidden. But Sikes finds no such respite, so much has he affronted the conscience, which, for Dickens, offers a means of constructing identity. When he clubs Nancy to death, she is "a ghastly figure to look upon" (*OT,* 303), and as a spectral objectification of his elemental conscience, the "eyes," she pursues him through the countryside and back to London, where Sikes, seeing "the eyes again!" (*OT,* 328), loses his balance and hangs himself. She is the nightmare he wishes to eradicate but cannot; his final words are not a confession but an "unearthly screech" (*OT,* 328), an expression at the edges of language that points to the collapse of any capacity to create fictional bulwarks against decay and death.

As he flees London, Sikes is pursued by "some fearful thing" (*OT,* 328) whose impersonality, though connected with Nancy, suggests the dissolution of individuality and language into a spectral nature that accompanies death:

> Every object before him, substance or shadow, still or moving, took the semblance of some fearful thing; but these fears were nothing compared to the sense that haunted him of that morning's ghastly figure following at his heels. He could trace its shadow in the gloom, supply the smallest item of the outline, and note how stiff and solemn it seemed to stalk along. He could hear its garments rustling in the leaves; and every breath of wind came laden with that last low cry. If he stopped it did the same. If he ran, it followed—not running too: that would have been a relief: but like a corpse endowed with the mere machinery of life, and borne on one slow melancholy wind that never rose or fell. (*OT,* 307–8)

Like Brontë's Heathcliff when nearing death, Sikes reads nature in radically analogical terms. Everything is Nancy, only this disembodied fear is stripped of gender, reduced to an "it," which suggests the collapse of theatricalities on which illusions of identity are constructed as if to conceal the absence (in Nancy's case, the physical obliteration) of human attributes. Heathcliff pursues a union beyond gender opposition; Sikes flees the collapse of all opposition into the spectral "it," which reflects the destruction of gender, indeed, of every fiction on which society is built. Yet flight merely magnifies the "it" that, ornamenting the trees with its "garments," parodies the association of femininity with "original nature" and ornamentation, whether of the prostitute or the idyllic angel.

Sikes experiences a nature animated by the madness he projects onto it, much as, on a trivial level, Mrs. Corney projects her grotesque repressed passion and "sad recollections" (*OT,* 142) of Mr. Corney onto a teapot, which, more successfully than Sikes's animated nature, creates an analogical stability. Sikes's inability to create such fictional stability—he has outraged his own nature and hence turned himself into a monster even in Bates's eyes (*OT,* 325)—is evidenced by his ill success in fleeing from himself and "those widely staring eyes, so lustreless and so glassy" (*OT,* 308). He throws himself into putting out a fire, the embodiment of his own destructive passion, during which "he shouted ... till he was hoarse; and, flying from memory and himself, plunged into the thickest of the throng" (*OT,* 309). But he cannot escape memory and himself.

Jacob's Island, the cynosure of London's putrefaction, is linked with the law courts by images of decay and theatricality, of which the participants themselves are unconscious: "Like a field of corn moved by an angry wind" (*OT,* 326), the crowd pursues Sikes as he tries to swing across Folly Ditch: "The houses on the opposite side of the ditch had been entered by the mob; sashes were thrown up, or torn bodily out; there were tiers and tiers of faces in every window" (*OT,* 327). The backs of the houses contain "crazy wooden galleries" (*OT,* 321). In Burke's *Reflections,* the Assembly become "comedians" before "a riotous audience," but "inverted" (Burke's term) order prevails in all things, for "the gallery is in place of the house."[5] Similarly, on Jacob's Island, instinct has turned society into a vast theater. London's hierarchies collapse into indistinguishable "faces" that find escape from memory and individuality in a blood lust. Sikes, in contrast, is forced to play the role of scapegoat.

At his trial, likewise, Fagin is surrounded "by a firmament, all bright with gleaming eyes" (*OT,* 339), a parodic master-trope that fixes him in its collective vision. Here, writing, drawing, and the theatrical intersect. Fagin instinctively seeks limited visual control by focusing on the newspaper artist (Dickens himself, in his earlier career as a court reporter?) who is sketching his face. His fixation is all that seems to prevent his collapse into absolute insanity: "He wondered whether it was like, and looked on when the artist broke his pencil-point, and made another with his knife, as any idle spectator might have done" (*OT,* 340). Like Brownlow vis-à-vis Agnes Fleming, he ponders a likeness in portraiture, but one he cannot see, as if to retard the "one oppressive, overwhelming sense of the grave that opened at his feet" (*OT,* 340). But he cannot close the abyss. With no view of or control over the face being sketched in the gallery, he fixes his gaze on other externals, like the fashion of the judge's robe. Before the narrator can "paint" his ending

(*OT,* 350), Oliver must witness society's expunging of this "stain" who is now bereft of every control over his identity. Fagin is transposed into a role he can neither manipulate nor fully understand, for, in the judicial labyrinth, he is powerless. Instead, he becomes the helpless observer of faces that demand his blood. In the condemned cell he tries to make sense of fragmentary words and impressions that, in his growing madness, he can do no more than repeat: "To be hanged by the neck, till he was dead—that was the end. To be hanged by the neck till he was dead" (*OT,* 343). Dickens manipulates reader sympathy for the condemned man "with a countenace more like that of a snared beast than the face of a man" (*OT,* 345) who, in a parody of the Crucifixion, will be publicly sacrificed to a mob whose frightfulness is evident in its levity:

> Day was dawning when they again emerged. A great multitude had already assembled; the windows were filled with people, smoking and playing cards to beguile the time; the crowd were pushing, quarrelling, and joking. Everything told of life and animation, but one dark cluster of objects in the very centre of all—the black stage, the cross-beam, the rope, and all the hideous apparatus of death. (*OT,* 347)

Utilitarianism is the abstraction that characterizes society in *Hard Times.*[6] The novelist confronts the experiential field; the peril is in mistaking that new language for reality itself, like the utilitarians did. Utilitarianism ostensibly detaches fictions from things but itself is a fiction. Rejecting realism in favor of rational "reality," it reduces people to parts, workers to "hands."[7] It replaces the memory with infinite repetitions of unaltering signs, inventing a past that affords the illusion of control and finality. Hence Bitzer and Bounderby can conceal and reinvent their parentage, while Gradgrind imposes his ideology on his wife's domestic sphere. Utilitarian Coketown is built upon words that limit meaning to the conscious and the quantifiable. In the schoolroom, taste has become merely another fact, reduced like everything else to "combinations and modifications (in primary colours) of mathematical figures which are susceptible of proof and demonstration."[8] Dickens's narrator, too, is impoverished by the reduction of fancy, for instance in this overwrought rhetorical analogy:

> Say, good M'Choakumchild. When from thy boiling store thou shalt fill each jar brimful by-and-by, dost thou think that thou wilt always kill outright the robber Fancy lurking within—or sometimes only maim and distort him? (*HT,* 6)

Naming has become a method of limiting and controlling the imagination; hence Sissy is told to call herself Cecilia and is rebuked for fancying that a room should be carpeted with "representations" of flowers. Language becomes a means of escaping, not confronting, reality. Tom's imperfect education in the "mechanical" and "mathematical" generates self-loathing and cynicism, while Louisa discovers an outlet in the seductive fictions of James Harthouse. The aesthetic, represented by Sleary's Circus, is reduced to something like a peep show in Tom's and Louisa's furtive metonymic visions. The "grovelling sensualities" that open Tom to Harthouse's manipulations are foreshadowed in his "abasement" before the peephole at the circus. Moreover, his catching but a "hoof" (*HT*, 9) of the circus horse points to his tendency, like the speaker's in Blake's "London," to see only marks, not whole beings. Louisa strains "with all her might" (*HT*, 9) to connect vision with meaning, but cannot. Instead, she later is released from fact into a forbidden world whose locus, Bounderby's mock-Edenic garden, parodies the broken myths of Coketown. This adumbrates the cost of failure to create meaning from the tension generated by the direct impingement of emplotments on the experiential field, from which realism arises. By failing to confront reality creatively, utilitarianism's limited lingual matrix merely mutilates humanity and nurtures savagery. Thus the narrator's rhetorical question when comparing the town ("of unnatural red and black like the painted face of a savage") (*HT*, 17) with Tom and Louisa: "Is it possible, I wonder, that there was any analogy between the case of the Coketown population and the case of the little Gradgrinds?" (*HT*, 19). Tom's savagery is visually apparent at the end of *Hard Times* when he is disguised by the circus people in "comic livery" that suggests animality (*HT*, 215). Unable to play with his belief in nothing like Harthouse, to create a simulacrum of autonomy, Tom proceeds from cynical relativism to savage nihilism. He lands in a psychological state beyond good and evil yet is wracked by repressed guilt. His cynical moral arithmetic takes utilitarian rationalism to its logical extreme. Tom denies responsibility: the old categories of good and evil have been defanged by a system that translates everything into formulas that cannot be judged, only interpreted. Tom's simultaneous rejection and embrace of rational laws suggests that he realizes their inadequacy but has nothing with which to replace them. Rational fictions are the supremely ironic products of a utilitarian project that mistrusts art yet opens the abyss.

The circus represents a theatrical alternative to utilitarianism, whose abstractions deny the uneasy complexities associated with realism. The narrator's idealization of the circus people is belied by their factual poverty and pathos; for instance, Jupe has beaten Merrylegs bloody. Sissy's refusal to believe he deserted her reflects a loving heart but also a denial of fact, the inverse of the utilitarians' insistence on facts alone.

Thus, in a different way, gaps remain unbridged. The circus is more desirable than Coketown yet still stunted. Its imaginative limitation is mirrored in the slurred language of its circus master and a denial of brute reality that mirrors the denial of wonder in industrial Coketown. Just as nature is reduced to a shop sign in *Our Mutual Friend*, here the nearly banished impractical art realm finds residence at a tavern named the Pegasus Arms, an ironic reference to an ancient symbol of poetic inspiration. Behind that sign are the squalid quarters of Sissy and her departed father and dog. Here, it is ironically Gradgrind who, in taking in Sissy, offers a practical sympathy that no one else, not the circus people and least of all Bounderby, can provide. For all its imaginative qualities, the circus can offer, at best, only a diversion from the world, not a solution to its problems. Thus, it serves something like the function of the Maylies' country home in *Oliver Twist*, which, for all its Wordsworthian splendor, offers no real alternative to Jacob's Island.

Vision, Language, and Control

In presenting Oliver's appearance before Fang, Dickens plays with the relation between books (and words) and truth. It is a pattern we have noted before in this study: language must be marshaled to create visual belief, but the impulse to see too far is perilous. Spoken words evade narrative closure; written language is necessary to stabilize the flux of experiences, yet, as Dr. Manette discovers, the once truthful text may falsify if disinterred and appropriated. Language can either falsify or affirm identity, point towards stability or indicate a loss of control. The desire for a union of pictorial and linguistic truth is inherent in the novel, yet the novel's goal is to reflect a historical field in which everything is in flux. There are some characters, like Brownlow, who seek to reify an ideal from a portrait. Then there is the idyllic realm associated with Rose Maylie, into which the spectral and diseased nevertheless come: here, too, a visual field reflects Dickens's narrative desire that Oliver reconcile visual and lingual truths. The idyllic nearly seems self-contained, not metonymic (what Roman Jakobson regards as the "fundamental trope of 'realistic' prose."[9]

Brownlow's projection of desire onto the portrait of Agnes Fleming awakens an astonishment he initially cannot articulate:

"There is something in that boy's face," said the old gentleman to himself as he walked slowly away: tapping his chin with the cover of the book, in a thoughtful manner; "something that touches and interests me. *Can* he be innocent?" (*OT*, 63)

Only later, after Oliver's illness, does Brownlow consciously connect the face with the painting, but even then he focuses on the implausibility of the comparison:

> He pointed hastily to the picture above Oliver's head; and then to the boy's face. There was its living copy. The eyes, the head, the mouth; every feature was the same. The expression was, for the instant, so precisely alike, that the minutest line seemed copied with a startling accuracy. (*OT*, 72)

"Some mistake," he tells Mrs. Bedwin. In *Oliver Twist,* Dickens suggests that the heart is key to provisional identity. But Brownlow has put a coffin around his heart, distanced its affections just as surely as the mother does her daughter's death by calling it a play. Thus, even after he sees the affinity, he stops short of asking the obvious further question. In fact, Brownlow has the portrait removed from above Oliver's bed because, "as it seemed to worry you, perhaps it might prevent your getting well, you know" (*OT*, 81). But Brownlow's is the disposition in need of soothing. He needs to believe Oliver is as innocent as the memory he associates with the portrait. If Oliver looks like the portrait of the young woman, this must reflect a moral affinity. But what about a world in which the moral and the aesthetic are detached from each other? The fear that fiction is *merely* fictive encourages denial, then engagement with reality. Brownlow's real anxiety is that, should Oliver prove corrupt, so must the woman who inspired the portrait. Moreover, life may be more complex and shaded than this simplistic opposition suggests. What is more real about Agnes, Edward Leeford's "guilty love" (*OT*, 317) or the beautiful portrait? In sexuality, childbirth, and death she crossed into the labyrinth. Later on, Losberne insists that Rose and her adoptive mother hear Oliver's history. Brownlow immediately does no such thing, but, like Grimwig, treats him as a kind of experimental object. This, too, represents a hesitation before memory that Brownlow must overcome if he is to understand Oliver's narrative. But lost signs and confessions—Oliver's, Dick's—underscore the precariousness of identity. Oliver's disappearance proves that he "is an impostor" (*OT*, 108), but this separates him from the broader aims and impulses on which character is predicated. Instead, Oliver is judged by a single (apparent) act, the obverse of Rose Maylie's refusal to judge him according to any practical criteria. Brownlow flees his house and its unresolved ambiguities for the West Indies, where he seeks to unravel the mysterious resemblance between the portrait and the boy, tracking down visible proofs that will verify resemblances between the memory of Edward Leeford, the portrait of Agnes Fleming, and Oliver Twist, and rescue all from apparent infection. Art will rescue life. Dickens, too, wants "to shew, in little Oliver, the principle of Good surviving through every adverse circumstance, and triumphing at last" (*OT*, xxv). That is, his text will present visual assurance through realistic discourse. Thus Brownlow is Dickens's mask. Both investigate the outer world to verify a univocal truth experience continually undercuts.

Brownlow uses books to test Oliver's honesty, but in truth they remove him from reality, in contrast to Fagin's literature, which takes Oliver close to the abyss. During the theft, his reading merely abstracts him from the thieves:

> It was plain, from his utter abstraction, that he saw not the book-stall, nor the street, nor the boys, nor, in short, anything but the book itself. (*OT*, 60)

He has difficulty reading the society outside his carefully regulated rooms, where his book-lined shelves, like Edgar Linton's in *Wuthering Heights*, are bulwarks against experience. On the other hand, the mother's "play" and Fagin's *Newgate Calendar* are too close to unmediated reality to reassure. Novelistic realism inhabits a middle space between monstrous energies and the ideal; Dickens ironically uses realism to explore a society (and his own desires) in which the capacity to mediate these oppositions is tenuous.

Oliver has a radically different experience with the written word when, kidnapped by Nancy and Sikes, his tenuously established bourgeois identity is imperiled:

> In another moment, he was dragged into a labyrinth of dark narrow courts: and forced along them, at a pace which rendered the few cries he dared to give utterance to, wholly unintelligible. (*OT*, 94)

Language and perception seem to dissolve; later, from his garret window, Oliver can see nothing but "a confused and crowded mass of house-tops, blackened chimneys, and gable-ends" (*OT*, 111). As with Charles Darnay in La Force prison, the accidentals begin to overpower the essentials. The Newgate stories Oliver reads reflect Dickens's desire, stated in the "Author's Preface to the Third Edition," to counter criminal romance with a "miserable reality" (*OT*, xxvi) that inoculates the reader against admiration for depravity. Fagin tries to infect Oliver with "stories of robberies" (*OT*, 115) to "blacken" his soul and "change its hue forever" (*OT*, 115). These dangerous stories offer an artistic immediacy to life absent in Brownlow's books.[10] Yet despite this intent, Fagin's *Newgate* volume helps inoculate Oliver against depravity. From reading its theatrically stylized stories of condemned criminals, Oliver receives a "paroxysm of fear" (*OT*, 124) that at once terrifies him and helps him define himself by realizing what he does not want to be. Oliver's innate strength enables him to be saved by the book, where lives are translated into art that terrifies rather than romanticizes. Moreover, words become visualized and hence true in their emotional effects, which reifies an art that grabs the emotions yet has a moral end and does not merely make the criminal seem attractive:

> It was a history of the lives and trials of great criminals; and the pages were soiled and thumbed with use. Here, he read of dreadful crimes that made the blood run cold; of secret murders that had been committed by the lonely wayside: and bodies hidden from the eye of man in deep pits and wells: which would not keep them down, deep as they were, but had yielded them up at last, after many years, and so maddened the murderers with the sight, that in their horror they had confessed their guilt, and yelled for the gibbet to end their agony. ... The terrible descriptions were so real and vivid, that the sallow pages seemed to turn red with gore; and the words upon them, to be sounded in his ears, as if they were whispered, in hollow murmurs, by the spirits of the dead. (*OT*, 124)

This is quite unlike the "beautiful writing" of Brownlow's world.[11] The criminals' need to confess when maddened by the "sight" of "bodies hidden from the eye of man" points to the need people have to use words as bulwarks against the transfixion or dissolution of identity. In *Great Expectations,* Pip, in contrast, is revolted by Wopsle's identification of the criminal George Barnwell with his "unoffending self." Far from inoculating Pip from criminality, however, the story of George Barnwell becomes him: "At once ferocious and maudlin, I was made to murder my uncle with no extenuating circumstances whatever."[12] Words, like the mother's "play," are the last redoubt before terror and nothingness. Yet such visualization, as I noted, is perilous. In reading Fagin's book, Oliver magnifies the stain of criminality that Fagin has introduced into him, and thereby is able to distance himself from it. This evolving text codifies the "glorious reputation" (*OT*, 283) sought by young criminals as, in their way, they seek stability. Still fundamentally innocent, Oliver seeks a different stability; his terror of "dreadful crimes" inoculates him against corruption and prepares him for his introduction to Rose Maylie's idyll two chapters later where, symbolically, his monstrous potential is projected onto the frothing Monks, who lurks on the periphery of his consciousness.

Bleak House closes with Esther's insistence on the aesthetic fineness of Allan and the widowed Ada, and her own lack of beauty:

> But I know that my dearest little pets are very pretty, and that my darling is very beautiful, and that my husband is very handsome, and that my guardian has the brightest and most benevolent face that ever was seen, and that they can very well do without much beauty in me—even supposing—.[13]

In being less, she is more; in affirming the beauties of others she creates a fiction that nurtures. Yet her statement is also disturbing, the "even supposing—" setting up a central indeterminacy at the novel's end centering on an anxiety towards the beautiful, to whose loss Esther has professed an indifference already undercut by her strange fascination with others' reactions to that loss, especially Guppy's. Esther embodies the bifurcation between lingual and visual assurances at the heart of realism's crisis and opportunity; the objective, third-person narrator seems to bridge the gap but, like Inspector Bucket, is suspect. She is not physically beautiful but will be surrounded by beautiful people in a "rustic cottage" with "pretty objects" and "pretty rooms" in a nature at once "tranquil" and "beautiful" (*BH*, 912). It is a lesser place full of "doll's rooms," just as her nicknames are diminutives.[14] Esther declares, "*My* little tastes and fancies" (*BH*, 912) are reflected in the new Bleak House. But her Yorkshire home is a surprise into whose design she has no input. She declares she is "just the same as ever": "Dame Trot, Dame Durden, Little Woman—all just the same as ever; and I answer, 'Yes, dear guardian!' just the same" (*BH*, 934). Yet this insistence on sameness when things clearly are not the same forces us, more than Esther, to wonder. She offers others, like Ada Clare, an emotional stability that their beauty can't afford them. They in turn give her the illusion of security.[15] Woodcourt, too, assures her, following her illness, that, were she to look in the glass, she would be "prettier than you ever were" (*BH*, 935). John Jarndyce creates an idyll in the little Bleak House; Esther, on a more personal level, creates an aesthetic certitude in which reductive nicknames paradoxically become terms of validation, and where even the loss of language in Caddy's "deaf and dumb" little girl becomes an emblem of human interrelatedness through "arts" that soften "affliction":

> I had almost forgotten Caddy's poor little girl. She is not such a mite now; but she is deaf and dumb. I believe there never was a better mother than Caddy, who learns, in her scanty intervals of leisure, innumerable deaf and dumb arts, to soften the affliction of her child. (*BH*, 933)

Yet, underlying all this is a radical uncertainty about beauty, which affords a socially approved space for women. The loss of this space in

Esther's case is connected with a broader question of meaning, for which the Chancery case is the appropriate unstable metaphor.

In *Bleak House,* Esther seeks visual stabilizations that will reify her identity, but she lives in a milieu where this is nearly impossible. Moreover, she experiences the loss of clear connections between signs and things, ornaments and realities. Indeed, even what seems real in the visible world is deceptive. Esther's initially positive, idyllic view of Chesney Wold, where heavenly wings seem to sweep "on benignant errands through the summer air" (*BH*, 300), is at variance with the third-person "view in Indian ink" from the window of the childless Lady Dedlock (*BH*, 56). Not having experienced disfigurement or the abject "terror" of herself as the "danger and the possible disgrace of my own mother, and of a proud family name" (*BH*, 569), Esther is apt to see angels where others see darkness and corpses. Her first sighting of Lady Dedlock in church, "which smelt as earthy as a grave" (*BH*, 301), occurs during her first visit to Boythorn's "serene and peaceful" estate, whose "undisturbed repose" (*BH*, 304) belies the legal conflict between him and Dedlock over a walkway. She has no idea of her relationship to Lady Dedlock, yet is disturbed by a resemblance she cannot explain, which causes her instinctively to recall her buried doll, the symbol of a lost childhood. Her insistence on an idyllic reading of the contiguous estates is shaken at church by the fragmented mirror of Lady Dedlock's face. Esther does not have the detective's obsession that leads Tulkinghorn and Bucket to their reconstructions of fragmentary evidence. But she experiences "strangeness," a sense of dislocation:

> But why her face should be, in a confused way, like a broken glass to me, in which I saw scraps of old remembrances; and why I should be so fluttered and troubled (for I was still) by having casually met her eyes, I could not think. (*BH*, 304)

She sees a likeness with her deceased aunt, but avoids drawing a conclusion:

> This made me think, did Lady Dedlock's face accidentally resemble my godmother's? It might be that it did, a little; but the expression was so different, and the stern decision which had worn into my godmother's face, like weather into rocks, was so completely wanting in the face before me, that it could not be that resemblance which had struck me. (*BH*, 305)

The emphasis on the momentary and strange nature of the experience points to its parodic epiphanic nature. She is among signs that seem impenetrable, yet also strangely readable:

"And yet *I—I*, little Esther Summerson, a child who lived a life apart, and on whose birthday there was no rejoicing—seemed to arise before my own eyes, evoked out of the past by some power in this fashionable lady." (*BH*, 305)

Like Guppy when he first sees Lady Dedlock's portrait, Esther cannot pursue the fragments she sees to their logical conclusions. This is left to the inexorable misogynist Tulkinghorn, who reduces the female body to fragments to possess and be nourished by.

The "spot and time" (*BH*, 485) with which Esther associates her premonition of the illness that disfigures her, and makes visual assurance of identity all the more difficult, alludes to Wordsworth's *The Prelude*, book 12. But her "spot" and "time" do not offer her the "renovating virtue" and creative control over identity that Wordsworth implies. Wordsworth's "moments," which "Are scattered everywhere, taking their date / From our first childhood," have the memory of childhood oneness with nature as their basis, but Esther must negotiate life without this memory that nurtures "A sensitive being, a *creative* soul." [16] Esther's past is nearly blank, and her ability to refashion memory to affirm a complex, evolving self is very much in doubt. In becoming different, she may become trapped in temporal stages that are discrete and incoherent, though linked to a melancholy childhood deprived of liberating myths. Her recognition of two Esthers may enable her to reinvent herself, or it may point to a loss of control over her identity. Dickens hopes for the first, but the very ideality of the novel's conclusion suggests his anxiety that the second is the likelier possibility. Esther's disease forces her to redefine herself (and be redefined by others) owing to her disfigurement. She must construct a fiction of self based on others' willingness to accept that in her changed state she is still the same. Esther hopes, in other words, that her imaginative sympathy is present in others. Yet most other characters in *Bleak House* are egotists; society itself is based on indifference and destructive legal objectivity. Dickens increasingly feared that identity would simply break down, once stripped of its language and social connections. [17]

During her illness, Esther experiences a loss of clear chronological divisions, which takes her to the edge of death. This is suggested by the "dark lake" she seems to have crossed:

I lay ill through several weeks, and the usual tenor of my life became like an old remembrance. But this was not the effect of time, so much as of the change in all my habits, made by the helplessness and inaction of a sick room. Before I had been confined to it many days, everything else seemed to have retired into a remote distance, where there was little or no separation between the various stages of my life which had been really divided by years. In falling ill, I seemed to have crossed a dark lake, and to have left all my experiences, mingled together by the great distance, on the healthy shore. (*BH*, 543)

She will have to reconstruct the stages of a life that needs cohesive memory if her identity is to approach stability. But now those stages seem to exist contemporaneously. In her delirium, she is "at once a child, an elder girl, and the little woman I had been so happy as" (*BH*, 543): having lost the mental constructions of time and space, the separation of self into selves that creates an illusion of orderly progress, she becomes distressed by a "great black space" where "there was a flaming necklace, or ring, or starry circle of some kind, of which *I* was one of the beads!" She seems to labor "up colossal staircases, ever striving to reach the top, and ever turned, as I have seen a worm in a garden path, by some obstruction, and labouring again" (*BH*, 544). This unidentified obstruction symbolizes her inability to emplot her past in a realistic fiction of selfhood. Instead, she may collapse into disorganized memories that have no originating purpose, fictive or substantive. The opposite of social sympathy and realism is the discrete bead and the horrific sense that it was "inexplicable agony and misery to be part of the dreadful thing" (*BH*, 544). In her delirium, she fears that all her stages have merely been repetitions, like Ricard Carstone's life, which is fundamentally a repetition of mad Tom Jarndyce's. Hence her prayer to be "taken off from the rest" of the beads. Her nearly fungible nicknames have enabled her to evade the lack of cohesion between her name, her past, and an evolving personality.[18]

At Boythorn's country home, where she stays to recuperate, Esther carefully controls the unveiling of her new face, taking the curtain away from the glass on her dressing table as if unveiling a portrait whose field she must control spatially and emotionally: "Then I put my hair aside and looked at the reflection in the mirror, encouraged by seeing how placidly it looked at me" (*BH*, 559). The monstrous turns out to be placid, as Esther reverses the transfixion in appearances of Frankenstein's monster: "If a good fairy had built the house for me with a wave of her wand, and I had been a princess and her favoured godchild, I could not have been more considered in it" (*BH*, 558). Dickens's interest in *Frankenstein* is evident in his depiction of Esther's insecurity about others' reactions. She reverses the daemon's rejection as a monster by little William, for instance, when she shows the "little loss of mine" (*BH*, 560) to a child, who is "not the less fond of me" (*BH*, 562). Her calm reaction to her change contrasts with the monster's self-loathing, though later on Lady

Dedlock's revelation that she is Esther's mother awakens an "augmented terror of myself" (*BH*, 571) because her mother affirms consanguinity yet requires her to conceal it so that Esther loses the public confirmation that might reassure her.

When she visits Jenny's cottage, Esther and Ada cover the dead infant with a handkerchief, the same one Lady Dedlock takes when she discovers Esther's illness. Like Esther's and her mother's veils, it symbolizes the mysterious signs in a world where unreal things are often more substantial than real ones. By covering the dead baby, Esther symbolically buries and ornaments it. This foreshadows her anxiety later on about the loss of feminine ornamentation. The handkerchief is the emblem of sympathetic acts superior to all ornamentation; hence Lady Dedlock's compulsion to hide it near her dead heart. Like Desdemona's (*Bleak House* has a parodic Othello theme centering especially around the Snagsbys), it symbolizes the indeterminacy of signs employed to create forms of belief and connection. It is invested with different meanings, yet it means nothing in itself as it passes from person to person; thus, it is emblematic of the system of disengaged signs on which society rests in *Bleak House*. Esther's gift of the handkerchief is a selfless act; around it, the mother builds a shrine with its "little bunch of sweet herbs" (*BH*, 162), but for Lady Dedlock it suggests the child she has discovered yet buried.

In *Great Expectations,* the possibility of transforming language into visualized belief (the task of the realistic novel) is even more tenuous. Pip comes into the world alienated, like the monster in *Frankenstein,* from knowledge of his parents, whom he must invent by transforming letters on their tombstones into mental hieroglyphs. The tombstones are the almost unreadable signs of lives he cannot accurately reconstruct and hence must invent. His sister evidently has told him nothing about his family, so Pip, like Mary Shelley, seeks them through their tombs, amidst a waste marshland that seems the antithesis of the beautiful nature that Wordsworth—a major influence on Dickens—associates with restorative memories. Pip's creation of visual images from these tombstones points to a desire for meaning but foreshadows a tendency to create meaning separate from any reality. He visualizations are based on "hieroglyphic" words that have no basis in experience, even experience retold by others. In contrast, the "lying" epitaph that Joe carves for his abusive father is valorized by the heart, which, for Dickens, is the glue that makes the middle space of realism possible. Like Hamlet (Shakespeare's play forms an important subtext in *Great Expectations*), he seeks the father's ghost; Magwitch appears and awakens terror. The shapes of his brothers' graves suggest that they were "born on their backs with their hands in their trousers pockets," ominously suggesting powerlessness and onanism (*GE*, 35).

His "first most vivid and broad impression of the identity of things" (*GE*, 35) occurs the afternoon the escaped convict terrifies him, demanding a file and food. But this identity of things points to Pip's fundamental insecurity. As Keats defines it, identity is a complex of individualizing features that comprise character, the product of suffering and experience whose materials are the heart, the intelligence, and the world. But identity also means sameness. Thus, Pip is torn between the desire to be unique and the need to belong. He struggles to create an identity based on difference and hierarchy, yet is continually affronted by guilt and criminality, which suggest a chthonic uniformity that transfixes language and meaning. As he grows up, he is constantly reminded of identity as sameness, as in the repeated reappearances of the "file," like the file of soldiers and the file with which the convict stirs his drink. He dreams of "the file coming at me out of a door," but is unable to see who holds it and screams himself awake (*GE*, 108). Bereft of a stabilizing origin, the file is the unstable locus of spectral fear that everything must collapse into analogical sameness. Pip associates it with the natural energy of Joe's hearth, but also with criminality; it frees a prisoner, but metaphorically organizes soldiers into a unit; it is overtly phallic, yet is used to sunder. The file symbolizes the inscrutability of the providential order that Pip endeavors to locate and appropriate. Experience threatens to lose itself in visual and lingual repetitions of the object Pip associates with his criminality; like the "odious casts" (*GE*, 223), likenesses Jaggers has made of clients after their executions, these likenesses threaten him with an inescapable identity. He is trapped between origins that must be invented and an identity he may lose control of.

As Joe confirms (*GE*, 105), Pip named himself, yet his manner of describing this is strangely circular:

> My father's name being Pirrip, and my Christian name Philip, my infant tongue could make of both names nothing longer or more explicit than Pip. So, I called myself Pip, and came to be called Pip. (*GE*, 35)

Joe seeks his name in identity with letters, signaling a fluid attitude towards language when he picks his initials out of something Pip has written: "One, two, three. Why, here's three Js, and three Os, and three J-O, Joes in it, Pip!" (*GE*, 75). Pip takes the slate and asks him to spell "Gargery" (he cannot), but does not correct his misspelling. This adumbrates the conflict between univocal language and meaning anterior to language that characterizes Dickens's own anxiety. The task of finding the middle space between self-referential univocality and the real—in effect, the task of incorporating Magwitch into Pip's text—is nearly daunting. Pip's spelling lesson confirms his desire to control the sign so that appearances do not collapse into sameness, but this is delusory, for finally, like all manipulations of signs separate from nature, it is self-referential.

His counterfeit selves decay and finally collapse when Magwitch, the signifier whose sign cannot be embellished, emerges from the shadowy past and reveals himself. Like Pip, Magwitch tried to discover thaumaturgic significance in the act of naming:

> I know'd my name to be Magwitch, chrisen'd Abel. How did I know it? Much as I know'd the birds' names in the hedges to be chaffinch, sparrer, thrush. I might have thought it was all lies together, only as the birds' names come out true, I supposed mine did. (*GE*, 360)

But he has no control over his naming, which does not "come out true"; for instance, his outcast status belies his name (Abel). Again, the variance between essence and naming reveals a narrative anxiety about language's capacity adequately to represent real experience. He supposes the naming was all lies, but he remains locked within signs he barely comprehends. Magwitch confusedly believes that language should point to truth, but suspects there is a lack of correlation between the two. Recognition of incompatibility between the name and the thing is not enough to create an alternative identity. Yet the name has become the thing by twisting the heart and mind to suit the human fiction. Magwitch believes he is a criminal because society has categorized him as one; a phrenologist (who reduces human nature to an allegorical reading of the head's appearance) once concluded he was "a terrible hardened one," but "had better a measured my stomach" (*GE*, 361). The body becomes a trope but, like language, it falls short as a sign of essence in the limited gaze of scientism. Yet that limited field is enticing, given the emotional and social instability that eats at every organizational endeavor. Magwitch's remote-control creation of a gentleman in Pip is his endeavor to master his environment, though through another person, for, unlike Compeyson, he cannot appear to be a gentleman himself. Thus, he becomes Pip's absentee father, God, and master-trope, though his creation seeks his benefactor in more acceptable places.

Pip's univocal "gentleman" exterior makes him resemble both monster and creator in *Frankenstein*. [19] But his constructed identity is counterfeit, a metaphor used throughout *Great Expectations* to depict the detachment of language and naming from reality.[20] Pip recalls that he swindled himself:

Surely a curious thing. That I should innocently take a bad half-crown of
somebody else's manufacture is reasonable enough; but that I should know-
ingly reckon the spurious coin of my own make, as good money! (*GE*, 247)

Yet society valorizes, indeed is built upon, counterfeit fictions that evade
any real attempt to represent what is, instead of what some class takes
reality to be. How one speaks (one's grasp of official language) becomes
the index of worth, just as bumps on the head do for the phrenologist.
Verbal and nonverbal languages alike lie, yet lies are also essential to art
that represents the real. This is art's conundrum. At his trial, it is assumed
that Magwitch, not Compeyson, is the main perpetrator because of the
way he looks and speaks. His desire during the struggle in the marshes to
tear Compeyson's face off to show the beast beneath adumbrates the
desire that language and essence be one and the same:

He's a liar born, and he'll die a liar. Look at his face; ain't it written there?
Let him turn those eyes of his on me. I defy him to do it. (*GE*, 68)

He assumes that others can read the specious "writing" he sees in Compeyson's face. We live in a cave of illusions, Estella suggests in chapter
38, contrasting the "dark confinement" of her rooms with the daylight
outside (*GE*, 324). What lies under the fictions of identity may be too
depressing to contemplate. Life is a series of illusions constructed of
words, attitudes, and myths, but we are always relatively in darkness.

In his *Inferno*, Dante offers an instructive parallel to what Dickens
means by counterfeit identities, suggesting a connection between
language that engages nature and valid art. The counterfeiter simulates
nature to escape engaging its flux. Yet, in doing so he also loses its beauties. Dante questions mimesis itself: counterfeiters are merely imitators
of imitators of truth because they create not from nature but from a
manipulation of appearances. The dropsical Master Adam, an arch-coun-
terfeiter Dante likens to Narcissus, is doomed to parody forever the
stamping of false coins by striking and being struck by Sinon the Greek,
the liar who hoodwinked the Trojans into bringing the horse within their
walls. Thus Dante connects counterfeiting money and language, which
he associates with self-love and, through an allusion to Cinyras, with
incest. What Master Adam most misses is the real nature he forgets when
counterfeiting:

The little brooks that from the green hills of Casentino run down into the
Arno, making their channels cool and moist ... the image of them parches
me far more than the malady that wastes my features.[21]

Pip's dislike of echoes (Biddy's, Trabb's boy's) is related to his fear that his identity as a gentleman is empty, that he is merely tricked out in signs that point to nothing real, while in truth Newgate is "in my breath and on my clothes" (*GE*, 284). Hence his anger at Biddy in chapter 19 for repeating what he tells her. To evade the "nameless" shadow, he creates a gentlemanly "human nature" as a perverse bulwark; in this system, it is Biddy who displays a bad nature by mockingly suggesting that he might not return to visit Joe. "Echoes" point both to the emptiness of words detached from the heart and to the possibility that life is merely a series of repetitions where, as Estella puts it, we "have no choice" and "are not free to follow our own devices" (*GE*, 285).

Far from staking out a middle space that emplots the real, Pip constructs a fairy tale that disintegrates. Thus his assumption, based on visual, not verbal, assurances, that Miss Havisham is his benefactor, who "had adopted Estella, she had as good as adopted me, and it could not fail to be her intention to bring us together" (*GE*, 253). At first she seems "the witch of the place," but soon she is a "patroness" of his romance with a "princess," Estella. Life will have closure, purpose, and meaning, and Pip will control all three. Of course, he discovers he is the subject of others' fictions, above all Magwitch's and Miss Havisham's, who has raised Estella to wreak revenge on all men for Compeyson's betrayal. Initially he recognizes his fictions as such, inventing for Mrs. Joe a "very tall and dark" (*GE*, 96) Miss Havisham who sits in a "black velvet coach" through whose window Estella hands her "cake and wine ... on a gold plate" (*GE*, 97). But more than he first realizes, Pip is attracted to a world where time is stopped, nature is shut out, and the past is frozen; its generative cause, Compeyson, is the absent deity behind the metonymic phenomena. It is, in sum, a parody of realism. Rejections merely exacerbate his desire to participate in a fantasy that potentially enables him to withdraw from shame, conflict, and reality altogether, in a place where memory, if painful, is at least predicated on a single, stable origin.

When Pip leaves Miss Havisham for what he thinks is the last time, after she begs his forgiveness, he sees her apparition in the ruined brewery:

> I fancied that I saw Miss Havisham hanging to the beam. So strong was the impression, that I stood under the beam shuddering from head to foot before I knew it was a fancy—though to be sure I was there in an instant. (*GE*, 413)

He returns, and the struggle he has putting out Miss Havisham's burning dress parodies the struggles between Compeyson and Magwitch:

> I still held her forcibly down with all my strength, like a prisoner who might escape; and I doubt if I even knew who she was, or why we had struggled, or that she had been in flames, or that the flames were out, until I saw the patches of tinder that had been her garments, no longer alight but falling in a black shower around us. (*GE*, 414)

The hanged goddess who mesmerizes and repels, she has been the ground on which Pip constructed his fictions. But now, like her garments, these fictions are in ashes. At the brink of death, she asks Pip to write down words that are neither fictive nor evasive: "Take the pencil and write under my name, 'I forgive her'" (*GE*, 415). But Pip cannot do so, for his hands, like his psyche, are too scarred. His inability to write down Miss Havisham's words points to a deeper anxiety about translating reality into its adequate representation.

Orlick's accusation that Pip "did for" his "shrew sister" is factually but not psychologically absurd: "Old Orlick bullied and beat, eh? Now you pays for it. You done it; now you pays for it" (*GE*, 437). Pip was guilty but not remorseful about his sister's injury; fear, not pity and sympathy, motivated his "unspeakable trouble" as to whether he "should at last dissolve that spell of childhood and tell Joe all that story" (*GE*, 148–49). The problem, again, is to translate internal realization into objective emplotment, which entails disclosing his (unwitting) supplying of the weapon in a spectacle of shame and confession. Orlick's connection to Mrs. Joe is revealed in another hieroglyph, this one unrecognizable, the "curious T" the brain-injured woman draws and which represents the hammer he attacked her with. Now she is passive and apparently conciliatory towards Orlick, unable to assault anyone with whip or words—in other words, the embodiment of Pip's desire for closure and control. Compeyson, Orlick tells Pip at the limekiln, "writes fifty hands," while Pip writes but one hand, a "sneaking" one all the same (*GE*, 438). Pip counters the world's inscrutable signs with secretive, univocal strategies, but he is endangered by physical erasure and verbal misrepresentation. Control of his text requires public communication as well as engagement with the real. Anxieties about writing, sex, and identity meet in the hands, which are further injured by Orlick at the limekiln. Jaggers, like Pilate, continually washes his hands, as if to eradicate the "filth and fat and blood and foam" (*GE*, 189) with which he is associated. Joe, on the other hand, shapes nature into artifacts with his hands and evades being bound to words, unless it is the doggerel poetry (a "lie," yet true in a deeper sense) that valorizes the "hart" over his father's and Pumblechook's failings.[22] Pip's problem, which adumbrates the realistic novelist's, is so to marshal language that the word and nature can coexist in a creative, ironic tension. But this may be a dream, like the maternal-paternal Joe.

In the confrontation at the limekiln, where identities and bodies alike can vanish with no trace, Pip glimpses a potential lost futurity. Now he realizes that love makes it possible to free himself from his ghosts. The novel questions the degree to which he can do this. But in articulating to himself how he does not want to be remembered, Pip realizes the importance of sympathetic remembrance, the only source of personal meaning and an afterlife. Pip "writes" his own death:

> Joe and Biddy would never know how sorry I had been that night, none would ever know what I had suffered, how true I had meant to be, what an agony I had passed through. The death close before me was terrible, but far more terrible than death was the dread of being misremembered after death. (*GE*, 436)

Thanks to his rescue, Pip avoids this misremembrance. But he also is unable to give his story an idyllic conclusion, as the novel's endings illustrate.

Pip's illness is comparable to Esther's as a centrally defining event. Surely he can reinvent his past, we are enticed to believe. After all, Magwitch's trial occurs during April, the time of rebirth, and he dies revivified by Pip's news that his daughter Estella "is living now. She is a lady and very beautiful. And I love her!" (*GE*, 470). But this reflects Pip's desire for a happy ending. His feverish dreams suggest both enclosure and the desire for transformation. Pip confronts "impossible existences" over which he has no control: he was "a brick in the house wall" yet entreated "to be released from the giddy place where the engineers had set" him. He was "a steel beam of a vast engine," yet he implored "to have the engine stopped" (*GE*, 471–72). Esther Summerson's dream of being one of the beads on a "flaming necklace" signaled the near collapse of her identity. In his delirium, Pip experiences an entrapment in oppositions from which there appears to be no release. Yet his dreams also suggest that a radical revaluation holds a key to breaking down the iron chain of causality from which dialectical opposition offers at best illusory egress, for also in his dreams, Pip struggles with "real people, in the belief that they were murderers," who turn out to mean to do him good. Rather than struggle, Pip "would then sink exhausted in their arms." In all kinds of "extraordinary transformations of the human face ... there was an extraordinary tendency in all these people, sooner or later, to settle down into the likeness of Joe" (*GE*, 472). Murderers turn out to be maternal, and people become the maternal-paternal figure of Joe. Pip experiences the regenerative "identity" of things in a human heart that transcends the world and rational intelligence, two of the three things Keats associated with soul-making. Yet Joe as a maternal-paternal figure is not an option; indeed, as Pip grows stronger, the tie between Joe's innocent heart and his more experienced one grows weaker. Eventually he must seek meaning with Estella, who has been nurtured to regard gender in violent oppositional terms. Here, it seems to me, is represented Dickens's anxiety about his own craft. Joe occupies in Pip's imagination the very middle space towards which authorial desire—autobiographical and realistic—yearns. Yet this space is within, and the difficulties of objectifying it in art are nearly insuperable.

By returning to the ruins of Satis house, Pip seeks regeneration, but in neither ending can this reexamination of the wasted Eden free him.[23] In the second and more ambiguous ending, what hope there is for a future with Estella is dominated by the past's shadows:

> I took her hand in mine, and we went out of the ruined place; and, as the morning mists had risen long ago when I first left the forge, so, the evening mists were rising now, and in all the broad expanse of tranquil light they showed to me, I saw no shadow of another parting from her. (*GE*, 493)

Pip does not experience the sort of idyllic escape Oliver Twist does; even an eccentric domestic idyll like Wemmick's seems impossible. In one sense, *Great Expectations* comes full circle, from shadows to shadows, tombstone to tombstone, parting to parting. Pip sets his nephew, Joe's and Biddy's son, on his parents' tombstone, just as Magwitch set him up on it years before. By alluding again to Milton's characterization of Adam and Eve's banishment from Eden ("The world was all before them"), as he does when recalling his departure from Joe's forge, Pip reinforces a tension between repetitions that imprison and the desire that this time the rising mists will lead to a better issue. The novel comes full circle, with just an ambiguous hint that he and Estella can be freed and united. Pip's ability to "bend the eternal shape of the past" is limited, as it must be in a life where we are the sums of our experiences. Yet he lives to tell his story to Estella and to young Pip. His story cannot have an idyllic conclusion, for experience has ravaged him. Yet he has accepted responsibility and learned.

Counterfeit Men: Skimpole and Harthouse

In *Bleak House,* Skimpole illustrates Dickens's mistrust of art for art's sake. With "no head for detail" and "no idea of time" (*BH*, 199), Skimpole represents an irresponsible aesthetic completely at odds with what Dickens thought a novel ought to be; in his world, "there should be no brambles of sordid realities" (*BH*, 122). But realities are what the Dickensian novel engages. Skimpole exudes a frozen youthfulness: he "had more the appearance, in all respects, of a damaged young man, than a well-preserved elderly one" (*BH*, 118). This contrasts with the contemporaneous stages of life in Esther's delirium in that it is a facade against time and change that ignores the terrors faced by other characters in *Bleak House.* He declares to his "enchanted" listeners that the world "should be strewn with roses; it should lie through bowers, where there was no spring, autumn, nor winter, but perpetual summer. Age or change should never wither it. The base word money should never be breathed near it!" (*BH*, 122). Yet this parodic idyll resembles too much the idyll Esther moves to when she marries Woodcourt; its self-evident blowsiness is merely closer to sordid reality—even if Skimpole, like old Turveydrop, ignores this—than little Bleak House. Dickens scorns this "mere child in the world" (*BH*, 119); even Esther gives up on him.

In perhaps his most revealing speech, Skimpole evades sympathy by viewing slaves as aesthetic objects:

> Take an extreme case. Take the case of the Slaves on American plantations. I dare say they are worked hard, I dare say they don't altogether like it, I dare say theirs is an unpleasant experience on the whole; but, they people the landscape for me, they give it a poetry for me, and perhaps that is one of the pleasanter objects of their existence. I am very sensible of it, if it be, and I shouldn't wonder if it were! (*BH*, 307)

Of course, they are not likely to be aware of the aesthetic pleasure they give Europeans in paintings. Skimpole "dares" to acknowledge that slaves live miserable lives, but their essence is aesthetic and hence their suffering does not matter. Simply by recreating life as a beautiful picture, Skimpole ignores ethical responsibility and guilt. His inhumanity is revealed by his heartless removal from Bleak House of the sick Jo, who, coming from the slums, is bereft of picturesque poetry. Up close, he resists the aesthetic play Skimpole can apply to slaves thousands of miles away. Moreover, Jo's infirm grasp of language (e.g., calling an "inquest" an "Inkwhich" [*BH*, 687]) may on some level remind Skimpole of the emptiness behind his apparent control over language.

At Skimpole's house, the only (debased) poetry is in his own apartment, which "was a palace to the rest of the house" (*BH*, 656), its "shabby luxury" (*BH*, 650) a constant reminder of the reality it is supposed to shut out. Thus it is hierarchical and oppressive. Skimpole's daughters, Arethusa, Laura, and Kitty (Beauty, Sentiment, and Comedy), are merely aesthetic signs, "their father's playthings in his idlest hours" (*BH*, 654), kept like beautiful toys with their poor families upstairs. Reduced to allegorical signs, which in and of themselves are inimical to realism, they deny reality yet display it. Their lingual tags do less to conceal their blowsiness than Esther's handkerchief does to ornament death.

In *Hard Times*, James Harthouse, likewise a parodic artist, manipulates signs at will until vanquished by Sissy Jupe. Like Steerforth in *David Copperfield*, he is incapable of reformation because his ironic readings are all manipulation. Yet his knowing is as limited as Skimpole's professed childishness. Dickens presents him as the modern embodiment of the devil in combining the ironist's ability to manipulate appearances, destroy them, and build them anew, all the while seeming to adhere to a belief system, except when, as in his manipulations of Louisa, it suits him to show his hand. Like Goethe's Mephistopheles, he assumes a modern guise:[24]

> When the Devil goeth about like a roaring lion, he goeth about in a shape by which few but savages and hunters are attracted. But, when he is trimmed, smoothed, and varnished, according to the mode; when he is aweary of vice, and aweary of virtue, used up as to brimstone, and used up as to bliss ... then ... he is the very Devil. (*HT*, 137)

Harthouse cannot understand human complexity or love. But he can appeal simultaneously to the utilitarians, whose language he cynically replicates, and to Tom and Louisa, who resent their emotional repressions. He is agreeable and amiable; he fits in. He is able to manipulate people because, guiltlessly, he believes in nothing, including himself. He approaches life as a perverse theater in which people are merely fungible roles. "Having found out everything to be worth nothing," Harthouse is "equally ready for anything" (*HT*, 94). He is adept at dissecting a social fiction, but he is a void. At first, Harthouse cannot read Louisa, but soon he establishes a secretive familiarity. Once he realizes that "this whelp [Tom] is the only creature she cares for" (*HT*, 100), the stage is set for his double seduction. He tells Louisa that he is "quite as much attached" to utilitarian ideas as if he believed in them:

> I have not so much as the slightest predilection left. I assure you I attach not the least importance to any opinions ... any set of ideas will do just as much good as any other set, and just as much harm as any other set. (*HT*, 99)

Harthouse's "as if" is decisive. A simile, more than a dynamic metaphor, suggests a stable analogy between the literal and the figurative. But Harthouse's simile reverses the relation between the literal and the figurative, positing belief as equivalent to self-referential fictions. He even reveals his strategy to Louisa to build her confidence in him.

While he realizes that Louisa lives a lie of propriety, his reading of her is as limited as Mrs. Sparsit's. Harthouse can manipulate a two-dimensional concept of the heart, but not the heart itself. Like Mephistopheles, he thinks that people will always remain the way they are because, like the utilitarians, he acknowledges only a concept of humanity. Near the end of his stay, he tells Sissy Jupe, "I have had no particularly evil intentions" (*HT*, 177). But this does not point to any self-knowledge. He is more rationally self-conscious than Bitzer, and a much better manipulator of language, but he understands the human heart no better. The archdestructor of words is a prisoner of appearances. This is most evident in his attempted seduction of Louisa in Bounderby's parodic garden. We, along with Mrs. Sparsit, become voyeurs as, like Milton's Satan, Harthouse uses every lingual power to seduce her, including a noticeably prosaic reduction of *carpe diem* that parodies *Paradise Lost*:

> But we have so little time to make so much of, and I have come so far, and am altogether so devoted, and distracted. There never was a slave at once so devoted and ill-used by his mistress. To look for your sunny welcome that has warmed me into life, and to be received in your frozen manner, is heart-rending. (*HT*, 161)

Louisa plays Eve's role. Mrs. Sparsit, through whose vantage we witness the scene, reenacts the Satan who, prior to his verbal seductions, is stunned by Eve. Harthouse parodies Satan's empty rhetoric, Mrs. Sparsit the visual seduction which is Satan's and Eve's weakness. As so often is the case, in other words, Dickens foregrounds the bifurcation between visual and lingual fields, which are both detached from experience and entoiled in fictive strategies. Harthouse succumbs to Eve's error in mistaking rhetoric for truth: he thinks that because Louisa says she will follow him into Coketown, she must; he is so agitated when she fails to appear on cue that he cannot read his newspaper. When confronted by Sissy, he generates a phony courtesy, a form of the indifference he connects with "high-breeding" and "conviction"(*HT*, 174). But she is impervious to his flattery (*HT*, 238), while he is rendered almost inarticulate and childish ("He bit his lip") by her mysterious power. He leaves Coketown.

Harthouse's reduction of people to game pieces is equivalent to the laissez-faire dictum that no one has responsibility for anyone else:

> Where was the great difference between the two schools, when each chained her down to material realities, and inspired her with no faith in anything else? What was there in her soul for James Harthouse to destroy, which Thomas Gradgrind had nurtured there in its state of innocence! (*HT*, 127)

Thus, Louisa is at once fallen and unfallen: her seduction by Harthouse has no literal sexual consequence. The embodiment of sexual purity, Sissy momentarily mortifies his vanity and plants in him "a secret sense of having failed and been ridiculous" (*HT*, 179). But to appear ridiculous is to be guilty of an aesthetic, not a moral, failure. She succeeds in touching Harthouse "in the cavity where his heart should have been" (*HT*, 176) because Dickens endows her with a childlike imagination and love, a residue of Wordsworthian natural piety that Coketown can sustain only in a girl who carries an elysian inviolability. She offers the starkest contrast to Harthouse, who is "incapable of any Arcadian proceeding whatever" (*HT*, 130) and whose overly-refined self-consciousness has led him to reduce even conscience to a concept. Her love, trust, and fancy make her Dickens's illustration of the social values missing, ignored, or repressed in Coketown. Harthouse's veneer, once penetrated, reveals a nonentity that, unable to commit to anything, merely disintegrates and, with associative transposition, will be reconstituted elsewhere, ironically amidst the Egyptian pyramids, those symbols of historicity and, for Samuel Johnson, of the vanity of human wishes:

> The defeat may now be considered perfectly accomplished. Only a poor girl—only a stroller—only James Harthouse made nothing of—only James Harthouse a Great Pyramid of failure. The Great Pyramid put it into his head to go up the Nile. (*HT*, 179)

Idyllic Women

The sort of "massive self-confidence" in nineteenth-century realism that, according to George Levine, implies a "radical doubt,"[25] is evident in Dickens's idealization of Rose Maylie, whose very surname ("May lie") suggests the untenable nature of the idyllic escape she represents.[26] Her "artless loveliness" connects her with the naive as defined by Schiller and Rousseau. Harry Maylie associates her with "the young, the beautiful, and good" (*OT*, 220), and similarly Nancy, when she meets Rose at her hotel, calls her "young, and good, and beautiful" (*OT*, 258). In both cases, Goethe's standard formulation, the "good, the true, the beautiful," is altered so that the "true" is replaced by the "young," the one portion of the formulation which (as Rose's near death reminds us) is transitory, even in an idyllic realm abstracted from historical flux. In the meeting at London Bridge, Brownlow offers Nancy a venue into Rose's idyllic world, "a quiet asylum, either in England, or, if you fear to remain here, in some foreign country" (*OT*, 296). Yet she cannot live in what Harry calls the "bright home of lasting rest" (*OT*, 220), which is aesthetically pacifying yet incompatible with modern life. Rose points to the dichotomy when, refusing Harry's first proposal, she tells him, "Look into the world; think how many hearts you would be proud to gain, are there" (*OT*, 221).

When Harry Maylie rejects society's dialectic for a new "rank and station" as a county vicar amidst the "smiling fields and waving trees in England's richest county" (*OT*, 338), he accepts a domestic idyll and a village church. Yet in Chertsey, the Wordsworthian effusions are undercut by the eruptions of Monks and Fagin, and by Rose's nearly fatal illness. The narrator nevertheless insists on affirming nature:

> Men who look on nature, and their fellow-men, and cry that all is dark and gloomy, are in the right; but the sombre colours are reflections from their own jaundiced eyes and hearts. The real hues are delicate, and need a clearer vision. (*OT*, 215)

How can men who cry that "all is dark and gloomy" be "in the right" if nature's "real hues are delicate"? The answer is suggested by Oliver's strange dream, which follows this passage, in which "reality and imagination become so strangely blended that it is afterwards almost a matter of impossibility to separate the two" (*OT*, 216). Rose's illness, unlike Esther Summerson's in *Bleak House*, does not deprive her of her beauty; nor does she have, like Esther, daemonic doubles. But Oliver Twist does, in Monks, Fagin, and Sikes.

In *Hard Times*, Dickens valorizes sympathy, love, and quasi-Christian faith, ideals so diffuse as to arouse the suspicion that his imprecision signals a hesitation to embrace what may turn out to be evanescent. The abyss always looms: Mrs. Sparsit envisages Louisa descending the stairs into darkness; the workers buried in tenements are released down ladders that disgorge the dead into the "labyrinth of narrow courts upon courts" (*HT*, 48). In contrast, the naive energy of Sissy, whose restorative influence enables her to "shine like a beautiful light" (*HT*, 172) upon Louisa's darkness after she flees Harthouse's attempted seduction, seems like wish fulfillment. Dickens's own sense of abandonment is reflected in Louisa's alienation from childhood dreams, beliefs, and fears, the "drying up of every spring and fountain in her young heart as it gushed out" (*HT*, 151). The awareness of memory's loss does not ensure that it can be reclaimed through another's influence. Yet in the novel's idyllic coda Louisa, though herself infertile, participates in Sissy's ideally extended childlike innocence. By loving Sissy's children, she grows "learned in childish lore; thinking no innocent and pretty face ever to be despised" (*HT*, 226). But this is precarious. If no "innocent and pretty face" is "ever to be despised," what happens when visual ugliness is at variance with inner beauty, or vice versa? This issue, of course, is central to *Frankenstein* and *Bleak House*. The feminized aesthetic realm, like Sleary's circus, is questionable. Dickens implicitly questions its relevance even as the narrator asserts its power to transform personality through touch, sight, and projected memories of innocence. The narrator's hope that psychological mutilation will cease occurs in an idyllic wish-projection, which leaves it to the reader whether the imagination and the intellect can exist in balance:

> Dear reader! It rests with you and me, whether, in our two fields of action, similar things shall be or not. Let them be! We shall sit with lighter bosoms on the hearth, to see the ashes of our fires turn grey and cold. (*HT*, 227)

Idyllic Conclusions: *Oliver Twist* and *Bleak House*

In his idyllic conclusions Dickens questions the relevance of univocality to realism yet desires closure all the same. We are left at the end of *Oliver Twist* with a choice between Fagin's manic delusions of escape emanating from his "belief" in Oliver's acting, and Oliver's infuriatingly pious "Let me say a prayer. Do!" (*OT*, 346), and between Sikes's horrifying trip to the country pursued by Nancy's eyes and Harry Maylie's country parsonage. Dickens suggests that the restful idyllic and the energetic London worlds are irreconcilable; his association of "woman's original nature" (*OT*, 254) with childlike nature likewise suggests an opposition between Edenic aesthetic rest and a fallen, sexually confused society bereft of a positive paternity and organized by pasteboard. Oliver Twist gravitates between these worlds, eventually finding rest in the idyllic upper-class world with its book-lined walls that seem like bulwarks against the circumambient flux. In this alternative world the narrator would "paint" Rose Maylie "the life and joy of the fire-side circle and the lively summer group" and "her and her dead sister's child happy in their mutual love" (*OT*, 350). Yet, Dickens suggests, beautiful painting and writing remain threatened by infernal art and social chaos. Brownlow's study is but a barely credible extension of Rose's aesthetic near-autonomy into London.

Dickens is finally at an impasse in reconciling the two worlds of *Oliver Twist*, the idyllic in which reality is denied, and the labyrinthine, in which reality is warped by theatrical strategies. Agnes's "weak and erring" (*OT*, 350) legacy is reversed, as Brownlow, having adopted Oliver, seeks to supply him with the childhood of which he has been deprived. It is a happy ending, but one that creates dissatisfaction:

> How Mr. Brownlow went on, from day to day, filling the mind of his adopted child with stores of knowledge, and becoming attached to him, more and more, as his nature developed itself, and shewed the thriving seeds of all he wished him to become ... these are all matters which need not to be told. (*OT*, 350)

Perhaps Dickens suspected that they need not be told because they could not, except in an idyllic realm that no longer could be the locus of valid fiction.

In *Bleak House,* Dickens displays his interest in the degree to which people try to fix the past in a particular form. Such efforts parallel the novelist's attempts to fix meaning in his word matrix which, to the degree that it suggests finality, is false. This in turn entails a creative means of organizing experience, for in creating character and context, the realistic novel must represent time. It is necessary, Nietzsche argues, to forget the past. Yet at the same time, as White puts it, "Out of the capacity to remember the past ... all specifically *human* constructions arise."[27] But this can be destructive, whether it entails a projection of innocence into the past (a form of anarchism),[28] that seemingly reflects history or human nature, yet is really a fictional construct detached from experience. Miss Havisham remembers too well; Pip thinks he flees his past but really is bound by it. In *Bleak House,* Chesney Wold embodies two frozen pasts: Lord Dedlock's family tradition (and curse) and the one Lady Dedlock invents to escape a past which catches up to her. Like Oscar Wilde does in *The Picture of Dorian Gray*, Dickens uses the family portrait gallery as an emblem of the inability to evade the past and apply it creatively to life. The sunlight projects a simulacrum of animation onto the portraits, which seem to mock the living when "strange movements" cause them to "thaw":

> Down into the bosom of a stony shepherdess there steals a fleck of light and warmth, that would have done it good, a hundred years ago. One ancestress of Volumnia, in high-heeled shoes, very like her—casting the shadow of that

virgin event before her full two centuries—shoots out into a halo and becomes a saint. (*BH*, 620–21)

Their illusory life is projected from the outside. Like corpses momentarily galvanized, they must have thought of the "gap that they would make in this domain when they were gone." The narrator gives their "gap" a momentary memory, but they "pass from my world, as I pass from theirs, now closing the reverberating door; so leave no blank to miss them, and so die" (*BH*, 620). After death, the individual can only live on in the memories of others; yet in the Dedlocks' world only false fictions are embraced as bulwarks against dissolution. Indeed, the narrator must provide the blank with which to memorialize and miss them: once he is gone, there is only nonmeaning. So there is not even a sense of disconnection that requires the creation of a beneficent fiction that gives life coherence. The paintings are meaningless to all but the narrator and the reader, though barnyard animals, being "artists," might be able to do something with them.

Bleak House concludes with a series of univocal narrative possibilities that events explode; they illustrate once again Dickens's desire for closure, yet his realization that realism precludes this.[29] Old Turveydrop's wish to rise above an England that has "degenerated very much," whose gentlemen have been replaced by "a race of weavers" (*BH*, 246), adumbrates an attitude antithetical to realism. The exploitative old dancing master wants his son to "polish—polish!—polish!" (*BH*, 246). Dickens clearly disapproves; but Dickens, it could be said, at once polishes and subverts his own conclusion.[30] If he is drawn to the idyll in which actuality and the ideal are reconciled, he also displays an anxiety towards his own medium. To polish a text is to give it a meretricious ending. Yet what is idyllic closure but such a false appearance? Polished prose, polished plot, polished ending: Dickens's anxiety towards these is encoded above all in his interpenetrating, but never reconciled, narratives. Behind Turveydrop's deportment and tight cravat is a rotting corpse that, like Krook's, disintegrates.

The ludicrousness of the idyllic is evident in the narrator's description of a moonlight pastoral London, in which, we soon discover, Tulkinghorn's murder has occurred:

> Not only is it a still night on dusty high roads and on hill-summits, whence a wide expanse of country may be seen in repose, quieter and quieter as it spreads away into a fringe of trees against the sky, with the grey ghost of a bloom upon them; not only is it a still night in gardens and in woods, and on the river where the water-meadows are fresh and green. ... but even on this stranger's wilderness of London there is some rest. Its steeples and towers,

and its one great dome, grow more ethereal; its smoky house-tops lose their grossness, in the pale effulgence; the noises that arise from the streets are fewer and are softened, and the footsteps on the pavements pass more tranquilly away. In these fields of Mr. Tulkinghorn's inhabiting, where the shepherds play on Chancery pipes that have no stop, and keep their sheep in the fold by hook and by crook until they have shorn them exceeding close, every noise is merged, this moonlight night, into a distant ringing hum, as if the city were a vast glass, vibrating. (*BH*, 719)

The stillness of this ironic London pastoral belies the activity that violently ends Tulkinghorn's life and later shakes the static fictions of Chancery. Like the paintings at Chesney Wold, the appearance of London can be manipulated by the narrator to appear quite different than the muddy place in chapter 1. Yet the imposition of idyllic rest on this setting is comically inappropriate, above all in the thought of the crafty Tulkinghorn and his fellow attorneys as shepherds that "play on Chancery pipes" in a synaesthetic idyll in which "every noise is merged" (*BH*, 719). Implicitly Dickens denies any possibility of a univocal ending, which the unironic idyllic-pastoral represents: signs are disconnected from any stable reference. Any attempt to recognize experience absolutely is false; rather, it is possible only to present a matrix of words that suggests experience yet calls attention to its own inadequacy. There is no God, whatever the ostensible statements may be: instead, there are only parodic substitutes like John Jarndyce or Inspector Bucket, whose inadequacies or inexorableness merely call attention to the degree to which signs and essences are detached. Hence Tulkinghorn's allegorical, pointing Roman is inherently meaningless, though for now, in its current matrix of realistic meaning (its previous context was domestic), it parodies the legal fiction over which he presides. The Roman suggests the absence of transcendence, as do Tulkinghorn's boxes with their "transcendent names" (*BH*, 182):

For many years the persistent Roman has been pointing, with no particular meaning, from that ceiling. It is not likely that he has any new meaning in him to-night. Once pointing, always pointing—like any Roman, or even Briton, with a single idea. (*BH*, 720)

This "single idea" can be any obsession that reduces meaning to a mere shell, like Tulkinghorn's strange desire to discover Lady Dedlock's past and confront her with it. Yet the idyll is likewise a single idea based on a reconciliation of is and ought, the real and the ideal. The end of *Bleak House*, like the allegorical Roman, points nowhere, yet Dickens wishes it

to point somewhere. In this desire lies the novel's inherent inconsistency
and fascination.

Bucket, too, points quite often as he reconstructs meaning from clues,
unravelling Tulkinghorn's murder and imaginatively entering Lady
Dedlock's mind as if to foreknow her actions like the parodic deity (and
artist) he is.[31] He reflects Dickens's desire for practical meaning that reconciles art and life. Yet he is scary and inexorable. Bucket is able mentally to rise above London and attain a narrative perspective approaching
that of the third-person narrator, creating and pointing to conclusions:

> The Augurs of the Detective Temple invariably predict, that when Mr. Bucket
> and that finger are in much conference, a terrible avenger will be heard of
> before long. (*BH*, 768)

In a world bereft of unifying meaning, he, like Jarndyce, offers a kind of
providential vision:

> There, he mounts a high tower in his mind, and looks out far and wide. Many
> solitary figures he perceives, creeping through the streets; many solitary
> figures out on heaths, and roads, and lying under haystacks. But the figure he
> seeks is not among them. Other solitaries he perceives in nooks of bridges,
> looking over; and in shadowed places down by the river's level; and a dark,
> dark, shapeless object drifting with the tide, more solitary than all, clings with
> a drowning hold on his attention.
>
> Where is she? Living or dead, where is she? If, as he folds the handkerchief
> and carefully puts it up, it were able, with an enchanted power, to bring
> before him the place where she found it, and the night landscape near the
> cottage where it covered the little child, would he descry her there? (*BH*, 824)

The inherently meaningless handkerchief connects a dead baby with
Esther and her mother, and thus points somewhere in the narrator's (and
Bucket's) matrix. Bucket's construction blends almost seamlessly with
the third-person narrator's:

> On the waste, where the brick-kilns are burning with a pale blue fire ...
> traversing this deserted, blighted spot there is a lonely figure with the sad
> world to itself, pelted by the snow and driven by the wind, and cast out, it
> would seem, from all companionship. It is the figure of a woman, too; but it
> is miserably dressed, and no such clothes ever came through the hall, and out
> at the great door, of the Dedlock mansion. (*BH*, 824)

Accompanying Bucket on his detective mission, Esther is led finally to
the *Nullpunkt* of London, the graveyard where Nemo, "no one," is

buried.[32] His name also suggests the Greek *nemos*, meaning glade, an open space in a forest that evokes the pastoral idyll of which his life, reduced to nothing, was the antitype. Bucket's practical imagination leads him to reveal Lady Dedlock's past to Sir Leicester and to become Dickens's mask in revealing to Esther the reality behind Skimpole's poetry, the physical dissolution at the heart of illusory idylls, which nonetheless must be valorized. Yet as Skimpole's accomplice in removing Jo from Bleak House and pushing him along out of London, Bucket is a terrible avenger, objective and practical in his reconstructions and readings of evidence. He is the inverse Carlylean sansculotte, the instrument of social power who tears the wrappings from society to reveal an underlying power and reconstitute it, against which Esther is silent and powerless. If meaning is to be created from this doubleness, it is up to the reader.

6

George Eliot's Visions: Idealism and Realism

In the two novels I shall discuss, *Silas Marner* and *Middlemarch*, George Eliot employs realism to reconstruct English provincial society of the turn of the nineteenth century and the time leading up to the first Reform Bill of 1832 from the vantages of 1861 and 1871–72. This enables her to distance current change through "histories" of unhistorical lives, much as Mary Shelley distances terror through her story. But just where are Eliot's terrors, the energies, destructive and creative, that rage in perceptual and historical fields in other novelists we have discussed? Austen, a Burkean without the *frisson*, simply distances war and revolution from her realistic field while slyly acknowledging their existence. Very much the contextualist, George Eliot places her characters in societies that limit individual transcendence yet also offer Virgil's hand, so to speak, not the Medusa death-stare, the petrifying monstrosity glimpsed by Burke, Shelley, Wilde, and Conrad. Instead of the abyss, we have in *Middlemarch* a vision of life as a middle state in which meaning is incomplete yet in progress. Fragments indeed there are—fragments of ancient Rome, of Casaubon's Gog and Magog, which threaten to overwhelm Dorothea—but it is possible to create meaning. In Dorothea Brooke's perceptions, we have not an abyss or horror but a more domesticated "blankness" that must be filled. We do not know what lies within Silas Marner's cataleptic *Nullpunkt*; mysteries remain, though it is important that we translate ourselves into another person's point of vision. There is limited disorder in the political-historical sphere—in Brooke's election campaign, for instance—but Eliot shoves historical chaos out of her historical field, replacing it with a social "web" that both limits aspiration and provides a kind of assurance. Hayden White writes that Nietzsche thought that the historical field should "be regarded, in the same way that the perceptual field is, as an occasion for image making, not as matter for conceptualization."[1] Like Herder, Eliot judges no one (or claims she doesn't) in the endeavor to understand others without constricting preconceptions. "For admission to the realist novel," George Levine writes in *The Realistic Imagination*, "the monstrous energies must be dammed."[2] For Eliot, as for Hardy, the monstrous has been domesticated as conceptualization and idealism.

Gotthold Ephraim Lessing, Susan Gustavson writes, was interested in the "instability and openness of representation" and thus investigated poetry, which "encourages excursis," while visual art "stifles creative response."[3] So is Eliot, for whom Lessing is a subtext in *Middlemarch*. Like Charlotte Brontë, she explores and places idealistic strategies aimed at controlling the visual through univocal language. Realism's goal, I noted in the preceding chapter, is to create images that make the reader see without closing off mystery. The novelist or character must learn to mediate the visual within a fluid verbal field without being transfixed in the process. Eliot underscores the dangers of visual placements generated from within and without, and undercuts them through verisimilar multiplicity that parodies lingual idealism. Thus, the cataleptic Silas Marner, his life frozen by a providential univocality he physically parodies yet cannot control, becomes silent statuary that encourages, yet resists, interpretation; he adumbrates the central problem of realism in order to hold the reader's vision in a fiction of reality between the extremes of abstraction and chaos (or blankness). Similarly, in *Middlemarch*, Dorothea Brooke is the object of aesthetic placement from without, idealistic shortsightedness from within. Naumann tries to reduce her to a visual field as an "antique form animated by Christian sentiment," and Casaubon nearly inscribes her within his reduction of myth to historical explanation. That is, she is assaulted by visual and verbal univocalities, which she must learn to subsume under a tragic realism grounded in belief and sympathy. This entails reconciling art with the lowly and abject (Lessing's concern as well) so that the experiential field extends across the full fabric of society. *Silas Marner*, it seems to me, adumbrates this ambition, as the narrator embraces a rural society with a parodic providential vision that delineates the limits of the known (that is, affirms mystery while suggesting there is a rational explanation beyond the text) and supersedes the Romantic-Wordsworthian register in which Eppie is bound.

Especially during his cataleptic fits, Silas Marner seems a mystery, a *Nullpunkt* around which people generate fictions. Thus, he symbolizes the problem of art itself to create verisimilitude from blankness (the clean page, but also the absence of ulteriority). Like Dorothea Brooke, whose need to cover "blankness" the narrator continually stresses, he becomes a nexus of others' misreadings owing to his transfixion (he rejects the past by burying himself in routine; she constricts the future to her idealism). The seizures are transfixions that open him to readings based on visual impressions (he does not, of course, speak). As if enchanted by an "invisible wand" into "a graven image, with wide but sightless eyes," he becomes a repository for the "vagueness and mystery" that people need to make life bearable.[4] Yet Silas remembers nothing of his experiences— what Macey calls his soul's going "to school in this shell-less state" (*SM*, 55)—because, paradoxically, mystery requires the language and conscious vision which, if reduced to univocality, merely transfixes us. The mythmaking impulse covers blankness with meaning, as if to avoid facing directly the question of whether the vision beyond this world is sightless and all meaning is in the shell, while the kernel is merely empty, or worse.[5] So Silas is apparently a "graven" gap between experience and its emplotment from which people can create fictions (or "mists," Nietzsche calls them in "The Use and Abuse of History") to suit their liking; yet he also adumbrates the possibility of nonmeaning, being, in this shell-less state, hard, univocal, reduced to a visual instant from which he must escape into society. Indeed, in associating the Evil One (Macey's "those who could teach them more than their neighbors" [*SM*, 55]) and God (Dolly Winthrop's "Them above us" [*SM*, 204]) with multiplicity, the people of Raveloe instinctively resist Silas's parodic marmoreal univocality.

In *Silas Marner,* the agents of univocality include the Lantern Yard Brethren and Nancy Lammeter, who discern God's meaning in "lots" which, Eliot suggests, are merely chance (or human device) disguised as providential order. Literal or figurative shortsightedness unites those unable to rise above themselves.[6] Yet they visualize meaning and language in radically delimited explanations of mystery. The Lantern Yard Brethren pursue "hard words" that confirm a punishing God. Their "mastering purpose," like Bulstrode's in *Middlemarch*, arises from the desire to discern a providential order; thus the mysterious is delimited in metonymic organizations and symbols. Macey separates expression ("body") from thing ("soul") to explain Silas's seizures, assuming that the "kernal" of his experience is somewhere out there, while the motionless body is merely empty, not the bodily sign of this higher (or infernal) mystery. The Brethren, in contrast, insist that what is visible must point directly to the truth it symbolizes: thus, Silas seems to have raided the congregation's till, if there is visible evidence he has done so, which his supposedly devil-inspired silence confirms. The visual is true even if words cannot verify this, indeed, especially if words are absent. The absence of any spiritual vision during Silas's "outward trance"

suggests that a stably definable Satan (not "those who could teach them")
must be behind it. They create assurance, not myth, from mystery.
Similarly, Nancy imagines a controlled future in her courtship of
Godfrey, creating an "inward drama" free of nuance, organicism, and
sympathy (*SM*, 151). Her "high reason," merely the inverse of Godfrey's
lawlessness ("God free"), is at odds with a society where "things *will*
change." Her refusal to adopt a baby when she learns she cannot bear one
is a fatalistic closing off of future possibility masquerading as
providential control. The unused baby clothes she keeps in the drawer are
visual emblems of a suppressed "longing for what was not given" (*SM*,
215). Nancy, too, manipulates the visual, by insisting that Priscilla wear
an identical dress (*SM*, 150–51), for instance, or by (as her homely sister
recalls) avoiding whippings as a child by looking "prim and innicent as a
daisy" (*SM*, 150). Her wish, as Priscilla puts it, to "see the men
mastered" (*SM*, 150) locates her field of control in the visual. Silas, in
turn, condemns "a God of lies" (*SM*, 61), but he too has subordinated
himself to chance, especially the visual lots through which God
ostensibly speaks. His lingual incapacity is suggested by his weaving as
much as by his cataleptic speechlessness. Until Eppie gradually
incorporates him into nature and society, he is the parodic artist bound to
a transfixed state at the peripheries of self-expression, without the
capacity to use the gaps between memory and emplotment to free himself
from a psychological state his catalepsy mirrors. Like Miss Havisham, he
is bound to a single event and suffused with resentment; an end in itself,
the event cannot be transformed, but merely repeated. In other words, he
has experienced, like Esther Summerson or Pip, the collapse of moveable
fictions. Time is a series of temporal instances that merely repeat each
other:

> He seemed to weave, like the spider, from pure impulse, without reflection.
> Every man's work, pursued steadily, tends in this way to become an end in
> itself. (*SM*, 64)[7]

Because it does not reach out into a wider community, his weaving is
merely onanistic:

> The same sort of process has perhaps been undergone by wiser men, when
> they have been cut off from faith and love—only, instead of a loom and a
> heap of guineas, they have had some erudite research, some ingenious
> project, or some well-knit theory. (*SM*, 68–69)

Thus, Eliot suggests a connection between weaving and other forms of
intellectual organization, like Casaubon's. Weaving is a metaphor for the

fabric of social life and the production of fictions, in which the lifeless is given the appearance of animation. Hence, what McLaverty terms Silas's fetishist treating of objects "as though they have a life like his own" (*SM*, 329) points to the artist's function in manipulating nuances of details to create "life," verisimilitude. Yet Silas's fictions, like his reassembled pot, (his "memorial") point to their own inadequacy (*SM*, 69). Every night Silas reenacts his onanistic love-worship of gold, the hard object that creates at best collapsible fictions that freeze him in parodic repetitions of relationships between self and other:

> He loved them all. He spread them out in heaps and bathed his hands in them; then he counted them and set them up in regular piles, and felt their rounded outline between his thumb and fingers, and thought fondly of the guineas that were only half-earned by the work in his loom, as if they had been unborn children. (*SM*, 70)

In *The Gay Science,* Nietzsche suggests that "logic is a tyrannical moment within the human power of rhetorical play." For George Eliot, this logic is aesthetic as well as moral-theological, and is connected with the need for a stable substitute for the absent God. Hans Kellner writes that Vico made "the point that logic is not a truth behind events, but rather an event itself, a deed, a created thing."[8] Eliot reacts to a world in which transcendental truth is absent, and in which the author must provide the master-trope that subsumes comedy, irony, and tragedy alike. Like Dickens, Eliot valorizes sympathy as the godlike unifying emotion but struggles to reify, yet question, the need for a unifying voice, which, if care is not taken, may solidify into that "tyrannical moment" of the ideal, which contradicts realism and the open-ended freedom it entails. So realism must communicate a deed in such a way that language does not harden. This I take to be the point behind Macey's story in *Silas Marner* about the botched wedding ceremony, which he recounts at the Rainbow tavern in chapter 6. In a sense, all three topics in this pivotal scene are about the search for "ghosts," the "truth behind events," and the dangers inherent in pursuing this search too far. Macey recounts how his elderly predecessor mistook husband for wife in reading the wedding vows:

> "Wilt thou have this man to thy wedded wife?" says he, and then he says, "Wilt thou have this woman to thy wedded husband?" says he. (*SM*, 101)

No one in the congregation noticed the error, including Mr. Lammeter and his bride. Macey recalls being troubled by the variance between words and deed, ceremony and marriage:

Is't the meanin' or the words as makes folks fast i' wedlock? For the parson meant right, and the bride and bridegroom meant right. But then, when I come to think on it, meanin' goes but a little way i' most things, for you may mean to stick things together and your glue may be bad, and then where are you? (101)

The minister's answer to this conundrum, that "it's neither the meaning nor the words—it's the re*ges*ter does it—that's the glue" (*SM*, 102), places in a tangible object, the parish register, the verbal trace of what a marriage is. For Eliot, as for Goethe, the deed precedes the word: thus, the register has truth only to the extent that it reifies actions, intentions, and choices. The mistake here is in the language, which is irreducible yet subject to a liberating play which exists independently of the truth of the marriage itself. To insist too much on terminology, Eliot suggests, is to be implicated in the hard logic that seeks meaning within itself, and thus makes logic the master, for truth is in human actions and sympathies, not in the search for a secret code that makes language and logic the determinants of deeds. Man and woman are confused in the wedding ceremony. Meanings, like masculine and feminine functions, are fragments "glued" together; perhaps it's best that the glue *be* bad, for the consequence of attaching meanings too successfully is a lie that has the appearance of truth. Nancy Lammeter's parents were married whether or not Drumlow's words were a bit off base; its success or failure was a question of actions, not words or writing. Nancy's marriage to Godfrey may be ceremonially accurate but is marred in its action. Truth is somewhere other than in literal words; Drumlow's humor in having the "re*ges*ter" "do" truth suggests, as Susan Cohen argues, that truth is in an "authoritative" piece of writing linked with activity. What is written does not make a marriage, Eliot suggests, but merely codifies the ceremony.[9]

The other conversations at the Rainbow, about the Red Durham and Cliff's ghost, continue this basic theme, illustrating the middle space of realism that Eliot champions better than any of her univocal pronouncements (the Wordsworthian overlay on Eppie, or chapter 17 of *Adam Bede*) possibly can.[10] The landlord's "analogical argument" (*SM*, 105) places him rather comically as a parodic deity amidst the claims of logic, language, reporting and seeing, from which beliefs are created or mysteries maintained. The blacksmith Dowlas, the logician in the group, insists that meaning derives from quantifiable experience: the ghost is either there or not. The possibility of another, creative rhetorical space, in which the ghost is both there and not there, is not a possibility to him. John Snell, the landlord, maintains a neutrality amidst conflicting arguments ("You're both right and you're both wrong" is his refrain), while Dowlas insists that the "gho'ses" of Cliff's Holiday should show themselves so that the actual truth about the legend will be clear. Much as Forster's Margaret Schlegel resists defining proportion too closely, he declares about the existence or nonexistence of ghosts, "I'm for holding with both sides; for, as I say, the truth lies between 'em" (*SM*, 105). But he makes no effort to define this truth.

Dowlas scoffs at Bob the butcher's banter about the "fine beast" he has driven in, whose identity the farrier insists on establishing: "Was it a red Durham?" (*SM*, 96). The landlord mediates an increasingly angry exchange over whether the cow's importance is in its surface appearance (name, color, identification with the cow the farrier just "drenched") or in its being, the butcher says, "a lovely carkiss—and anybody as was reasonable, it 'ud bring tears into their eyes to look at it" (*SM*, 96). That is, the debate is over whether the animal's essence is in its visual sign or in the emotional effect it has on the beholder, where the naming itself is almost irrelevant, like the words in the wedding ceremony. Eliot suggests that the purpose of discourse is neither rational truth nor its complete evasion but a verbal play. But what of the ghost, which cannot be seen? Here Eliot adumbrates the search for meaning behind language and seeing, which is perilous, yet makes possible the social relations that nurture the individual in a broader social matrix. The facts about Cliff are fleeting and shrouded in myth. As with old Mr. Lammeter, who may or may not have been a shepherd, his origins are mysterious. The discussion nearly breaks down over another dispute about origins, what Kellner terms the "postulated 'before.'"[11] But if origins cannot be ignored, neither are they pursued to the end. The discussion threatens to break down when the butcher wonders if Dowlas will tell the truth if he goes alone to verify the existence of Cliff's ghost. Dowlas may be prone merely to see what he knows "a'ready," whether or not the ghost appears. When the issue becomes trust, Snell steps in with a politic equivocation, keeping the issue within verbal play that enables Cliff to remain a creative idea. Trust is the confluence of experience and the irrational, the ground on which mystery is explored but not stripped of its metaphor.

Eliot makes a similar point in characterizing Mary Garth in *Middlemarch*. Eliot, of course, fashions realistic texts whose purpose is to reify belief through verisimilitude. The problem is to find the mystery of the world in the visible, abject and imperfect though it may be. In her characterization of Mary Garth in the apple orchard, Edenic associations foreground their own fictionality in a narrative desire for unity between verbal and visual fields. Rembrandt, who painted both imperfection and its transcendence, is the pictorial realist linked to Mary's visual representation. But her "portrait" must be presented in prose, where symbols and mythical allusions are subordinated to a verisimilar matrix:

> Rembrandt would have painted her with pleasure, and would have made her
> broad features look out of the canvas with intelligent honesty. For honesty,
> truthtelling fairness, was Mary's reigning virtue: she neither tried to create
> illusions, nor indulged them for her own behoof.[12]

She is a plain realist, in contrast to Rosamond Vincy with her fairy tale
marital fictions. The apple orchard in which Farebrother meets her in
chapter 40 is neither transcendent nor characterized by the sterility of
Casaubon's garden two chapters later. Instead, it suggests a cancellation
of univocal theological and metaphorical trappings. Nor are we teased, as
in an analogous faux-Edenic scene in *Tess of the D'Urbervilles*, into
contemplating the mythic absurdity—the blankness, finally—that
underlies the construct. Eliot stresses Mary Garth's relative freedom from
analogies even as she deploys them to frame her character. She suggests
that we must read myths skeptically and ironically, creating from this
tension a freedom from reductive conclusions:

> They made a pretty picture in the western light which brought out the
> brightness of the apples on the old scant-leaved boughs—Mary in her
> lavender gingham and black ribbons holding a basket, while Letty in her
> well-worn nankin picked up the fallen apples. (*MM*, 397)

Just as the narrator has freed Mary from aesthetic reduction, she has
suggested an Edenic reading freed from its theological trappings; to cite
Levine, she has resacralized "a world from which God has been dismissed."[13] But while the garden for which Dorothea yearns encloses
temptation (she sees Will "receding into the distant world of warm activity and fellowship," for instance), Mary's is different. Only the morally
neutral apples are "fallen," and, as much as he loves her, the Reverend
Farebrother (far from playing the tempter) maintains his sympathetic distance and even solicitation for Fred: "Have you any message for your old
playfellow, Miss Garth?' said the Vicar, as he took a fragrant apple from
the basket which she held towards him" (*MM*, 398). To make Mary's
garden "fallen," Eliot implies, one must apply univocal (specifically,
Pauline) categories to it.

However, an even more intriguing instance of Eliot's desire for reify-
ing the visual in adequate language that suggests mystery yet resists univocal ulteriority occurs in her references to *Purgatorio* 7 in the Roman
chapters of *Middlemarch*. In Dante's famous scene, the transcendental is
present but beyond the visible sphere, just as the unifying master-trope is
for Eliot. Dorothea's "one beautiful ungloved hand pillowed her cheek"

(*MM*, 184), the pose in which Naumann first sees her, entails an allusion to the lines from canto 7 with which chapter 19 of the novel begins: "L'altra vedete ch'ha fatto alla guancia / Della sua palma, sospiro, letto" (*MM*, 219), "See the other that, sighing, has made a bed for his cheek with the palm of his hand," Sordello says, referring to Henry I's sorrow.[14] It is nighttime in the hollow where Dante and Virgil view Sordello, when those who ascend the Mount of Purgatory lose volition. Yet this stylized gesture of sorrow precedes renewed movement. The gesture is anticipatory, not frozen, and signals an energy working upwards, not a repressive form that extinguishes identity behind artistry. Those who are undergoing purgation recline in stylized poses that suggest art, yet transcend it, for nature and art are in harmony. Logic, rhetoric, and music are in equipoise, and the stylized gesture—the visual "moment"—while modified by desire, is almost self-sufficient. Heaven is above (just as Eden is behind Mary Garth's apple orchard), but the experience itself has a truth anterior to the ulteriority that lies beyond the visual image. If pain and desire exist, this moment is not frozen by the desire for immediate attainment of an ideal, whose realization finally lies outside human experience, indeed, outside language itself. This is indicated by Virgil (repeating essentially what he told Dante in the *Inferno*) when, praised by Sordello as the "glory of the Latins ... through whom our tongue showed forth its power," he responds, "I am Virgil, and for no other fault did I lose Heaven than for not having faith."[15] He did not know Christ and therefore cannot name Him. Henry I's classical gesture is adapted from the Byzantine iconography for grief yet surpasses its artistry through dynamic visualization and musicality. Nature surpasses the artificial colors with which she is "painted." While this is not the earthly paradise and contains its musical disharmonies (Rudolf the Emperor does not sing, for instance), there is a foretaste of the higher harmonies to come, for here even the grass and flowers sing their song to Mary: "Nature had not only painted there, but of the sweetness of a thousand scents she made there one unknown to us and blended."[16] Here the precious metals "gold and fine silver ... fresh emerald at the moment it is split" are unsullied and at one with the rest of nature.[17] A contrast to the stylized gesture occurs in chapter 1 when Dorothea puts "her cheek against her sister's arm caressingly." The subject, tellingly, is the emeralds to which she is drawn in a sort of "mystic religious joy" (*MM*, 14). They adumbrate a lost providential order, which later is traced in parodic theories about feminine beauty that fail to unite rest with motion, vision with language.[18]

Another subtext in the Roman chapters, as Wiesenfarth notes, is Lessing's *Laocoön*, through which Eliot valorizes realism. Lessing was concerned with the effects of visual (or plastic) and verbal art forms ("poetry"). His focus is on the different effects created by the Laocoön myth in the (misidentified) Roman statue and in Virgil. In Virgil's poetry, his agonized scream is acceptable because it is implicated in a relatively realistic mode in which personality is gradually uncovered in all its hues; thus one seemingly unheroic (or abject) act does not necessarily determine the entire personality. In a statue, on the other hand, it would, for statuary freezes a moment of absolute character significance, to which all beyond its field consequently is rendered subservient. This is analogous to Schiller's distinction in *Naive and Sentimental Poetry* between realism and idealism in character: the realist is judged according to aims and tendencies (as Lydgate wishes to be judged), the idealist according to a single moment (as Lydgate realizes he has been judged). In chapter 15, Lessing writes that, for the poet, "the action is visible and progressive," while for the visual artist "the action is visible and stationary, its different parts developing in co-existence in space."[19] Because the symbols of poetry are "indefinite and weak images" and "arbitrary," Lessing argues, the poet is able to create moments of illusion when "we believe that we feel the real impressions" of the objects of his ideas.[20] The danger is that the artist may merely reproduce details "without producing a trace of illusion," and aim instead at a didactic or scientific understanding that separates logic from rhetoric.[21] Instead, the poet should convert "a series of images scantily interwoven with feelings into a succession of feelings sparingly interlaced with images."[22] Eliot is less skeptical about the power of verisimilitude. Lessing is closer to Samuel Johnson's idea that the poet should "examine, not the individual, but the species" than to her novelistic realism. But in discussing the place of the grotesque and ugly in poetry (much as Schiller does the place of the lowly in realism), we find agreement with Eliot's belief that the novel must embrace the lowly, the imperfect, and the ugly.

The Nazarene painter Naumann wishes to subordinate Dorothea to a univocal interpretation, and in essence turn her into a stable representation controlled by "objectivist" aesthetics of the feminine. His art-worship, of course, is innocuous in itself, but then again it is not fundamentally different from other univocalities, for instance Causaubon's. His debate with Will Ladislaw about the representation of woman in art adumbrates the tension between realism and idealism that concerns Eliot and Lessing alike. Naumann's reductive aesthetic is evident at the Vatican in chapter 19, when he interprets Dorothea, whom he has never seen, as the embodiment of an ideal. As if to create a fluid contrast to Naumann, the narrator calls into question narrative assumptions with the reminder that, when these events occurred forty years ago, even Hazlitt "mistook the flower-flushed tomb of the ascended Virgin for an ornamental vase due to the painter's fancy" (*MM*, 183). To impose a stable, unexplored aesthetic reading, this suggests, is to retreat into limited finality. Yet in evoking Hazlitt, the narrator reminds us of the doubleness that at once decenters and makes possible a more complex reading. Hazlitt was incorrect, but without his error a better approximation to the truth might not have been realized. [23]

Naumann tries to force a unity between passion and spirit, making his subject a symbol of some greater truth that lies outside her apparent paradoxes. Yet by referring her to something beyond herself, he lessens who she actually is. The paradox of the ideal is that it reduces the individual while ostensibly connecting her with transcendental origins; the paradox of the real is that the individual attains greater fullness in defeat or limitation to the actual. Naumann wishes to paint Dorothea as "an antique form animated by Christian sentiment—a sort of Christian Antigone—sensuous force controlled by spiritual passion" (*MM*, 185). He finally decides to use her as a model for Santa Clara (ironically, the patron saint of eyesight), "leaning so, with your cheek against your hand" (*MM*, 249), that is, frozen in an idealized moment, a parody of Dante, to do justice to which (to cite Schiller's definition of realism in *Naive and Sentimental Poetry*) "one must limit oneself to particular occurrences" in life.[24] Naumann's aesthetic rules reduce her to a set of binary oppositions that suggest not a repose, as in Schiller's description of the *Juno Ludovici* in the *Aesthetic Education*, but a struggle between irreconcilable drives, each one ("sensuous force," "spiritual passion") a paradox that belies his desire for a univocal interpretive moment. One would ordinarily speak of "sensuous passion" and "spiritual (or moral) force," but Naumann underscores his aesthetic incoherence by an insistence on projecting objective meaning onto the subjective female body. Reading her dress, he intuits her Puritanical alienation amidst a "vast wreck of ambitious ideals, sensuous and spiritual, mixed confusedly with the signs of breathing forgetfulness and degradation" (*MM*, 188). Yet by capturing her in a moment of painting, he ensures that she will remain a classical gesture of sorrow, not a living woman. Like St. John Rivers in *Jane Eyre*, therefore, he seeks to translate a stabilized visual field into a conceptual artwork that cancels the divisions inherent in human personality; thus Dorothea is yoked to a historical idea. The visual field is intended to do realism's work in containing multiplicity. However, in reality, its language, because its logic is not an event per se but instead a search for truth beyond events, merely yokes that multiplicity to an originating cause and thereby mutilates it. All realism is metonymic in that its total field plays with the idea of a master-trope, be it an authorial providence or a positive field outside the novel's range. But to insist on subordinating life to an idea is to guarantee the mutilation to which Naumann in effect would subject Dorothea, at least in concept (but Casaubon's attempts to do so— on both sides of the grave—are hardly conceptual). If Naumann can read surfaces, he cannot sympathetically transport himself into another's center of self. For all his talk about the "ideal in the real," he rejects the real; his aesthetic is far from "wi-ide," as he puts it, since its unities are false. His shortsightedness induces him to project onto Dorothea a naiveté that is the product of masculine desire. Like Pater (from Eliot's perspective), he valorizes impression over fact as an excuse to bury the object of appreciation in multiple parables that confine rather than open.

Will Ladislaw, in contrast, espouses realism, though at this stage it is less a realized experience than a callow assertion. Unlike Naumann, he comprehends that genuine art must represent people capable of change— indeed, who are amidst change. Echoing Lessing, he tells Naumann:

> Language gives a fuller image, which is all the better for being vague. After all, the true seeing is within; and painting stares at you with an insistent imperfection. I feel that especially about representations of women. As if a woman were a mere coloured superficies! You must wait for movement and tone. There is a difference in their very breathing: they change from moment to moment. (*MM*, 186)

It is not in the single moment that identity is to be found but in the development of consciousness through time, "from moment to moment." This, as well as anything, defines what realism does. Yet if, as Will says, "language is a finer medium" (*MM*, 186) than painting or Plastik, it is clear that he, too, still views Dorothea as an artistic object to be enfolded in language, as she embodies something close to Friedrich Schiller's realist, whose character must be evaluated "not in any particular act, but only in the whole sum of his life."[25] He views woman from the outside in, as it were, as an object of aesthetic appreciation whose "movement and tone" are better described through language, which can capture change better than the visual arts, which reduce her further to a mere "superficies." Will understands the need to get beneath the surface, but he has not learned that this entails sympathetic projection. He mentally binds Dorothea to a text whose realism is but a more subtle method of control.

The secretive Bulstrode likewise tries to control his life and others' with reductive and ultimately ineffectual providential fictions. The consequence, as with Godfrey's and Nancy's secrecies in *Silas Marner*, is a complete loss of control as well as a subjection to what Gilbert and

Gubar call feminist revenge, that is, inscription within the very sort of feminine aesthetic Naumann tries to impose on Dorothea.[26] Thus, the narrator parodies the monstrous ideal whereby characters (or authors, for that matter) flee history and experience. The secrecy that characterizes the strategies of control (Casaubon's, Naumann's, Bulstrode's) parodies the evasiveness practiced by women like Rosamond, who must create imaginative spaces for themselves within a restrictive society whose maternal voice likewise is bent on controlling the signs of female identity. Bulstrode is unable to cope with the enforced passivity that is women's lot, once his fictive providence is exploded and he must, like women, cope with a society that allows only limited illusions of control.

Bulstrode's is a primitive religion of fear, which, the narrator states, "remains nearly at the level of the savage" (*MM*, 607). Underlying this is an egoistic evasiveness rather like Rosamond's, who also gets power through secretive emotional manipulations. His providence is a projection of desire onto a fictive objectivity, the displacement of the subjective ego onto an invented deity whose masculinity creates the illusion of control. But his providence, like Godfrey Cass's in *Silas Marner*, merely imprisons him in circumstance. Not only does he create a manly "robust belief" out of unstable materials, projecting his fear of the feminine onto a God of fear; he also becomes the parodic God, a bully of humility who attempts to stage-manage Middlemarch society. His providence has its deflating counterpart in Raffles's "providential thing," which collapses into Mr. Brooke's "that sort of thing"; yet Raffles is no fiction but rather a revealer of actions who explodes Bulstrode's efforts to maintain mastery over the past to evade guilt and create a new identity. Even after his complicity in Raffles's death, Bulstrode continues to think he can master his destiny when, in fact, he is about to find his "vampire's feast in the sense of mastery" (*MM*, 153) translated into exclusion, not just from Middlemarch but from the text itself, from which he disappears after his final withholding of information about himself in chapter 85. He is erased from the "Finale," which, though containing melancholy futures for the main characters, at least provides them with limits that are not limits.

After his public disclosure and humiliation, Bulstrode collapses into a parodic neurasthenia, weeping "like a woman" (*MM*, 612) and suffering, as Lydgate puts it, "some little nervous shock" (*MM*, 736). Bulstrode passively waits for his wife to discover his disgrace rather than communicating it directly, again parodying feminine evasive strategies. He sits at home, "alleging nervous susceptibility to sounds and movements" (*MM*, 735), while he lets his wife interpret the visual picture he presents. Eliot's revenge on the man who tried to write others' lives is to have him be completely written off by polite society and at the mercy of his wife, who finally plays the forgiving God who transcends language to offer a replacement for Bulstrode's punishing patriarchal construct:

> He dared not look up at her. He sat with his eyes bent down, and as she went towards him she thought he looked smaller—he seemed so withered and shrunken. (*MM*, 740–41)

After she says,"Look up, Nicholas," "he burst out crying and they cried together, she sitting at his side" (*MM*, 741). But she controls the visual field while he withers in his withholding of language.

Lydgate's flight from the real, his search for an archetypal trope or "primitive tissue," is disguised as a direct engagement with the real; but his providential scientism finally is as unsuccessful as Bulstrode's religion. In seeking a structure of life as comprehensible as the proportions of the materials from which a house is constructed, he, like Victor Frankenstein, seeks unity through usurpation of the feminine; this contrasts with Silas Marner who, in adopting and raising Eppie, combines masculine and feminine, thought and feeling, in a way that approaches a cancellation of destructive oppositions. Middlemarch's power is stronger than his idealism. His attempt to trope the human body eventually is parodied by his treatise on gout, the rich man's disease. The basil plant with which he later compares Rosamond, the one that feeds on a dead man's brains, symbolizes the end of his aspirations in its parody of the "archetypal plant" that Goethe, like he, pursued. He is, in fact, coopted by the minutiae of life that his scientific pursuits have led him to ignore:

> We may handle even extreme opinions with impunity while our furniture, our dinner-giving, and preference for armorial bearings in our own case, link us indissolubly with the established order. (*MM*, 340)

If Bulstrode's masculinism is parodied by his protofeminine neurasthenia, Lydgate finds himself the creature of the very social and aesthetic field he has denied. Rosamond, in contrast, has a better grasp of the real (though finally she, too, is the prisoner of her delusions), what the narrator terms a "remarkably detailed and realistic imagination when the foundation had been once presupposed" (*MM*, 115).

In his pursuit of the French actress Laure, Lydgate created an ideal passive but passionate woman to serve his every emotional need:

> She was a Provencale, with dark eyes, a Greek profile, and rounded majestic form, having that sort of beauty which carries a sweet matronliness even in youth, and her voice was a soft cooing. (*MM*, 148)

If Naumann wishes to capture a limited moment in painting Dorothea, he does not mistake his appropriation in the studio for the actual world. But Lydgate falls prey to a deceptive aesthetics that denies volition to the female, even while he pursues (yet thinks he stands apart from) women whose wills exceed his own. He is at heart a masochist drawn to selfish women whom he perversely tries to ward off as scientific objects (his "remote impersonal passion for her beauty" [*MM*, 150]) even while subconsciously he surrenders to the stage violence, which becomes real. After helping Laure, following the staged "accident" that kills her husband, he pursues her to Lyons, where she declares "*I meant to do it*." The ideal construction is confronted with the actual, palpable act, and Lydgate becomes disillusioned with women, deciding (rather like Teufelsdroeckh in *Sartor Resartus*) that "henceforth he would take a strictly scientific view of woman, entertaining no expectations, but such as were justified beforehand" (*MM*, 151). But life is irrational, not impersonal and scientific. The real is subjective, though its subjectivity may peer through masks of objectivity.

Rosamond, of course, is not interested in worshiping "the more impersonal ends of his profession and his scientific study" (*MM*, 572). His metaphors dissolve under an awareness of her "terrible tenacity" and a "blank unreflecting" mental surface (*MM*, 572). So, after her betrayals and Raffles's death, he replaces her with a protoreligious adoration of Dorothea Brooke, a "Virgin Mary" exercising some "heroic hallucination" (*MM*, 578). Dorothea learns to temper her idealism with realism; Lydgate, a far weaker person, finally is reduced to wishing that he might be judged according to (to cite Schiller) "the entire context of his life" rather than according to "individual actions" that "will bear the *whole* character of moral independence and freedom";[27] that is, he wants to be judged as a realist, not an idealist, even though his life has been grounded (and continues to be) on assumptions about masculinist ambition and feminine function every bit as idealistic as Naumann's aesthetic of the feminine. This is clear in his interview with Dorothea in chapter 76:

> Lydgate turned, remembering where he was, and saw Dorothea's face looking up at him with a sweet trustful gravity. The presence of a noble nature, generous in its wishes, ardent in its charity, changes the lights for us: we begin to see things again in their larger, quieter masses, and to believe that we too can be seen and judged in the wholeness of our character. (*MM*, 751–52)

Yet Lydgate is aware that society judges him now according to a single apparent act, his complicity in a questionable death. Dorothea's sympathy for him in chapter 76, which contrasts with his own lack of persistency in being "more" because Rosamond was "less" (*MM*, 748), reinvigorates him even though he realizes that his career is in ruins. Though "blighted—like a damaged ear of corn" (*MM*, 753), he is bedazzled by the vision of Dorothea as having "a heart large enough for the Virgin Mary." Ironically, like Naumann, he can conceive of her only in iconic Christian terms and, hence, enlivened only by *her* belief, cannot finally experience her all-embracing "generous sympathy" (*MM*, 752). Entrapped in an appearance of criminality, his "double" mirrored soul is twisted from futurity to the endless "repeating" of "things behind," to cite the epigram at the beginning of chapter 72 (*MM*, 723). However, there is no "endless vista of fair things before": Dorothea's belief and his "heroic hallucination" of her do not free him from repetitive entrapment.

In the course of *Middlemarch,* Dorothea learns the importance of sympathy, which is central to the realistic vision and counter to idealistic formulation. Upon hearing the rumors about Lydgate's complicity in Raffles's death, Dorothea tells Farebrother, "I will not believe it. Let us find out the truth and clear him!" (*MM*, 719). The truth she seeks is no more rational than the "ardent, theoretic impulse" that has gotten her into trouble before. But grounded in sympathy, it does practical good. Her problem, like Lessing's, is to negotiate the intersection between language and vision in such a way that belief is encouraged yet not allowed to freeze into the form suggested by the initiating vision of truth. Yet early on she cannot see the pedant that stands before her in Casaubon. Just before the disastrous Roman honeymoon, she indicates to Mr. Brooke the difficulty she has relating what she sees to its appropriate language:

> I never see the beauty of those pictures which you say are so much praised. They are a language I do not understand. I suppose there is some relation between pictures and nature which I am too ignorant to feel—just as you see what a Greek sentence stands for which means nothing to me. (*MM*, 77–78)

The relationship between "pictures" and "nature" is Dorothea's conundrum as well as the problem with the novel itself. Dorothea is in search of a metaphorical analogy, an "as if," yet at this stage thinks she can find it in a "Greek sentence," a Rosetta stone like Casaubon's "Key to All Mythologies," which merely needs translation to be understood. Words and experiences too easily diverge as people seek to escape life's pressures: the search for a simple translation exemplifies an escapism that disguises itself as engagement. In realism, the attempt is made to cancel the separation between visual and lingual effects, excursis and repression. The formulating gaze (St. John Rivers's, Naumann's, Robert

Lovelace's) is the thinly cloaked (and gender reversed) Medusa-stare from the abyss that cancels peripeteia and freezes creativity.

Belief is central to Dorothea's epiphany in chapter 80. This is evident in her belief in Lydgate and her projection of "impulses she had not known before" into Rosamond's "dream-world" (*MM*, 784). Belief, which is rooted in sympathy, operates as a providential master-trope that is anterior to both language and vision yet connected with both as the medium of fluid expression. The events of chapters 77–80 lead Dorothea to an epiphany that includes language and vision, feeling and intellect, and connects her with the life outside her window as she frees herself from univocal idealism and embraces what Caserio terms "the value of inhibition."[28] In discovering what seems to be an affair between Will Ladislaw and Rosamond Vincy, Dorothea confronts, like the reader, the inadequacies of visual representation alone: what words can contradict what seems to be a passionate encounter? Rosamond's words in chapter 81, "It was not as you thought," implicitly suggest the difficulty of reconciling language and vision. The effort to create belief by verbalizing visual images, the realist's task, implicitly militates against closure; indeed, any attempt at finality in reality is escapism. Dorothea's discovery (it is described as if it is an artistic tableau) is an ambiguous mistake that nevertheless propels her towards tragic insight. She has learned verbal indirection and a realism that can be the only (and fragile) vessel of the ideal. Confused, she confronts a hard vision of marital infidelity that parodies epiphanic insight:

> She found herself on the other side of the door without seeing anything re-markable, but immediately she heard a voice speaking in low tones which startled her as with a sense of dreaming in daylight, and advancing uncon-sciously a step or two beyond the projecting slab of a bookcase, she saw, in the terrible illumination of a certainty which filled up all outlines, something which made her pause motionless, without self-possession enough to speak.

> Seated with his back towards her on a sofa which stood against the wall on a line with the door by which she had entered, she saw Will Ladislaw: close by him and turned towards him with a flushed tearfulness which gave a new brilliancy to her face sat Rosamond, her bonnet hanging back, while Will leaning towards her clasped both her upraised hands in his and spoke with low-toned fervour. (*MM*, 764)

This has the air of an illusion: not only is the servant unsure whether Mrs. Lydgate is at home (*MM*, 763), she is afterwards unaware that Dorothea has left or that Will has been there and gone (*MM*, 769). The episode is begun and ended with the narrator's emphasis on Martha's "never knowing" (*MM*, 769), repeated in our never knowing generated by the narrator's withholding meaning or the illusion of meaning. Neither Dorothea (who may not be able to make out the words) nor the narrator (who can) informs us of what Will's "low-toned fervour" consists: we are as confused as Dorothea, and the "piece of furniture" that impedes our graceful exit is the text itself. The reader experiences something like Dorothea's confusion at witnessing events that visually seem to confirm her worst suspicions. The reader, too, is forced to overcome doubt, reject suspicion, and sympathetically embrace "those three." The ambiguity is not entirely reversed by Rosamond's assurances in chapter 81 (*MM*, 786), for the narrator withholds final determinacy, indeed (even if we accept as factual that Will resisted Rosamond's advances) plays with such withholding, as she does in chapter 83 with the refusal to communicate or create responsibility for Will's and Dorothea's kiss: "It was never known which lips were the first to move towards the other lips" (*MM*, 799). The point is that belief, like realism, entails a mistrust towards the purely visual.

Dorothea's climactic epiphany occurs before her visit to Rosamond, when she realizes that life will not yield her the fulfillment of a single ideal but must be approached with a dual vision that affirms belief and the loss of belief. The ideal is theoretical and absolute, but life itself is more difficult:

> There were two images—two living forms that tore her heart in two, as if it had been the heart of a mother who seems to see her child divided by the sword, and presses one bleeding half to her breast while her gaze goes forth in agony towards the half which is carried away by the lying woman that has never known the mother's pang. (*MM*, 775)

Here, experience and the visual are reconciled. If Rosamond remains the prisoner of her egoism until momentarily released by Dorothea's sympathy, Dorothea, turning away from scorn and jealousy, yearns for a "perfect Right" but links it to three specific humans, not to an ideal of humanity. Will, like Lydgate, wishes to be judged realistically by the tendency of his character, but he risks being enclosed in an ideal epiphanic moment (*MM*, 777). In the past, Dorothea contrasted the view of nature outside her door with the tomb in which she felt she was buried in her marriage to Casaubon, and she associated its freedom with Will Ladislaw. Now the vision is at once more tragic and more sympathetic. The Wordsworthian idea that comes to her aid is not the regenerative power of the child or of nature but the "still, sad suffering," not of humanity in general, but of specific humans; Eliot's citation of

Wordsworth's "Ode to Duty" at the beginning of chapter 80 is at once a homage to and a deviation from an idealism that still views humanity in too generic terms. Now it is different:

> in the field she could see figures moving—perhaps the shepherd with his dog. Far off in the bending sky was the pearly light; and she felt the largeness of the world and the waking of men to labour and endurance. She was a part of that involuntary, palpitating life, and could neither look out on it from her luxurious shelter as a mere spectator, not hide her eyes in selfish complaining. (*MM*, 777)

Significantly, her vision of the road beyond her curtains connects the abstract and visual with the abject. The visual is no longer an avenue of escape or self-delusion but leads her into further indeterminacy, where, nonetheless, a purpose may be found. This contrasts with Naumann's, Bulstrode's, and Lydgate's strategies for defining, delimiting, and controlling experience. She is, in the public eye "absorbed into the life of another" (*MM*, 822). This entails loss and limitation. Yet she gains success, having substituted fellow-feeling for egoistic idealism, which makes possible society's amelioration, beginning with limited, unhistorical acts.

7

Hardy's *Tess of the D'Urbervilles*: Realism as a Form of Idealism

How real is the real? I have investigated literary engagements with actuality whose emplotments are, at best, verisimilar, yet reveal that any realism is to some degree the fictive projection of authorial desire. In *Tess of the D'Urbervilles*, however, Hardy emphasizes the breakdown of the realistic middle space created between experience and its organizing tropes. He looks, as it were, towards the collapse of realism into kaleidoscopic visual moments in Conrad's *Heart of Darkness*. Realism's (or history's) inability to maintain fluidity between experience and containment leads, we have seen, to aesthetic or ideological escapes in pursuit of univocal meaning. History and nature are the unstable grounds on which characters try to create identity, yet they are stymied by forces they cannot control or, like Angel Clare, by ideological flights whose perversity they recognize too late. The novel becomes full of boundaries, margins, and doublings that fail to offer the creative aporias or transcendent moments that make stable meanings (or the appearances thereof) possible. Stages and crossings simply reify the implacable presence of pasts that, Like Tringham's genealogy or Angel's reminder of the D'Urberville coach, merely implicate characters in fatalities. The only escapes seem to be through preconscious oneness with nature, or through the sort of idealism Angel follows. History, Michel de Certeau writes, "is born in effect from the rupture that constitutes a past distinct from its current enterprise."[1] In realism too, meaning arises from a gap between production and the period known. In Hardy's novel many middle spaces are merely fatalistic stages along the way from the May Day dance to the black flag at Wintoncester. Nature, associated with the pretemporal, the naive, and Tess in her purest state, is colonized by those who, like Angel, stabilize mythic meaning in the act of cataloguing, explaining, and (in Angel's case) idealizing it. But such colonization cannot make possible the stable middle space, the fictive real. Interestingly, Hardy himself participates in such colonization, losing the boundary between nature (or experience) and organization as he mediates the nature he evokes through a concept of the real that threatens to efface the creative interplay between the signified and the absent from which the impression of the real arises.

Like Edmund Burke, Hardy recognizes the ambiguities of distinguishing "political" and "imaginative" interpretations of the past. This is evident in Angel's difficulties with Tess's ancestry:

> Politically I am skeptical as to the virtue of their being old. Some of the wise even among themselves "exclaim against their own succession," as Hamlet puts it, but lyrically, dramatically, and even historically, I am tenderly attached to them.[2]

Much later, having changed his mind in Brazil about Tess, Angel rethinks his earlier confusion:

> This historic interest of her family—that masterful line of d'Urbervilles— whom he had despised as a spent force, touched his sentiments now. Why had he not known the difference between the political value and the imaginative value of these things?" (423)

This reconsideration entails a valorization of realism over idealistic colonizations of the Other, now that, ironically, he has become the nearly dying Other. Realism is valorized by the imaginative and vice versa, while political—that is, ideological—readings are too unyielding to allow for disinterring the past in such a way that, to cite de Certeau, the "discourse about the dead" confronts origins yet maintains a tension, a rupture, between that postulated Other and reconstructions of it. Such reconstruction entails both myth and science, reductions of whatever was against which the mind plays to create verisimilar meaning. Hardy, though, is stymied by the disjunction between legend and criteriology, as well as experience and the naming of experience; his political naming entails Schiller's concepts of the real and the ideal, which he mistakes for an imaginative valorization of Tess, the "pure" woman. In other words, despite himself, he is implicated in Angel's confusion of political and imaginative values. Burke, you will recall, advocated a political interpretation of history grounded in aesthetics and the imaginative. His endeavor to parry the margins between historical flux and organization elicited differing rhetorical modes, a brief flight into Marie Antoinette, and the condemnation of revolution through the imposition of a theatricality metaphor. For Hardy and Angel, the fixation of the gaze on nature (and natural purity in Tess) is the supposed means of understanding, even giving meaning or consciousness to, the Other. Through striking imagery, Hardy describes nature, moving in and out of his landscapes with his prescient camera eye as if to fix through spatial movements the timeless and inchoate. But this, like Angel's visual strategies and his conceptions of the imaginative, are illusory deployments, of which Tess is the object and victim.

In Brazil, Angel experiences a conversion that impels him to reevaluate his assumptions about character:

What arrested him now as of value in life was less its beauty than its pathos. Having long discredited the old systems of mysticism, he now began to discredit the old appraisements of morality. He thought they wanted readjusting. Who was the moral man? Still more pertinently, who was the moral woman? The beauty or ugliness of a character lay not only in its achievements, but in its aims and impulses; its true history lay, not among things done, but among things willed. (421)

He thinks he discovers a viable alternative to the "hard logical deposit" (311) around which his destructive fictions about women have collected. Yet the hard logical deposit remains in the "aims and impulses," the realism (Hardy alludes to Schiller's *Naive and Sentimental Poetry*) Angel mistakes for something more authentic than judgments based on single failings that become merely metonymic reductions of the human. If Angel substantially changes, it is to become merely fatalistic like Tess, itself a sign of realistic "closeness to nature," according to Schiller. Thus, ironically, the concept-monger becomes the object of Hardy's external concept. Far from acting decisively to aid Tess after she murders Alec, he is as passive as she and as helpless before the grotesquely phallic "erection" (483), Stonehenge, where they accept her capture and sacrifice.

Aporia—what Hayden White terms "the favored stylistic device of Ironic language" in "realistic" fiction and skeptical, relativizing history—can impel the mind towards a reconstituted illusion based in part on forgetting.[3] But Tess can neither escape her past nor "annihilate" it (150), for society dictates a connection between moral consequence and temporal consciousness that makes forgetting an unacceptable act. Hardy's "President of the Immortals" is an ironic master-trope that cancels the capacity for creative irony, turning the creative play along the margins of life into exercises as feckless as all attempts to impose form and ideological closure on the inchoate and unconscious core of nature's meaning. Creative irony, of the sort that enables the interplay between form and chaos, word and vision, requires provisional belief in the reality of whatever is created therefrom, metaphorically so in the case of realism, metaphorically and scientifically in the case of history, which ostensibly refers to actual events outside the mythopoetic field. In *Tess*, nature is always looked at from above, or laterally, always from some vantage point of which we are continually aware, for the vision must continually shift to give apparent form to this formless object, which really is formless only in the mind. The literal nature Hardy depicts is the well-ordered English countryside, not the jungle experienced by Conrad, and thus what he and his narrator organize is less the actual, visible nature than a mental representation of an idea of nature that reflects the disappearance of mental margins in a universe where impressions take precedence over objective facts and interpretations. Thus nature shifts along with moods and stages, but offers nothing abiding; indeed, it suggests the transcendental meaninglessness of stages in the very contiguity between stage and mood. The New Forest leaves are "dead" (119) when Alec rapes Tess, but up till then nature has seemed fecund and luxuriant, the nearby "soft azure landscape" (77) of the Chase associated with "sylvan antiquity" (77). At Flintcomb Ash, in contrast, nature appears the cold, hardened reflection of Tess's abandonment and despair. In Brazil, nature is feverish and wet, the emblem of Angel's illness. In chapter 50, the landscape with its "couch-burning plots" (430) seems hellish, reflecting Tess's desperation as, tempted by Alec, who is "forking the same plot as herself," she is tempted to take up with him once more (431). Nature is black and primeval again at Stonehenge before the sunrise in chapter 57, bringing the novel full circle to the blackness surrounding her earlier sacrifice to Alec's lust in the New Forest. In chapter 59, everything seems suspended and motionless, reflecting the powerlessness of Angel and Liza-lu, those speechless gazers who seek to reinvent themselves, yet, one suspects, will merely replay Tess's transfixion in some form or other (488).

Margins for Hardy, I would suggest, are fictions as ephemeral as chapter headings: the real (even the word domesticates, like "abyss" or "horror"), like the ideal, is a construct, but one in which we wish to believe. The gap between the knowable and the unknowable, itself essentially empty, nevertheless is invested with purpose if not content, for from this gap we create meaning. But Hardy always reminds us that this is all a blank, like the hole in the cloud to which the epiphanic moment seems reduced in chapter 19. Kathleen Blake locates one of these instances where margins appear and recede:

A field-man is a personality afield; a field-woman is a portion of the field; she has somehow lost her own margin, imbibed the essence of her surrounding, and assimilated herself with it. (137–38)[4]

The focus on disappearing margins suggests that Hardy has more in common with Conrad—especially with Marlow's trip down the Congo—than may seem at first to be the case. The feminist approach to margins is clear enough: from a certain exterior, camera-angle vantage, the working woman seems reducible to nature, assimilated into her surroundings, and hence a creature of fate, while the male worker has a more discernible personality and more stable margins. The "field-man" has some control over his margins; the "field-woman," in contrast, "imbibes" her surroundings; she experiences a natural interpenetration of self and environment that gratifies. Tess, of course, has lost her marginlessness, as the result of the lingual, hence conscious, separateness provided by the Sixth Form education she received. "The Thinkable" has rendered her unable to forget, hence bound by the margins of a social discourse that condemns her for Alec's "seduction" and her illegitimate child. Hardy's contrast between male and female when it comes to margins reflects a misogynistic bias; to that degree Blake is correct. But there is more, a radical anxiety towards margins combined with an attraction towards unreflective natural "purity." Yet, at the same time he needs to assert margins and control through narrative discourse and a ratiocinative control that nevertheless falters, shifts, and reveals its inadequacy amidst the profusion of natural prose portraits and effusive literary and philosophical allusions. Conrad is more willing simply to let the margins drop so that he (and Marlow) can accept the need for limited, provisional meanings in a universe where the past cannot be forgotten preparatory to doing so.

Motion between margins is also of limited use. The narrator speaks of a "chasm" that divides Tess from "that previous self of hers" (119) after her rape in the New Forest. But she is fully implicated in the disinterred name, D'Urberville, appropriated by Alec's family, including its curse and retribution arising from socially constructed origins, her punishment for crimes committed by mailed ancestors in the shadowy past. Entoiled in a historical trace, which is given form by Alec's lust, Angel's idealism, and the narrator's metaphorical vision, she is pursued across formless space, as it were, by the forms others would impose on her and it. She is at once forced onto nature as essentially pure, yet is transfixed by the very setting of boundaries this entails. In this sense, her rape is reenacted throughout *Tess*, as she tries but is unable to create an identity through differentiation on her terms. Her tradition cannot become what de Certeau calls a "past object," for the margins continually fade and, though reinforced through verbal and visual strategy, merely reify her powerlessness, not her capacity for escape and freedom, even in the act of accepting death. She cannot control her narrative. Indeed, Hardy's narrative stresses her being both a natural and an abject object, that is, while stressing her essential closeness to nature, it defines her vis-à-vis it. Ostensibly her closeness to nature is indicated by the associations with birds, flies, and dying birds, or her passivity when ravished by Alec or when she later murders him. At the intersections between sleep and waking, where margins fade but epiphanies also are possible, she is merely the passive object, as when Prince is gored by the mail cart.

We are continually reminded of double naming and identity: Angel's perceptions of Tess before and after she recounts her history, the Durbeyfield-D'Urberville namings with all their ironies, and the double namings of geographical and historical places: the "Vale of Blakemore or Blackmoor" (48), Tess's original home, or the valley setting of Talbothays Dairy, "the verdant plain so well watered by the river Var or Froom" (156). Angles of vision shift—we see Blakemoor as a tourist might in chapter 2, objectively distanced—much as namings do, and we cannot help but detect a narrative wish for metaphorical meaning coupled with an awareness that any such attempt to stabilize experience must fail. Myths, too, seem broken, as alternative readings vie for space, and the suspicion develops that, behind the metaphors and allusions of Hardy's realism, all meaning finally is abderitic, so that, as Hayden White writes of Immanuel Kant, "all movement represents nothing more than a redisposition of primitive elements."[5] Thus for Alec, Pauline Christianity and pagan sensuality are merely different names for the same need to control Tess, while Angel's idealism is but a disguised form of the Christianity he thinks he has rejected.

Hardy presents a telling commentary on the elusiveness of meaning— which leads to the need to control, to conceptualize, to be monstrous—in the symbolisms surrounding Cross-in-Hand. Its essence is pain, imprisonment, and death, towards which all meanings in some way point. When Alec pressures Tess to swear on it that she will never tempt him (389), we see its essence enacted. But identifying its controlling myth is more difficult, for it is lost in the mists of history. Cross-in-Hand may mark a boundary, or it may be "the site of a miracle, or murder, or both" (373). Alec tells her the worn thing was once a holy cross; someone else tells her it marked the execution site of a criminal who sold his soul to the devil (391). Like Angel, with his confusions of political and imaginative values, we are left to contemplate the relation between naming and meaning. If it merely marks a boundary, then someone else, or something within all people, has necessitated its association with the terrible. But there is a generalized aesthetic effect, "a new kind of beauty, a negative beauty of tragic tone," which creates "something sinister, or solemn, according to mood, in the scene amid which it stands" (389).

Tess similarly is lost amidst others' aesthetic readings of her, like Angel's wish to see her as "impressing, interesting, pathetic," which contrasts with her recognition that her life, "just like thousands and thousands," is the reenactment of another's tale: "There is set down in some old book somebody just like me" (182). Angel's subsequent need to demonize her results from his inability to maintain that early fiction of innocence invented amidst the luxuriant countryside at Talbothays. At first, the "brimfulness of her nature" evident in her mouth (red, "as if it had been a snake's") and the "coiled-up cable" of her hair (231) strain for nontheological meaning, as Hardy's narrator suggests a univocal moment prior to theological codification "when the most spiritual beauty bespeaks itself flesh; and sex takes the outside place in the presentation" (231). The kernel and the shell interpenetrate in a sensual pagan transformation, until Tess's self-consciousness returns under Angel's gaze, awakening "an oddly compounded look of gladness, shyness, and surprise" (231). Yet Tess is always under Hardy's gaze; we already are aware of the "fallen" state engendered by Alec's ravishment. In other words, it is impossible to read this pre-Christian mythmaking without retroactively, as it were, applying categories that aren't directly stated. Tess, like Cross-in-Hand, like nature itself, must be read, gazed upon, or simply effaced. Even if her story is the repetition of some primordial event prior to consciousness and history, it must be told, and disguised as something unique in the telling. George Eliot convinces us that Mary Garth's garden displays a realism that transcends the fixating gaze of providential artistry; Hardy suggests here, and in the harp-playing scene, that the master-tropal ironic "gaze" is unavoidable, indeed, is the only means of creating the illusion of progress and meaning. Angel's problem is his lack of such irony: he, more than Tess, is the naif who moves from univocal reading to univocal reading until, chastened by Brazil, he at least conceives of a wider-ranging vision.

As an idealist who (to cite Schiller) "takes the grounds of his determinations from pure reason,"[6] Angel Clare recreates others to suit his preconceptions. Upon hearing the Orpheus-like tale of William Dewey's taming the bull with his fiddle, Angel's first impulse, as it is with Tess, is to use myth to escape the present: "It carries us back to mediaeval times, when faith was a living thing!" (165). The impulse to poetize at once distances experience and enables him to escape its (here, sexual) implications in a flight into history. He cannot believe Tess has had experiences, when she tries to broach the subject of her sexual encounter with Alec (240); to know otherwise would be to lose control of his creation:

> He expressed assent in loving satire, looking into her face. "My Tess has, no doubt, almost as many experiences as that wild convolvulus out there on the garden hedge, that opened itself this morning for the first time." (240)

At Talbothays Dairy, the mental obliteration of "the pitiable dummy known as Hodge" in favor of a differentiation of personalities replaces one stereotype with another. Hodge has ceased to exist:

> He had been disintegrated into a number of varied fellow-creatures—beings of many minds, beings infinite in difference; some happy, many serene, a few depressed, one here and there bright even to genius, some stupid, others wanton, others austere; some mutely Miltonic, some potentially Cromwellian. (173)

Yet the process of viewing complex human realism day by day does nothing to shake his need for stereotypes. "Hodge" is too simple, of course, but his replacement is an aesthetic dramatization of "men who had private views of each other, as he had of his friends" (173). Angel remains the outsider; the laborers are not his friends. His interpretation needs lapidary metaphor, philosophy, and allusion as far-ranging as Milton, Cromwell, Gray and Pascal to gain stability. Movement from the undifferentiated to differentiation needs verisimilar reification, especially since its originating mental act is the disintegration of a concept rather than any real loosening of margins (173). Angel's turning Tess into "a fresh and virginal daughter of Nature" (176) is the product of his unacknowledged desire for mastery which, like Alec's sensual kind, requires that Tess be his blank text. Like the "intellectual liberty" he seeks as a colonial farmer, she is virgin territory from which he creates meaning.

Angel differentiates Tess from the other milkmaids when he hears her say, "I don't know about ghosts ... but I do know that our souls can be made to go outside our bodies when we are alive" (175). His idealism attracts him to this suggestion of an otherworldly perspective. Tess desires to leave the body: look at the bright star long enough and you will "soon find you are hundreds and hundreds o' miles away from your body, which you don't seem to want at all" (175). Conscious that she is being observed, she traces "imaginary patterns on the tablecloth with her forefinger with the constraint of a domestic animal that perceives itself to be watched" (176). Her "imaginary patterns" represent the only text she can control, for her meaning is private. Yet even her drawing and nervousness contribute to the impression Angel creates of a "virginal daughter" against which reality cannot impinge, or if it does, with destructive consequences to his imaginary structure. Angel learns after some time and suffering in Brazil that "the magnitude of lives is not as to their external displacements, but as to their subjective experiences" (214). But like Mr. Darcy's change in *Pride and Prejudice*, his change goes on largely outside our gaze, unlike Tess's victimization. The "mighty personality" (214) is likewise a milkmaid, and somewhere within those bounds is the possibility of meaning. Meaning, J. Hillis Miller suggests, "is suspended within the intersection among the elements."[7] Yet in idealizing Tess, Angel seeks a stable, conscious, yet natural reading of a woman whose past, despite her hints that she has one, he will not explore. By explaining the milkmaid, he creates for her an origin and meaning that rest entirely on a single point, really: "virginal." Nature is anything but virginal, as he well knows, yet he tries to encode Tess with an idealism masquerading as realism, according to which character is judged by a single act or characteristic, not general aims and tendencies.

Tess's fantasy that she and Angel are alike (291), because of their sexual histories, immediately withers before his insistence that, having told her tale, she is another person altogether (298): "He looked upon her as a species of impostor; a guilty woman in the guise of an innocent one" (299). He thinks the "essence of things" changed when she contradicted his idealization (297), but in truth her essence has remained the same: he simply shifted mythic readings to protect himself from the confusion created by her refusal to suit his impression. Angel reads her according to theological categories he believes he has rejected but merely has translated to social codes of "decrepit wills, decrepit conduct" (302). The reader's complicity in placing her converges with Angel's mental transformation, so that "each diamond on her neck gave a sinister wink like a toad's" (293). The hard, almost unbreakable substance, like the shapeless thing called Cross-in-Hand, is not sufficient in and of itself; like Tess, it must be read and gazed upon, or forgotten altogether. And such forgetting is impossible, so by positing two Tesses, Angel insists actually on a historical continuum that ostensibly separates the fallen and unfallen Tess while implicitly linking the two in a cause-and-effect continuum. The Other is at the same time the essence behind her innocent guise; but the opposite could also be the case, for like the spiritual and fleshly Tess, these meanings interpenetrate, indeed, have no meaning until the insistence on double vision and historical objectification becomes paramount.

In chapter 19, where Angel plays his second-hand harp, he unconsciously creates an illusion of timelessness into which Tess is briefly
drawn. Yet time itself is a mental construct we must forget momentarily
to achieve transcendence. For the baby Sorrow, "eternal Time had been a
matter of days merely" (146), that is, unity is never conceived of and life
is a series of unreflective experiences. In the second-hand harp scene,
Hardy evinces a skepticism about the sort of transcendence celebrated by
Keats, Wordsworth, and Tennyson, suggesting that the spiritual and the
univocal are scientific or metaphorical constructs deployed to give meaning. Interestingly, Tess and Angel are close to unmediated experience; it
is the narrator—and hence the reader—who realizes that it is all a bit of a
sham, that Tess's moment of timelessness seems a shoddy instance of
Kant's belief that time and space are creations of the mind. At best we
can only emplot undifferentiated experience, conceptualize it as myths of
spirit intertwining the flesh, and dress this further with judgments about
sin, naturalness, or meaninglessness. In any case, the gaze creates
distance, just as it must when historicizing. As they fall in love, Tess and
Angel seem part of an intoxicating nature whose "rush of juices" and
"hiss of fertilization" seem to impregnate everything, sweeping humans,
animals, and vegetation alike into some proto-Keatsian synaesthetic unity
(207). But we are always aware that something is out of kilter, that
behind the unities are dissonances confirmed by the narrator's ironic tone
and information. The essence of transcendence is forgetting and remembering. The world's pain momentarily is given up as some primordial
unity anterior to division and consciousness is recalled. Tess has wanted
to believe that "to escape the past and all that appertained thereto was to
annihilate it" (150). Yet she cannot, for life is about inventing origins and
pursuing them. A failed Orpheus, Angel finally fails to create dreams
with his music to counter the "inquisitive eyes" that always return,
Lycius- (or farmer Groby-)like, to stymie her attempts to escape the past.
Here is the central faux-epiphanic episode that has garnered so much
critical study:

> The outskirt of the garden in which Tess found herself had been left
> uncultivated for some years, and was now damp and rank with juicy grass
> which sent up mists of pollen at a touch; and with tall blooming weeds
> emitting offensive smells—weeds whose red and yellow and purple hues
> formed a polychrome as dazzling as that of cultivated flowers. She went
> stealthily as a cat through this profusion of growth, gathering cuckoo-spittle
> on her skirts, cracking snails that were underfoot, staining her hands with
> thistle-milk and slug-slime, and rubbing off upon her naked arms sticky
> blights which, though snow-white on the apple-tree trunks, made madder
> stains on her skin; thus she drew quite near to Clare, still unobserved of him.

Tess was conscious of neither time nor space. The exaltation which she had described as being producible at will by gazing at a star came now without any determination of hers; she undulated upon the thin notes of the second-hand harp, and their harmonies passed like breezes through her, bringing tears into her eyes. The floating pollen seemed to be his notes made visible, and the dampness of the garden the weeping of the garden's sensibility. Though near nightfall, the rank-smelling weed-flowers glowed as if they would not close for intentness, and the waves of colors mixed with the waves of sound.

The light which still shone was derived mainly from a large hole in the western bank of cloud; it was like a piece of day left behind by accident, dusk having closed in elsewhere. (178–79)

"Raising up" does not create permanent facts or abiding illusions of facts. The narrator, too, participates in the onrush of sensation even as he undercuts this event.[8] Angel forgets conscious categorization, while Tess forgets the disparity between her self-image and her social identity. Momentarily, his poor playing "with a stark quality like that of nudity" (178) relieves her of the burden of consciousness that she is a fallen woman. Yet this is fundamentally unlike the apple orchard scene in *Middlemarch*, which exemplifies Eliot's wish to desacralize Christian associations preparative to valorizing a Rembrandtesque realism, which is fluid, not hard and providential. Hardy's narrator undercuts prelapsarian innocence and ideality by mentioning the "offensive smells" and the "sticky blights" associated with semen-like juices and pollen. Similarly, through luxuriant natural descriptions and the reference to synaesthetic "waves of colour mixed with the waves of sound" (179), we are reminded of a Romantic afflatus, specifically Keats's transcendental moments in such poems as "Ode to a Nightingale," which the episode calls into question—as does Keats, for that matter, but not in so absolute a way. Hardy's "waves of colour" and "waves of sound" emanate from an "accidental" hole (the light "was like a piece of day left behind by accident") that suggests not so much an abyss as the absence of any meaning beyond the phenomena themselves. It is the need to fill the hole, so to speak, that leads to transcendental idealisms like Angel's. This detail inserts a dissonance into this dazzling polychrome, combining "accident" with an origin that simply isn't there. Nothing is accidental, Hardy suggests, at least in the sense of operating outside natural law, or sometimes the mysterious rules established by the malevolent Immanent Will. The chapter, after all, opens with Tess's realizing that there is nothing accidental about the arrangement of her milking cows; instead, this results from Angel's intervention: "She felt that their order could not be the result of accident" (177). So too in the harp-playing moment, "raising up" reinforces the sense of causality, which she expresses in her belief soon afterwards that she is trapped in others' parts and "past doings" from which there is no escape. The epiphanic escape from time, space, and causation decays; the narrative itself undercuts synaesthetic moments, not, as in Tennyson's lyric 95 in *In Memoriam*, to emphasize the ineffability of the "strange" experience which "matter-moulded" words cannot communicate, but to gaze upon a hole into which transcendental meaning collapses. Meaning is the product of chance disguised as fate, from which we sometimes fool ourselves into believing we can escape into unconsciousness or philosophical reverie. [9]

In the remainder of this chapter I shall discuss Hardy's curious uses of the philosophical concept of realism as a means of characterizing Tess. In Tess, Hardy depicts not so much a real woman as an idealized conception of her: that is, his representation is several times removed from experience, codified in a philosophical matrix framed, as it were, by the prefaces in which he implicitly acknowledges the fictiveness of the purity he defends. Thus, he depicts Tess according to a philosophical concept of nature no less fictional than Angel's belief that she is a "fresh and virginal daughter of Nature" (176).[10] On this issue it is difficult to distinguish the narrator from Hardy, or Hardy from the naive but ostensibly self-conscious theorizing of a man like Angel, who discovers realism in woman, but only through the philosophical concept, not the real thing, which would be beyond language. Humma's statement that "Angel is not so much wrong to think of Tess as a pagan goddess as he is wrong to abstract the goddess from her earthly element" is typical of critical attempts to distinguish Angel from Hardy, who champions a natural realism that valorizes Tess's worth.[11] But Tess's "earthly element" is a fiction grounded in German aesthetics, which associates feminine value with the naive, the childlike, and the chthonic. It is only superficially at odds with Angel's inability to appreciate Tess's worth. The narrator sides with Tess against her male predators, yet he also delimits her:

> Women whose chief companions are the forms and forces of outdoor Nature retain in their souls far more of the Pagan fantasy of their remote forefathers than of the systematized religion taught their race at later date. (158)[12]

There is no indication that we are to place this ironically, as there is about Angel's hypocrisies concerning Tess's sexual history. The novel's sexuality, which led Henry James to term it "vile," reveals an at once liberated and enclosed authorial sensibility, for whom the desired womanly alternative to the "ache of modernism" (180) is a life free of abstraction. Though Hardy defends Tess's purity, the aesthetic categories he applies to do so place his creation at the mercy of ideas.

In *Literary Notebooks* entries of the same period in which *Tess* appeared, Hardy reveals an interest in Schiller, Schopenhauer, and Nietzsche, whose ideas he considers in light of his own about the connection between women and nature. In an 1891 entry he enters the following thoughts by Jouy:

> Women are childish, frivolous, & short sighted. ... Woman lives more in the present than man, & if it is tolerable, enjoys it more eagerly. ... Women fix their eyes upon what lies before them; we see far beyond, overlooking what is under our noses. ... Concrete things exercise a power over them, wh. is seldom counteracted by abstract principles of thought. ... Have never managed to produce a single achievement in the fine arts that is really great, genuine, or original. ... Never got beyond a subjective point of view. ... The vanity of women ... takes an entirely material direction(?)[13]

Jouy's gender categories parallel Schiller's, but with a more overtly misogynistic bias. Women live for the present, are attracted to concrete things, are objects of but cannot create great art, are subjective and prone to materialism, and vain: the lineaments of the personality Hardy defends in Tess are evident in these entries, though with a negative bias. "Materialists," Hardy notes, "hinder the due appreciation of the intellectual life."[14] It is noteworthy that Jouy links feminine materialism with resistance to chronology, while only men are capable of the great "single achievement" which requires concentration on "abstract principles of thought" (ideals) and the capacity to take the long view and exploit time. It is perilous to equate Hardy's journal entries with his beliefs, yet it is telling that his only editorial comment is the question mark following the observation about women's material basis.

Schiller popularized Rousseau's linking of the natural in women and children with an absence of pronounced self-consciousness. In the last section of *Naive and Sentimental Poetry*, Schiller argues that in a "century that is civilizing itself," an antagonism is developing between the realist, whose "fixed loyalty to the uniform testimony of the senses" indicates "a resigned submission to the necessity (but not the blind necessity) of nature," and the "sentimental" character, or idealist, who "presses on to the unconditioned in all its knowledge" and practices "a moral rigorism that insists upon the unconditioned in acts of the will."[15] The realist is essentially a fatalist while the idealist strives for moral freedom and autonomy. Schiller continues:

> In order to do justice to the realist, therefore, one must judge him according
> to the entire context of his life; for the idealist one must limit oneself to
> particular occurrences in it, but these must first be selected.[16]

Hardy was aware of Schiller's ideas about realism and idealism; they
are prominent in his 1892 preface to *Tess* and underlie his
characterization of Tess as caught between what she should be (naive)
and the divided person masculine idealists have made her.[17] Defending
his characterization, he cites a letter by Schiller to Goethe: Critics who
condemn a work of art for this or that transgression

> seek only their own ideas in a representation, and prize that which should be
> higher than what is. The cause of the dispute, therefore, lies in the very first
> principles, and it would be utterly impossible to come to an understanding
> with them. (38)

"That which should be higher" is the idealized conception, while "what
is" suggests realism. In quoting Schiller, Hardy associates his own
realism with Tess's purity. He denounces one critic, "a gentleman who
turned Christian for half-an-hour" (38), who condemned his work for its
immorality, turning on him Schiller's statement, "As soon as I observe
that any one, when judging of poetical representations, considers
anything more important than the inner Necessity and Truth, I have done
with him" (38). The critic becomes Angel Clare and Hardy becomes
figuratively the aggrieved Tess (Tess, *c'est moi*?) as he contrasts judging
character according to aims and tendencies with an idealism that
evaluates according to specific behaviors that may contradict general
tendencies. Religious and artistic idealists (the type who want a
"respectable story") miss art in their idea. Yet the realism Hardy affirms
is a conception that, like idealism, arises from modern self-
consciousness, though its object supposedly is anterior to that. It is telling
that, in the 1912 "General Preface" to the Wessex edition, Hardy denies
being limited to a "philosophy of life" and writes that "positive views on
the Whence and Wherefore of things have never been advanced by this
pen as a consistent philosophy." Instead of offering an "objectless
consistency," his sentiments have been "mere impressions of the
moment, and not convictions or arguments" (495). Yet, against this
supposed impressionism are undoubted assumptions about women's
connection with nature: thus Tess's seemingly sexually receptive "pouted
up deep red mouth" (52), in which description the margins between the
narrator and Alex fade. Hardy participates in this placement, projecting
its metonymic reductiveness through Alec and Angel. His Tess somehow
is really, in her essential form, purely nature, while they are guilty of

transfixing her with words. Yet his passionate defense of her in the prefaces merely reiterates his implication in that same transfixing of the feminine ideal according to a matrix of meaning that requires that she must be defended in the first place, or be the ground on which others generate the difference that enables identity's crisis and its reconstituted meaning. If Tess has fewer margins than men, indeed if the only margins she has are imposed on her by men, she is fertile ground on which to define a meaning through distancing. Nature lacks stable enough form, but she can be situated as an object, a metaphorical ant or a dying pheasant, the noble, pure, defiled victim of the modernity whose railroads impinge on the Wessex countryside.

Hardy's genius is evident in the fact that, despite (or perhaps because of) his confusion of artifice and nature, *Tess* is a profoundly interesting novel. He is influenced by philosophical ideas, and Tess's victimization should be evaluated in terms of the questionable assumptions that underlie them. Yet the novel remains rewarding on affective and intellectual levels. Hardy's conception of the nature to which the realist is close is much more complex and, of course, metaphorically interesting than Schiller's. Tess eludes the narrative placement that would make her merely the victim of nature or man. Our visual impressions, like the last view of Tess at Stonehenge at sunrise, transcend the simple critical judgment on which the narrator (and Hardy's shaping hand) seems to insist in foregrounding the sacrificial nature of Tess's fate. It is, of course, Hardy's visual power that many readers have admired, while much criticism has been leveled at his sometimes half-digested ideas and commentaries on action and character. To state that Tess can no longer experience childlike innocence owing to her psychic mutilation by society, or to have Angel (barely separate from the narrator) ruminate about Tennyson's lyric about defending childlike faith in *In Memoriam* (234), narrows effects that visually supersede such reductionism.[18] Yet the philosophical basis, or hard logical deposit, that generates the novel, is finally Tess's association, in her purest, most unmediated form, with a nature that, by definition, must lie outside categories of time, space, and language.

8
Oscar Wilde's *The Picture of Dorian Gray*: The Monstrous Portrait and Realism's Demise

At the center (or, to be sure, the attic) of *The Picture of Dorian Gray* is the portrait onto which two people, the painter Basil Hallward and his subject, Dorian Gray, project their desires for the permanence to be found in art. Yet, unforgotten though hidden away, like some denied conscience, the representation decays and mocks all attempts to deploy art to allay life's rush and decay. Realism, I have suggested, seeks a middle space between the real and its emplotment, and it uses language to reify belief in a visual field. But when the visual becomes the transfixing source of horror—the Medusa-stares from the abyss or the ideal—it becomes necessary to deploy language to conceal or at least tame the unspeakable, or to relegate what cannot be effaced from the mind to a hidden place from which, inevitably, it must emerge. Dorian's very body, of course, becomes a denial of the hidden portrait, changeless as it appears to be, regardless of the decay within. The body is a form of the falsifying word, in other words, creating a frozen reality to conceal the ongoing depravity that marks the hidden representation. It parodies the failure of realistic representation, which already is in crisis, given the realization that art really mirrors the spectator, not life. But objectifications (really subjectifications) of the self are dubious and unstable, given the crisis of language as an adequate means of representing the real. Too great an awareness that the real being emplotted is merely an emanation of an unstable subjectivity threatens the verisimilar with dissolution. What de Certeau suggests about history, that it should not allow reference to the real (documents, other facts) to be obliterated, is (as Conrad's Marlow recognizes) true of literary realism as well. Realism may be, as Roland Barthes suggests, merely a subjective fiction. But the loss of ability to suspend disbelief cancels the possibility of verisimilar belief, or at least forces the reader to grasp at belief within a text so unstable as to resist any such endeavor, so that it must, as it were, be hidden, or covered over with interpretive judgments that create stability even as they depict an unstable object. Once the capacity to generate meaning from the gap between the real and its organization dissipates, when all barriers between self and Other collapse, we are left somewhat as Emily Brontë's hapless Lockwood is when snow covers all the landmarks in *Wuthering Heights*: in this novel, Heathcliff's desideratum, the end of all differentiations, of self and other, male and female, place and place, adumbrates as well the end of realism, which must be rescued symbolically in the novel's second part.

In Wilde's novel, the possibility of verbal stability collapses into metaphorical-allegorical (Lord Henry and Basil) and ironic (Lord Henry) alternatives, verbal enemies of the middle space where realism thrives at the intersections of visual field, written word, and concept. Burkhardt thought that the allegorical "always destroys art and truth."[1] Basil's idealization of Dorian, like Lord Henry's wish to see him as a type of the New Hedonism, reduces particularity to the conceptual, and raises the boy to a parodic deity, a role he can sustain no more than Sibyl Vane can when Dorian turns this strategy on her. Yet equally damaging to Dorian, and to particularity and realism, is the entrapment of language in radical irony. Discussing the historian Burkhardt, Hayden White argues (and this could summarize Lord Henry perfectly) that irony "tends in the end to turn upon word play, to become a language about language, so as to dissolve the bewitchment of consciousness caused by language itself."[2] Assaulted by untenable conceptions and aloetic ironies, Dorian Gray desperately seeks aesthetic bulwarks against the dissolution of meaning but in the end is forced to confront utter decay and horror as the real itself perversely becomes his desideratum, the last redoubt of meaning amidst collapsing fictions that lead to the abyss. Dorian's appropriation of feminine ornamentation (Burke's strategy with manners and Marie) to distance terror arises from the same impulse that makes him wish to forget history, even as, offered perpetual life, he physically parodies the historical text frozen in time, rendered absurd by its changelessness. Increasingly, he sees only decay and cannot, like Carlyle in *Past and Present*, use fiction to clothe an organic and provisionally interpreted historical truth. Thus history must become a forgetting and a burial, behind scientific and objective fictions that are inherently lifeless.

Lord Henry Wotton is the exemplar of an irony whose essence is the opposite of the embodied "marvellous" Basil Hallward seeks, yet, in its self-contained witticisms, it is equally destructive to Dorian. Recall how, in the chapter on *Emma*, I suggested levels of delimitation, ranging from Mr. Woodhouse's cynical solipsism to Emma's delusions (based typically on visual incompetence), and to the narrator's virtual exclusion of the historical field in favor of a limited realism. All emplotment requires an ironic awareness of the tension between experience and its organization; the problem is determining when and how the delimitation this entails becomes simply inimical to the middle space in which realism thrives. An equivalent problem exists in tropal perceptions. Lord Henry seduces Dorian by suggesting that he can be the "visible symbol" of an age that needs "new sensations."[3] The trick is to avoid gazing too intently at the symbol, or grasping it as a finality, for to do either is to seek closure. As in Goethe's *Faust*, the peril lies in trying to stop the flow of time and losing oneself in a single aspect of experience. Lord Henry's philosophy is based on the rejection of renunciation, that mainstay of Victorian ethics, in favor of sensations that remove the New Man from the danger inherent in his epicurean project. Yet, as Wilde recognized in his early poem "Helas!" this attempt is fraught with peril: "To drift with every passion" may cause the loss of "a soul's inheritance." Moreover, this entails a loss of margins and borders, which are necessary to any endeavor to organize experience. For Lord Henry, language is a mere instrument, a congeries of aphorisms that have no meaning beyond themselves as he creates hermeneutic walls of nonmeaning, mist, and obfuscation. Belief is not part of his system (he is based on Goethe's Mephistopheles, the "spirit that denies"). He successfully excludes all reality, morality, or organizing purpose outside his carefully delimited borders. If Mr. Woodhouse is most effective in the library, Lord Henry is at his best at dinner party chitchat, where nothing means much beyond itself. In other words, he advocates a philosophy that melts boundaries in a series of sensations, but he remains inviolate himself. His symbol is not a visual allegory, as it is for Basil, but a collection of concepts in action, from whose consequences he is safe. Ellmann writes that Wilde "balanced two ideas which ... look contradictory. One is that art is disengaged from life, the other is that it is deeply incriminated with it."[4] This adumbrates, in effect, the crisis of realism in the latter part of the nineteenth century, which, like the crisis in historicism, arose from an ironic vision of life so intense that at best it could effect only demonic, or failed, epiphanies.[5] It becomes impossible to emplot reality in a believable way, for at the source of every such attempt is the fear or realization that everything is a sham.

Lord Henry's aesthetic, locked within a system of repetitions, is essentially a parody of the development in time that characterizes realism. The New Hedonism embraces sensation, but the practical consequence is the loss of definition, difference, and the creative fissures between self and other that enable the realist to anchor the visual field in language that prevents its petrifaction or subsumption under conceptual or chthonic uniformities. He advocates, in essence, changeless change, surrender to flux and fortune, yet calls it perfection. Thus, near the end of Dorian's failure to counter degeneration, Lord Henry tells him he has not changed: "You are quite flawless now" (209). Dorian knows he is "not the same" (209), but Henry, like Mephistopheles, only understands change conceptually, trapped as he is in a critical-ironic pose, just as Basil is in his idealism and Dorian in his imposition of univocal art on life. Lord Henry moves from drawing room to drawing room, irony to irony, unaffected by the morality he advises Dorian Gray to eschew. He thrives in a play of memory amidst subtle influences and sensual imaginings (209); he acquires superficial knowledge without nausea and evades the consequences of his words. But the price is monstrosity, for to do this he has rigorously delimited himself from all commitment and called this delimitation—and its symbol, Dorian—perfection. His aloetic irony is a perpetual creation and destruction without danger to him: covering knowledge with mists and repartee, he limits himself to a claustrophobic social milieu that has none of the permeability that exists between Austen's drawing rooms and something, always cloaked in delimiting but suggestive language, that exists beyond the text. Instead, language is not the trace of ceremonial, aesthetic, or moral purpose but perfect in its surface replication of visual and verbal enclosures. In chapter 17, refusing to define his belief, Lord Henry rejects the capacity of language to do justice to belief, and hence its capacity, through verbal textures, to occupy the middle space between concept and abyss:

"You are a sceptic"
"Never! Scepticism is the beginning of Faith."
"What are you?"
"To define is to limit."
"Give me a clue."
"Threads snap. You would lose your way in the labyrinth." (193)

For Lord Henry, names are infinitely alterable, which makes them as meaningless as unorganized sensations. Hence language creates self-contained perfections within narrow spaces but is powerless to name things-in-themselves (beliefs, knowledge, mystery) outside. This, in essence, is realism's dilemma, for belief, including belief in language, is in disarray and decay, as both Basil and Dorian discover. "To define is to limit," Lord Henry declares. "I hope Dorian has told you about my plan for rechristening everything," he tells Gladys (191). But this wish to rename, which adumbrates the decay between language (and sight) and the thing outside, suggests that words are meaningless, unless carefully infused with irony in a parodic idyllic sphere completely separate from infinitude and society alike. Lord Henry's witticisms are merely verbal games, simulacra of passion emptied of any purpose, freed from time and space yet offering no view into infinitude. They are, at best, intensifications arising from the novelty of the wit. Erskine believes that "the way of paradoxes is the way of truth. To test Reality we must see it on the tight-rope. When the Verities become acrobats we can judge them" (77). This sounds superficially like the credo of such Romantic ironists as Blake and Friedrich Schlegel. But for Lord Henry, verities, like memory and guilt, are merely fictions that, detached from experience, can be redefined or repudiated at will. Hence literature can no longer present horizontal and vertical textures of belief but at best reifies a "forest of symbols" (in the *symboliste* manner), that is, is simply another prison of language whose verisimilar fluidity is frozen, not in concepts, but in repetitions of sensations that convert "an appetite into an art," to cite Lord Henry's attitude towards romance. Thus, he insists that the book he gives Dorian (inspired for Wilde by Huysman's *A Rebours*) cannot have poisoned Dorian's soul, for true art, as self-enclosed as the social table, has no meaning beyond itself: "It is superbly sterile" (210). Yet art *does* affect action, Wilde suggests, if its effect is to turn all meaning, all passion, into mere repetition, which precludes eventually every endeavor to build personal or artistic texts over the real, parrying it in fluid recreations of past experiences that turn life into narrative, unrepetitive meaning. Secrecy, Basil tells Lord Henry, "seems to be the one thing that can make modern life mysterious or marvellous to us" (51). Analogously, Lord Henry's "mist" that "makes things wonderful" points to the necessity of cloaking, though for him the underlying meaning is empty, while Basil seeks the ideal. But the very need to discover yet hide the marvellous is a mark of the triumph of allegory over realistic fluidity, suggesting an ossification of the lingual and visual. Contextualism is impossible, for any opening entails the dissolution of all meaning into horror. Organicism is also impossible, as Dorian discovers in the family gallery, for the only integrative meaning collapses differentiation onto a unifying malady that unites generations. And the mechanistic aim to view life scientifically is equally feckless. Thus, realism is bifurcated into extremes of nonrepresentational irony and parodic tropes that fail to organize (or create bulwarks against) flux. If it must be protected with a mist or with secrecy, meaning is no longer capable of realistic revelation, but, like Marlow's meaning in *Heart of Darkness*, must itself become a mist, "enveloping the tale which brought it out."[6] Impressionism alone can save tale and meaning from the consequences of spectral display. Burkhardt, according to White, linked failures of perception and vision with "submission to the element of 'mystery,'" which allegory represents.[7] This, likewise, is a failure of realism, with which allegory sometimes works in uneasy subordination. Basil seeks to allegorize Dorian—freeze perception and vision—in a medium he thinks he controls, painting. Yet, he hesitates to show his masterpiece because, instinctively, he fears the disclosure that might strip his artifact of meaning (yet, finally, see it he must). The goal of realism, on the other hand, is at once containment of the monstrous (a hiding) and a revelation of a discourse through an activity that makes an experience (or recreation of experience) known. To justify itself, it must be public, not hidden, and, indeed, revelation of the concealed (Emma's complicity with Churchill, little Dick's or Kurtz's last words) is necessary to adumbrate the existence of further mysteries that won't be explored to their final, univocal bourns.

Basil's belief in Dorian as an "unseen ideal" who can fill the gap between ugly realism and void ideality (56) points to his incapacity to supply an adequate substitute for a literary realism that no longer suffices to cover the abyss. He seeks, through Dorian, "the harmony of soul and body" which "in our madness" we have "separated" (56), that is, a lost Edenic unity that the languid, richly odored, opium-tainted garden environment of his studio ironically belies. Unable to embrace the object of his desire as both surface and symbol, he seeks in his "artistic idolatry" a point of perfection (56). In *The Critic as Artist,* Gilbert echoes Lessing in saying, "The statue is concentrated to one moment of perfection" and "The image on the canvas possesses no spiritual element of growth and change":

> "Movement, that problem of the visible arts, can be truly realized by Literature alone. It is Literature that shows us the body in its swiftness and the soul in its unrest." (260)

Basil's failure to stabilize Dorian visually is related to the problem of art for art's sake in general: by failing to grapple with, and represent, life in all its chaotic complexity, it ironically accelerates the decay of self. Basil's belief that the artist should "put nothing of his own life" into art (56) opposes him to realism, ostensibly Wilde's credo as well. Yet, short of Lord Henry's cynicism, it is impossible to do so. What Basil seeks is not movement but perfection, the unity between classicism and modernity the modern age cannot provide. Schiller's wish for the artist to "spiritualize one's age," effect a third impulse or what Dorian terms a "new spirituality, of which a fine instinct for beauty was to be the dominant characteristic" (144), fails because the motionless movement Schiller sought to conserve through the visual arts is antithetical to modern multiplicity. Indeed, a flight from modernity's chaos of physical forces, which threaten us with solipsistic imprisonment or with dissolution, leads Basil to flee motion and change. He pursues the youth he idolizes and the portrait that expresses this, and he mistrusts Lord Henry's paradoxes, which seem the expression of rubbish, facts, and reality: "As long as I live, the personality of Dorian Gray will dominate me. You can't feel what I feel. You change too often" (57). But the principle of modern life, and of the novel, its characteristic representation prior to the cinema, is change, and irony must be incorporated into its representation. Far from having Lord Henry's prophylactic irony, Basil, on the brink of death after seeing the "foulness and horror" wrought on the surface of his portrait from within its "inner life" (164), retreats into Christianity. He begs Dorian to pray, telling him, "I worshipped you too much. I am punished for it. You worshipped yourself too much. We are both punished" (165).

Basil's horror upon seeing the decayed portrait is accentuated by the traces of its former beauty:

> There was still some gold in the thinning hair and some scarlet on the sensual mouth. The sodden eyes had kept something of the loveliness of their blue, the noble curves had not completely passed away from the chiselled nostrils and from plastic throat. Yes, it was Dorian himself. But who had done it? He seemed to recognize his own brushwork, and the frame was his own design. The idea was monstrous, yet he felt afraid. (163)

What George Levine calls realism's struggle "to reconstruct a world out of a world deconstructing,"[8] its endeavor to represent yet tame excess and monstrosity, breaks down when, once freed of mist and concealment, the naked, unalloyed visual field is displayed. Dorian's body, I suggested, is the symbolic word that conceals for a time—but not from him—the monstrosity raging within. Like Victor Frankenstein, Basil discovers that the beauty and proportion he sought is merely a ghastly, ineradicable representation of the decaying corpse towards which all life tends. His effort to reduce Dorian to visual statuary and then to painting has created an uncontrolled monstrosity that contrasts with the Paterian *Mona Lisa*, through whom all the maladies of life have passed, for the latter is an impressionistic moment, a subjective appreciation of the fluid artwork, while the former is a terrible emblem of the frozen imagination, the vampire replicated in his creation. Basil's desperate attempt to escape his false aestheticism into traditional Christianity is feckless: no more than Marlowe's Faustus can he wash away the "iniquities" (165) that he has cherished too much in their guise as the ideal of beauty. By now, Dorian, bitterly aware of the dysfunction inherent in his aesthetic construction, can only bitterly ask Basil, whom he is about to kill and reduce to a "thing," "Can't you see your ideal in it?" (164). In death, Basil, as a thing, is the parodic reflection of the motionless aesthetic object into which he projected himself.

Dorian has increasing difficulty constructing illusions, "mists" that hide decay and death. The disintegrating portrait, always present in his mind, mocks his attempts to do so. Hence, he pursues objectification of subjective instability to create the illusion of order yet is affronted with a decay parodied by the imperturbable perfection of his physical appearance. While the cyclical changes of nature, as well as the ravages of immoral conduct, are projected onto that which should be useless, that is, bereft of an end, Dorian inserts into life itself the artistry that should remain separate from life. This entails, as Rita Felski notes, the appropriation of feminine associations: "languidness, vanity, hypersensitivity, a love of fashion and ornamentation."[9] He is impelled to seek organizations outside himself to counter the monstrosity within, whose degenerative traces are evident in stories that his youthful appearance increasingly belies. He becomes, in other words, the rigid aesthetic object that conceals the Medusa-stare, yet he is fully, horrifically aware of the failure of action and word to stabilize the rot within. He cannot, like Emma, use game and irony to organize his life, or delude himself into thinking he can. The body parodies godlike objectivity, but likewise the scientific kind, and thus renders all objectivity impossible, forcing meaning from some objective truth onto personal sensations which, by nature, contain no inherent meaning and resist the imposition of the extrinsic sort.

Dorian tries to render life, not art, objective so that its form remains unchanging while the art piece hidden in the former schoolroom, the locus of past innocence, bears the progressive imprint of temporality and engagement in decadent life. Scientific objectivity, a parody of the artistic kind, is Dorian's unsuccessful means of coping with the inherently flawed endeavor to render void the old categories of subjective and objective, masculine and feminine, science and art, for he remains bound in a dialectic that promises either progress or decay, positive or regressive evolution, but progress all the same. Dorian himself does not have the self-distancing irony to maintain the pose of living life artistically, for, as Lord Henry eventually realizes, his endeavor to make his personality assume "the office of art" is blighted by its being premature: "The pulse and passion of youth were in him, but he was becoming self-conscious" (91). If Walter Pater's project is to draw the hard gemlike flame from life's Heraclitean flux, an endeavor parallel to Nietzsche's to explore beyond the outmoded dialectical categories, Dorian merely drifts, parodying the need for detachment with his heartless "scientific point of view" (174) that dehumanizes the living; he finds in multiple personalities (154) not the means to defeat fate but a trick whereby he masks from himself his degradation until it is too late. The goal for the ideal artist in Schiller's *Aesthetic Education*, that he admonish the age by bringing to it a universal truth rooted in the idea of Greece, has broken down in a world where, at best, an author must diffuse himself amidst cunning masks and, as Nietzsche suggests in *Beyond Good and Evil*, conceal himself within the protean fictions he sends out into the world. Nietszche asks half facetiously, "Does one not write books precisely to conceal what one harbors?"[10] Dorian projects his decay onto Basil's portrait to perpetuate his youth. His body will retain the timelessness of art, yet he cannot forget the moral decay that is parodied by the imperturbable perfection of his physical appearance.

In his *Birth of Tragedy,* Nietzsche cites the twin dangers of Socratic optimism, which entails imprisonment in rational fictions, and the Medusa-stare from the abyss, which leads the beholder to weave beneficent fictions, like the Greeks' "middle world" of mythic art: the abyss, if contemplated too long, destroys the capacity for word and illusion. Hence, we justify the world by viewing it as an "aesthetic phenomenon" and try to avoid illusions that are too unstable. The trick is to look into the mirror of the self yet not be enthralled by the reflection, instead being "at once subject and object, at once poet, actor, and spectator."[11] But herein lies tremendous peril, for what should be an ironic play of subjective projections into the world can break down. Lord Henry's Romantic-ironic repartee is a gilded cage of language whose simulacrum of meaning is in wit, paradox, and ultimate nonmeaning that hovers above the horrific and the unspeakable. By pursuing the "real secret" of life through beauty, in contrast, Dorian guarantees the effacement of "*Rouge* and *esprit*," the collapse of beauty and appearance into debasement and decay. Dorian is much too serious; the failure creatively to embrace ironic denial guarantees the collapse of all meaning.

Dorian projects onto Sibyl Vane a desire for feminine perfection that cloaks his disintegrating self as well as the brute realism towards which every immoral act impels him. He cannot transform her into an objectified "eternally feminine" (Goethe's term) because his "monstrous desires" lead to repetition and meaninglessness as the capacity to maintain illusions disintegrates and he is caught between the systole and diastole of objective displacements and their collapses.[12] Thus, she must remain theatrical art to be believable. The object of Dorian's endeavor to retrieve a lost innocence anterior to modern self-consciousness, Sibyl seems "quite unconscious of her power" (87): she is the sort of innocent, childlike, feminine genius that Schiller and Rousseau idealize. She seems to solve the problem of remaining autonomous despite the need to embrace importunate change and multiple identities. Having repudiated middle-class Victorian ideology yet remained bound within its matrix, Dorian projects his need for assurance and meaning onto her. She is the appearance he must control and render permanent, whatever the permutations of her roles, in order to escape the growing perception that he is hollow at the core, his soul a shadow "seated in the house of sin": "All the great heroines of the world in one" (88), she is an apparent quintessence, a unity of self, poetry, nature, and the Other, which stands in contrast to his growing sense of incoherence. Only the "white narcissus" at the center of his idealization suggests its solipsistic nature. The ugliness of her surroundings impinges on her as she loses the capacity to commit herself entirely to the manipulation of theatrical illusions. Her real passion makes the feigned kind seem "unreal" (109). Following her failure on the stage, Lord Henry tells Dorian they must leave the theater, for "it is not good for one's morals to see bad acting" (110–11). Love is no less a form of imitation than art. To her, it is something else, but what, she is unsure, for words cannot provide an adequate expression of a feeling beyond language:

> I might mimic a passion that I do not feel, but I cannot mimic one that burns me like fire. Oh, Dorian, Dorian, you understand now what it signifies? Even if I could do it, it would be profanation for me to play at being in love. You have made me see that. (112)

Those who can feign passion do not feel it; those who feel passion grow vulgar in the eyes of the beholder. Or as Lord Henry puts it,

> There is always something ridiculous about the emotions of people whom one has ceased to love. (113)

To counter the brute reality that impinges on his carefully constructed aesthetic spaces, Dorian desperately grasps multiple personalities and masks but does not possess enough of what Pater calls a "passionate coldness"[13] to stabilize his identity. Like Victor Frankenstein, he seeks meaning in aesthetic appearances, reification through portraits, though, characteristically, he has a vampire-like dread of mirrors as well as of the

decaying portrait in the old school room in the attic. Yet he is implicated
in an artifact of self that turns any self-contemplation into a transfixion
by the Medusa-stare engendered by others' metaphorical-allegorical and
radical ironic emplotments of himself. Thus, at the peripheries of visual
self-identification, he seeks traces of himself retrospectively, in family
portraits that contain dispersed characteristics that, taken together, merely
implicate him again in transfixion. These portraits offer him no more
help than those in Lord Dedlock's family gallery in *Bleak House*, for the
dispersed signs point consistently to a family curse—an unvarying
emplotment, like the Dedlock family curse—that seems confirmed over
and over in pictorial representations, which no verbal texturings can tame
or hide. Thus Dorian wonders if a "poisonous germ crept from body to
body till it had reached his own?" This "inheritance of sin and shame"
(154), copied over and over in the faces of his ancestors, is the Gothic
fate from which no mediation can free him, as he watches definitions and
barriers visually collapse into one single, unifying thread from which no
escape is possible. Even the crossing of gender barriers is less a
liberation than the collapse of all possibility of parrying the gaps between
experience and its reconstitution. This is evident in Dorian's reading of
his mother:

> He had got from her his beauty, and his passion for the beauty of others. She
> laughed at him in her loose Bacchante dress. There were vine leaves in her
> hair. The purple spilled from the cup she was holding. (155)

The Dionysian offers no escape, for Dorian is bound by what Nietzsche
terms a "nausea and disgust with life" that vitiates illusions of order or
escape. Nietzsche provocatively terms Christianity "a secret instinct of
annihilation, a principle of decay, diminution, and slander." [14] Dorian (his
very name suggests the drive for order and simple majesty) focuses on
the Dionysian in his mother's portrait, but far from experiencing a pain
that leads him beyond the *principium individuationis*, he merely
appropriates the appearance of intoxication, replacing "primordial unity"
with his own forced one. To cite Nietzsche's *Birth of Tragedy*, Dorian
fails to "solve the problem of how the 'lyrist' is possible as an artist—he
who, according to the experience of all ages, is continually saying 'I' and
running through the entire chromatic scale of his passions and desires." [15]

Unable to find redemption from the ego, Dorian transfers from art to
himself what Pater had thought possible to read in *La Gioconda*, "the
fancy of a perpetual life, sweeping together ten thousand experiences." [16]
This entails not a continuing dialectic between the ego and phenomena
but a confusion that belies the "fullness of experience of the modern

world" that Pater advocates. Dorian's discovery of the feminine in himself becomes a means of further confusion, not liberation, for he remains trapped in a gender dialectic that associates ornamentation with the feminine, essence with the masculine. He also tries to project himself onto "the whole of history" to make it "merely the record of his own life" (155). To do so, however, he turns not to history but to the strange *symboliste* novel, whose hero, like Volpone, has imaginatively metamorphosed himself, from Tiberius to Caligula to a horse and to Domitian, and finally, in a *frisson* of androgyny, to Elagabalus, who "painted his face with colours, and plied the distaff among the women" (155). As in Ben Jonson's *Volpone*, androgynous projections, far from effecting liberation and unity, merely imprison the personality in a degenerating fleshly dialectic, in which the soul merely shifts among embodiments of sexuality, parodying the drive to mastery by inverting it into a protofeminine passivity of appearance. In Jonson's play, Pythagoras's soul decays during its historical journey from its origin (Apollo) to Puritan and hermaphrodite. So too with Dorian's losing himself amidst aesthetic appearances: unable to read himself, bereft of language's capacity to emplot life's flux, he clothes himself in ornamentation, only to experience the disintegration of the identity he wishes to stabilize.

Lord Henry's "poisonous" book parodies realism in that it appeals to the purely visual, rather than both embracing and retreating from experience, and marshaling language to create belief in a stable yet dynamic visual field. Thus, like Mephistophilis's pageant of the Seven Deadly Sins in *Doctor Faustus*, it actually entices the reader away from language into a seductive visual field that presents the appearance of organization, but only the appearance. Behind the show is rot, which verisimilar language might show yet arrest. Seduction is through the eye, as Dickens's Harthouse knows, and this is done much more effectively if the instrument is physically a book but really a generator of illusions arising from a protean sensuality whose essential self-decay belies surface meaning. Dorian experiences an ostensibly controllable loss of shape and order in a textual titillation that bedazzles him with visual luxuriances:

> The Renaissance knew of strange manners of poisoning—poisoning by a helmet and a lighted torch, by an embroidered glove and a jewelled fan, by a gilded pomader and by an amber chain. Dorian Gray had been poisoned by a book. There were moments when he looked on evil simply as a mode through which he could realize his conception of the beautiful. (156–57)

Always, the "misshapen shadow" in the upstairs room absently smiles, the portrait that decays into the unspeakable that lies at the heart of his identity, which, like the devisualized "creature so foul to look at" in *Hard Times*, Stephen Blackpool's wife, is the polluted truth behind his fictive strategies to elude meaninglessness through visual reification in an age when realistic investiture is difficult, and only irony seems able to cast up a bulwark.

Nassaar's observation that "Henry Wotton, by substituting the word *sensations* for the word *impressions*, slightly but significantly alters Pater's doctrine," clarifies Dorian's inability to create the illusion of aesthetic unity to solidify himself amidst temporal decay.[17] Sensations, in contrast to impressions (as Pater defines them) resist emplotment because, by definition, they are self-surrenders to passion that (Dorian discovers) bring him face-to-face with brutal realities that even the opium dens cannot let him forget. Walter Pater advocates focusing on "experience itself" rather than "the fruit of experience," letting each impression drop in pursuit of the "fruit of a quickened, multiplied consciousness."[18] The gemlike impression, the result of *askesis,* or "girding of the loins," offers an adequate, though perilous and desperately arrived at, substitute for the transcendental and the eschatological. Dorian desires objectivity but is impelled into the wellpit of decay like Dickens's Lady Dedlock, and for much the same reason: the attempt to create a mask fails because the capacity to retreat entirely into a self-sustaining eyrie (idyllic, romantic, or scientific) is lacking, and so too is the ability to create fluid, verisimilar conceptions of self infused with subordinate moralities, aesthetics, or theologies. One is left with the mask alone, that is, less a lingual coming-to-terms with existence than a denial of words in favor of a desperately maintained, but fake, visual field. Lady Dedlock exists amidst silences and forced promises (by Esther) not to talk; Dorian thinks he can recreate the past by withholding language. The failure of language, the belief that meaning can be established through the visual field alone, ensures that Dorian spends his sensations onanistically among portraits, personalities, and experiences that can offer him no stability, however much he tries to make their lives his own (155). His multiplied consciousness is finally a dispersion, not a concentration, of self; yet his uncritical acceptance of the New Hedonism gives way to a murderous objectivity that parodies aestheticism. If Gwendolen in *The Importance of Being Earnest* can successfully play with sexual role reversals, Dorian cannot, for he does not live in a detached idyll, even at the opera, where he goes to escape his guilt following Sibyl's suicide.[19] Life and art inevitably converge, but there is no organizing fiction that can resacralize meaning or tame the abyss.

The last redoubt before the collapse of all meaning is a scientific objectivity that makes words substitutes for things, or what Nietzsche termed "fairy tales" of science.[20] Faced with the realization that realism is but a disguised form of desire—that inner and outer chaos merely mirror one another until we emplot them—the last, desperate endeavor to know entails a univocal language that rigorously clarifies inconsistency and marshals past phenomena into unified fields. Lurking behind "the scientific point of view" that enables Dorian to reduce Basil to a dead thing and blackmail Alan Campbell into chemically reducing him to bare traces, is Wilde's suspicion that aestheticism may be just a disguised avatar of Darwinism. Lord Henry states:

> But, as the nineteenth century has gone bankrupt through an over-expenditure of sympathy, I would suggest that we should appeal to Science to put us straight. The advantage of the emotions is that they lead us astray, and the advantage of Science is that it is not emotional. (78)

Yet only he is able to quash sympathy within his radically delimited space, while Dorian is overcome by guilt, try as he might to convince himself that he can turn off memory and guilt about Sibyl's suicide merely by deciding not to talk about it: "If one doesn't talk about a thing, it has never happened" (128). Yet everything, even the body, is a form of telling that bears the imprint of previous acts even if this is not immediately apparent. Moreover, the assertion of scientific objectivity is just that, an assertion, not a reified verbal structure with any pretense of horizontal or vertical textures: it is a display of the body, of attitude, based on a denial of language, the hope that, somehow, a proper stance towards the visual field will organize it. But it can do no such thing, for, bereft of language, living in a world where language and the real are detached, there is nothing to prevent the monstrous from emerging. Even regulated impressions, Marlow discovers in *Heart of Darkness*, are inadequate to stay the jungle and the horror; it is necessary to look away at some point and to tell and retell one's experience, to warn, perhaps, but mainly to stabilize the horror that the word alone can scarcely adumbrate. Dorian's inability completely to quash sympathy ensures his downfall; sympathy, like renunciation, recognizes paradox and thus breaks down the fiction of an aesthetically autonomous identity. The past does not disappear merely because one ceases to speak of it: it remains hidden in the recesses of the mind, ready like all experience to overwhelm and terrify. Scientific objectivity gets Dorian nowhere, as the juxtaposition between the spectral portrait and Campbell's chemicals suggests. He cannot forget the portrait, nor even Basil's body once it is reduced, for the act remains buried in his conscience, whether he denies it or not:

> If in some hideous dissecting-room or fetid laboratory you found this man
> lying on a leaden table with red gutters scooped out in it for the blood to flow
> through, you would simply look upon him as an admirable subject. You
> would not turn a hair. You would not believe that you were doing anything
> wrong. (173)

Merely recontextualize the act within a scientific discourse and locus and
it ceases to have meaning. Yet Campbell, incapable of this, commits
suicide, as Dorian soon will.

Dorian's passions are furtive and forbidden; behind the veil of beauty,
they rot his soul, just as physically they deface the closeted portrait.
Desperate to escape himself, he embraces an aesthetics of the ugly to
replace the "mist" that cannot make things "wonderful" any more. The
"intense actuality of impression" is "needed for forgetfulness," a function
"all the gracious shapes of Art" cannot provide (186). But things
increasingly appear to be horrible as his life collapses. He is reminded
more and more of the reality of ugliness (186), especially as the novel
approaches its climax, for instance outside the opium dens, just before he
encounters James Vane:

> From cell to cell of his brain crept the one thought; and the wild desire to live,
> most terrible of all man's appetites, quickened into force each trembling
> nerve and fibre. Ugliness that had once been hateful to him because it made
> things real, became dear to him now for that very reason. Ugliness was the
> one reality. (186)

Desiring to finalize perception and freeze time, Dorian both yields to and
resists temptation; despite having imposed an aesthetic structure on life,
he is unable fully to quell the past that keeps welling up, as when,
embodying actual life and the buried past, the aging face of James Vane
reappears at the country house to mock the aesthetic "mask of youth" that
cannot save him. As the fictive union between act and actor, aesthetic
appearance and intention, breaks down—even denial of self becomes a
stratagem born of "curiosity," a parody of Arnold's term for the pursuit
of new knowledge—he is faced (like Emma Bovary at Vaubyessard)
with the spectre of the real staring through the window:

> He remembered that, pressed against the window of the conservatory, like a
> white handkerchief, he had seen the face of James Vane watching him. (196)

The handkerchief, the sign of dandiacal appearance that has comprised
his aesthetic construction of self, can no longer hide the misshapen brood
but becomes the metonymic shroud of the corpse whose appearance

precedes his own final mutilation, in evening dress, "withered, wrinkled, and loathsome of visage," recognizable only by the rings that betoken at once artifice, false union, and the failed endeavor to erase time, growth, and memory in a New Hedonism which, like Mephistopheles' promises of infinitely permuted experiences, represents the crisis of temptation in the modern age. Dorian cannot avoid the consequences of his acts, symbolized by the "loathsome red dew" that glistens on the hand in his portrait and, more tellingly, by the "torn curtain" through which it peers, much like the veil the youthful hierophant in Schiller's "Das Verschleierte Bild zu Sais" pulls aside in order to look at truth, only to find disillusionment and death (214).

9

Symbols, Ornaments, and Things
in Joseph Conrad's *Heart of Darkness*

In *Heart of Darkness,* Conrad's questionings of visual stability accompany a radical doubt about Western civilization itself. In his Africa, the West's symbols decay; by the time Marlow returns to Brussels, his perspective is decentered, though he keeps his sanity. Now, as he gazes at the Intended's portrait, he questions whether even the sunlight lies:

> I know that the sunlight can be made to lie too, yet one felt that no manipulation of light and pose could have conveyed the delicate shade of truthfulness upon those features.[1]

Yet this delicate truthfulness dissolves when his memories of Kurtz seem to overpower the Intended as the dusk grows. Marlow has learned that memory may be an accursed inheritance, not the source of regeneration. In his journey up the Congo, the trees that "patiently" (70) watch him seem to mock any endeavor to turn fragmentary experience into stable meaning. He is saved by his distancing of events and memories to mediate the terrible vision that threatens "to devour all the earth with all its mankind" (74). This entails a disillusioned yet necessary irony, for Africa dissolves the West's oppositions, confusing meaning and, particularly upsetting to Marlow, gender.[2] His capacity for ironic distancing is especially tested when, approaching Kurtz's compound, he must decide whether the heads stuck on fence poles are symbols or ornaments. To rescue the possibility of meaning, and deal with Kurtz's gender ambiguity, he affirms that heads are symbols, not ornaments, thus maintaining limited control over meaning.

Marlow commences his tale with a historical reconstruction of the Roman conquest of Britain, whose darkness paralleled Africa's:[3]

Imagine the feelings of a commander of a fine—what d'ye call 'em?—trireme in the Mediterranean, ordered suddenly to the north. ... Imagine him here—the very end of the world, a sea the colour of lead, a sky the colour of smoke, a kind of ship about as rigid as a concertina—and going up this river with stores, or orders, or what you like. Sandbanks, marshes, forests, savages,—precious little to eat fit for a civilised man, nothing but Thames water to drink. No Falernian wine here, no going ashore. Here and there a military camp lost in a wilderness, like a needle in a bundle of hay—cold, fog, tempests, disease, exile, and death—death skulking in the air, in the water, in the bush. (5–6)

The cruising yawl is situated between a sea "inscrutable as Destiny" (5) and an England whose history Marlow unravels to invent an equivalency with the Africa he experienced years before. Marlow constructs meaning by dressing the darkness with impressionistic meanings. But does memory unwrap something real from "thick cerements" with the aid of fictional techniques, as Thomas Carlyle suggests it should in *Past and Present*, or is it a mostly fictive colonization of the past that enables colonizations in the present? Stripping civilization's tentative wrapping may reveal a reinvigorated symbolism or simply nothing. Carlyle's Samson disinters St. Edmund: in touching the linen wrappings, his "sinful hand" seems to reinvigorate the monastery's faith.[4] But Marlow fears that such explorations may reveal the unspeakable thing for which the body is a nonsignifying ornament whose end is to be devoured.

Civilization is a flicker of light; if real, it is surely transitory. And light can be made to lie:

Light came out of this river since—you say Knights? Yes; but it is like a running blaze on a plain, like a flash of lightning in the clouds. We live in the flicker—may it last as long as the old earth keeps rolling! But darkness was here yesterday. (5)

Marlow grasps at meaning by visualizing and repeating it. Yet doubt underlies this: the "may it last" allows at best the repetition of events in the face of circumambient darkness. He precedes his affirmation with syntactical breaks ("Light came out of this river since—you say Knights?"; or later, "An appeal to me in this fiendish row—is there?" [37]), whose effect is to decenter the initial apparent certitude. Whatever his doubts, Marlow continues verbally-visually to reify his (and England's) past to project meaning into civilization's flicker, which, in memory's space, affords a limited assurance of repetition. Sticking to "surface-truth" (37) ensures some stability.

Marlow resents that his Aunt got him the job in Africa:

The men said, "My dear fellow," and did nothing. Then—would you believe it?—I tried the women. I, Charlie Marlow, set the women to work—to get a job. Heavens! Well, you see, the notion drove me. (8)

Her influence lingers in Africa: the brickmaker tells Marlow he is one of the "new gang—the gang of virtue": "Light dawned upon me. My dear aunt's influential acquaintances were producing an unexpected effect upon that young man" (26). The aunt's influence is diffused through men; the suspicion grows that the feminine is all-powerful—hence Marlow's dull anger towards the Intended and his projection of the chthonic feminine onto the jungle. His anxiety, like Frankenstein's, arises from a fear of death; his fictive reductions of women are evasions of it.

He is a participant in the colonial project he sardonically deplores. In *Great Expectations*, people measured Magwitch's cranium to confirm his criminality: society projects a pseudo-psychological myth on him. Similarly, in *Jane Eyre,* St. John Rivers reads Jane's head like a phrenologist, interpreting her plainness and lack of degradation as signs of renunciation. At his job interview, Marlow is measured by an alienist who reads skulls like books to discover their hidden truths in the "interests of science" (11). The calipers scientifically measure identity. But identity can only be suggested through analogies, not measured. The alienist wishes to make mystery comprehensible, just as the Europeans study, divide, and conquer Africa. His instrument parodies Jehovah's measuring (and creating) of the world. But as he sardonically suggests, his measurement precedes uncreation, the disembodiment of the sign, death. Nietzsche writes in *The Birth of Tragedy* that "Socratic" positivism upholds rationalist myths "with trembling hands."[5] Creating his mock-religious fairy tale of science, the alienist hints at conclusions he has never seen, since none of his subjects has returned to "confess":

"Oh, I never see them," he remarked; "and, moreover, the changes take place inside, you know." He smiled, as if at some quiet joke. "So you are going out there. Famous. Interesting, too. ... I have a little theory which you messieurs who go out there must help me to prove. This is my share in the advantages my country shall reap from the possession of such a magnificent dependency. The mere wealth I leave to others. Pardon my questions, but you are the first Englishman coming under my observation." (11)

Marlow denies being a typical Englishman: "If I were ... I wouldn't be talking like this with you." (12). He thinks he is different, but the alienist suggests that he is the same as the other colonialists, which will become evident in Africa if he fails to stay calm. The doctor smiles, jokes, and evades as he hints at, yet withholds, the consequences of being "out there" (12), playing with Marlow much as Marlow will play with Kurtz. Colonialism constructs autonomy and redefines another culture: physical appropriation begins with a mental act. Thus, the alienist appropriates knowledge, his "share in the advantages" (12) of imperial exploitation, as a palimpsest of physical power. Marlow's need for symbolical analogy is evident in his journey down the west coast of Africa, which thrusts him into isolation and sameness punctuated by bursts of "wild vitality" (14). His most memorable encounter is not with the occasional native boat with its "intense energy of movement" (14) but with the French warship whose ensign ("limp like a rag") and ineffective six-inch guns suggest imperialism's futility:

> Pop, would go one of the six-inch guns; a small flame would dart and vanish, a little white smoke would disappear, a tiny projectile would give a feeble screech—and nothing happened. (14)

Marlow displaces his anxiety onto a ship whose ineffectiveness seems curiously sexual.

On shore, his parodic "pilgrimage among hints for nightmares" (17) commences with his walking by a "vast artificial hole" at the coastal station, whose brutality he domesticates with disapprobation, a literary allusion to Dante's *Inferno*, and a turning away. The dehumanized "moribund shapes" (17) that crouch passively in this landscape relegate the products of masculine violence to a feminized space:

> Black shapes crouched, lay, sat between the trees, leaning against the trunks, clinging to the earth, half coming out, half effaced within the dim light, in all the attitudes of pain, abandonment, and despair. ... They were dying slowly—it was very clear. They were not enemies, they were not criminals, they were nothing earthly now—nothing but black shadows of disease and starvation, lying confusedly in the greenish gloom. (17)

Marlow's reduction of the natives to the impersonal "moribund shapes" and "black shadows" reflects his wish to make the insane explicable. To humanize the Africans (as he started to do with the "black fellows" off the coast [13]) would be to accept more fully his role in exploitation and murder.

In the narrow ravine, Marlow is affronted by "some picture of a massacre or a pestilence" (18). Onto this hillside scar, which contains phallic "imported drainage pipes" that have tumbled in and serve no purpose (17), he projects Dante's hellish circles: "My purpose was to stroll into the shade for a moment; but no sooner within than it seemed to me I had stepped into the gloomy circle of some Inferno" (17). This is not the later locus of "wild and passionate uproar" (37) but a quieter violence that coexists with elements of narrative structure (Dante, circularity, the story itself). The source of evil is a devouring feminine, which, later on, Marlow stabilizes in the outstretched arms of the helmeted dark woman. The Africans are sucked into passive death in a reversal of birth, entering a hole that foreshadows Marlow's journey up the "immense snake uncoiled" (8), the Congo, the symbolic birth canal that devours phallicism. He refuses to loiter because the workers' effacement to shapes and shadows mocks the controlling categories of language and myth that would classify and visualize the unspeakable.

The parodic "miracle" (18) of the place is the Chief Accountant, hollow within yet inviolate, unfazed by the impenetrable jungle, the big flies, and the groans of the dying man he ignores as he applies himself calmly to the figures with which he organizes colonialism. He is an ornament who requires no transfer to symbol, for to read him ironically is to read him literally: he is what he appears to be. He is autonomous and apparently freed from the horrific things that threaten effacement. Marlow is ironically seduced by him; but the accountant cannot be seduced into noticing the dying man:

> I respected the fellow. Yes; I respected his collars, his vast cuffs, his brushed hair. His appearance was certainly that of a hairdresser's dummy; but in the great demoralisation of the land he kept up his appearance. That's backbone. His starched collars and got-up fronts were achievements of character. (18)

Marlow's allegiances to visible reality and a saving "efficiency" enable him to avoid Kurtz's dissolution of the self. This is evident in his trip up the Congo:

> I had to keep a look-out for the signs of dead wood we could cut up in the night for next day's steaming. When you have to attend to things of that sort, to the mere incidents of the surface, the reality—the reality, I tell you—fades. The inner truth is hidden—luckily, luckily. But I felt it all the same; I felt often its mysterious stillness watching me at my monkey tricks. (34)

He has left the plausible comforts of European civilization to experience "the night of first ages, of those ages that are gone, leaving hardly a sign—and no memories" (36). Without signs, there can be no definable memories. A man must meet truth "stripped of its cloak of time" with "his own true stuff—with his own inborn strength. Principles? Principles won't do. Acquisitions, clothes, pretty rags—rags that would fly off at the first good shake." (37) Time, like civilization, is a human invention subject to decay: "The mind of man is capable of anything—because everything is in it, all the past as well as all the future" (37). But Marlow does not really pursue truth to the limit; he sticks to verbal and visual rags. Marlow's "deliberate belief" (37) entails a self-conscious awareness of lies and a saving disillusionment.[6] Conrad's language "muffles" in its "adjectival insistence upon inexpressible and incomprehensible mystery," F. R. Leavis writes.[7] But for Marlow (and for Conrad), such mufflings stabilize horrifying memories and decaying words.

Marlow's need for "rivets" (30) to hold his riverboat together is connected with his need for "redeeming facts" (23) to provide limited meaning in a world without "external checks" (22). He needs figurative rivets to reify memories that lose shape in recollection like rotting hippo meat. If it lies, as to some degree it must, language has a "taint of death," and (another play on death) it "appal[s]" (27). Language too is like rotting hippo meat; however, throwing it overboard, like the "pilgrims" do with the natives' food, is not an option. European society consists of lies and forgettings: without the consciousness that lies are lies, it is possible, like Kurtz, to follow an idealism that is merely the inverse of savagery. Language decays; it barely creates the illusion of stability over chaos, but there is no alternative to it. Marlow wants to recreate experi-ences that horrify, but retelling them offers a degree of reassurance. Sitting in the darkness like a Buddha, he is, like Kurtz, a voice, but a voice that stabilizes events. His anxiety about making memories visible, hence stable, is evident when he asks his listeners on the *Nellie,* "Do you see him? Do you see the story? Do you see anything?" (27). After all, "we live, as we dream—alone" (28).

In *Past and Present,* Carlyle reconstructs twelfth-century St. Edmundsbury with spare facts vivified with fictions that unwrap the past from its "thick cerements" and create "a green solid place, that grew corn and several other things."[8] Through such means, a substitute for lost speech is possible. Conrad seems less confident that this is possible, for Africa, indeed, everything anterior to civilization is like an ocean, an ineffability beyond meaning and opposition. Marlow recalls the "splashes and snorts" on the Congo that "reached us from afar, as though an ichthyosaurus had been taking a bath of glitter in the great river" (30). This shifting, ocean-like jungle is beyond verbal meaning, but must be organized nevertheless:

> The great wall of vegetation, an exuberant and entangled mass of trunks, branches, leaves, boughs, festoons, motionless in the moonlight, was like a rioting invasion of soundless life, a rolling wave of plants, piled up, crested, ready to topple over the creek, to sweep every little man of us out of his little existence. And it moved not. (30)

Like the dinosaur that symbolizes the dissolution of order at the start of *Bleak House*, Marlow's ichthyosaurus signifies the savagery that underlies "universal genius" (Kurtz). Yet it is also something around which meaning can coalesce, at least in memory. Fictionalization is twice foregrounded, yet it offers a cynosure to the sea-like jungle.[9] Marlow grasps meaning even as memory disintegrates. But his "dream-sensation" (27) is suffused with absurdity:

> No relation of a dream can convey the dream-sensation, that commingling of absurdity, surprise, and bewilderment in a tremor of struggling revolt, that notion of being captured by the incredible which is of the very essence of dreams. (27)

He confronts the incredible by doing his job (also Carlyle's solution to the open-endedness of the ideal and of the "Everlasting No"). In recollecting his journey towards the inner station, Marlow describes the jungle's motionlessness and silence, which are succeeded by screams, violence, and chaos. In this impressionistic setting, the white fog functions as a shutter that frames the momentary impression:

> When the sun rose there was a white fog, very warm and clammy, and more blinding than the night. It did not shift or drive; it was just there, standing all round you like something solid. At eight or nine, perhaps, it lifted as a shutter lifts. We had a glimpse of the towering multitude of trees, of the immense matted jungle, with the blazing little ball of the sun hanging over it—all perfectly still—and then the white shutter came down again, smoothly, as if sliding in greased grooves. (40)

Shortly afterwards, however, the "fool-helmsman" throws open the boat's shutter to fire at a very different scene, where the veil has been removed from the apparent peacefulness:

> I made out, deep in the tangled gloom, naked breasts, arms, legs, glaring eyes—the bush was swarming with human limbs in movement, glistening, of bronze colour. The twigs shook, swayed, and rustled, and arrows flew out of them, and then the shutter came to. (46)

The helmsman is speared before his shutter descends. The jungle cannot be restrained and, once the melee begins, "I might just as well have ordered a tree not to sway in the wind" as quiet the helmsman (46).

Near Kurtz's compound, Marlow discovers a hut with its mysterious book, *An Inquiry into some Points of Seamanship*, "by a man Towser, Towson—some such name" (38). Its mysterious notes in "cipher" (39) (really Russian script) seem like symbolic bulwarks. Like language itself, the book is fragile: Marlow must handle it "with the greatest possible tenderness, lest it should dissolve in my hands" (38). Its Russian owner can survive because he wants "nothing"; a "simple man" (64), he is thoughtless and "unreflecting" (55). If Marlow sees savages in the surrounding wilderness, the "childish" (116) Russian sees merely his own reflection, "simple people" (64). The danger for him is the Europeans, who are apt to hang him. A parodic Rousseauan noble savage, he is inviolate, like the Chief Accountant, owing to an insanity that parodies the saner forms of autonomy associated with Western colonialism. He is such a phenomenon that Marlow sometimes must "ask myself whether I had ever really seen him" (65). But he is able to parlay a few bullets, a pair of shoes, and Towson's *Inquiry* into a bulwark against the wilderness:

> I rooted out an old pair [of shoes], at which he looked with admiration before tucking it under his left arm. One of his pockets (bright red) was bulging with cartridges, from the other (dark blue) peeped "Towson's Inquiry," etc., etc. He seemed to think himself excellently well equipped for a renewed encounter with the wilderness. (64)

Marlow needs a limited mystery that, like the cyphers in Towson's *Inquiry*, affirms a "deliberate belief" (37) rooted in words and "inheritance" (36). He is threatened by the emptiness of which rage and violence are the inarticulate signs that precede nonmeaning. He has penetrated the "edge of a black and incomprehensible frenzy" (36) where memory and its enveloping sign nearly disappear, like the first "ages that are gone, leaving hardly a sign—and no memories" (36). In his *Reflections,* Burke anxiously grasps a national "inheritance" grounded in property and tradition. But a disillusioned Marlow recalls "an accursed inheritance, to be subdued at the cost of profound anguish and of excessive toil" (36).

Kurtz's attempts to find assurance in noble words fail because he does not have, like Marlow, the ironic illusion that separates the beautiful from the chthonic. Marlow hears "him—it—this voice—other voices" (49):

> The memory of that time itself lingers around me, impalpable, like a dying vibration of one immense jabber, silly, atrocious, sordid, savage, or simply mean, without any kind of sense. Voices, voices—even the girl herself—now—. (49)

Gender itself breaks down as "him" decays to "it" and the jungle's voices incorporate "this girl," Kurtz's Intended. Marlow finds refuge in his impressionistic adjectives, vocational practicality, and reassuring historical repetitions; yet doublings like "voices, voices" and "things—things" suggest that repetitions may collapse into self-referential emptiness. Kurtz has moved from idealism to savagery; his essay for the "International Society for the Suppression of Savage Customs" (50) offers no defense because its "unbounded power of eloquence" (51) is a mere "magic current of phrases" (51) that, like the "voices, voices," offer mere univocal (not ironic) repetition against the jungle's power. The analogy between Kurtz's eloquence—a "flash of lightning in a serene sky" (51)—and civilization's "flash of lightning in the clouds" (5) seems to undermine civilization itself. Kurtz had no irony. His peroration made Marlow "tingle with enthusiasm" and gave him "the notion of an exotic Immensity ruled by an august Benevolence" (51). Kurtz adorned himself with ornamental words, but they were no defense against the jungle. Marlow, the frame narrator asserts, finds "the meaning of an episode" outside the shell, not inside it: it envelops his tale "only as a glow brings out a haze, in the likeness of one of those misty halos that sometimes are made visible by the spectral illumination of moonshine" (5). Marlow is torn by a dilemma: to read the symbol too closely or to associate meaning with the hidden may guarantee its disappearance in a transfixing horror; to grasp purely ornamental meaning does not solve the problem either, for there is a deeper truth he cannot avoid. So Marlow's tale avoids the seaman's "direct simplicity" (5) and reverses the relations of kernel and husk in a radical revaluation of interpretive meaning. The key to this is indirection, limitation, and mistiness, something J. Hillis Miller has analyzed in some detail. The story's meaning is neither the kernel nor the husk, but the haze generated by the operation of moon and atmospherics on the latter's appearance. Oscar Wilde suggests that interpreters who either "go beneath the surface" or "read the symbols" do so at their peril.[10] Conrad is aware of a similar danger. Marlow parries the dangers represented by surface and kernel by mystifying the first and using the second to take him away from, rather than into, the horrific mystery towards which the symbol points.[11]

Marlow's focus on the need to see and generate sight in his audience arises from his desire to provide analogical yet misty meaning for a "droll" life, which is a "mysterious arrangement of merciless logic for a futile purpose" (71). "The appalling face of a glimpsed truth" (72) and the "inappreciable moment of time in which we step over the threshold of the invisible" (72) acquire substance and misty safety through ironic language, which enwraps the preternaturally eloquent Kurtz, who is the cynosure of a "shower" of demythologized "small flies." He is "at least seven feet long" but emaciated and, as his name suggests, "short" (60).

He is a presence, but merely as a voice. To the mad Russian he is the generator of visual things (56) both pure and depraved, echoes of echoes, indeed, whatever one wishes to see. From Kurtz's death, Marlow recalls, he created a "moral victory" (72), and a parodic cynosure of loyalty in his memory of Kurtz. Marlow encases Kurtz's horror in a prophylactic, ironic memory that gains provisional stability in the retelling to other men. Echoes gain meaning in their repetition, even if one knows they are echoes, for if the good, the true, and the beautiful are fictions constructed over an abyss that always uncovers itself, one needs echoes on which to build disillusioned visions. Hence, in the Intended's voice, Marlow "heard once more, not his own voice, but the echo of his magnificent eloquence thrown to me from a soul as translucently pure as a cliff of crystal" (72).

F. R. Leavis objects to a "cheapening" of the tone in *Heart of Darkness* when we encounter "an adjectival and worse than supererogatory insistence on 'unspeakable rites,' 'unspeakable secrets,' 'monstrous passions,' 'inconceivable mystery,' and so on."[12] But this adjectival inadequacy is exactly the point, for it saves Marlow as surely as his impressionistic mufflings do. Kurtz's mysterious secret includes love's unspeakable rites, from which Marlow is protected by his impressionism and his projection of the chthonic feminine onto Africa. The Russian cannot describe precisely what he learned from Kurtz:

> "We talked of everything," he said, quite transported at the recollection. "I forgot there was such a thing as sleep. The night did not seem to last an hour. Everything! Everything! ... Of love, too." "Ah, he talked to you of love!" I said, much amused. "It isn't what you think," he cried, almost passionately. "He made me see things—things." (56)

The "thingness" of knowledge is central to Kurtz's flight into idealism and its savage inverse. To gain this knowledge, Marlow would have to confront the unspeakable, whose domesticated verbal sign, "the horror" (71) cancels articulated meaning. But he turns away.

Kurtz, in contrast, has kicked "the very earth to pieces" to satisfy "monstrous passions" (112). He trades Western idealism for an *ars erotica* of forbidden knowledge from which the "harlequin" is immune. The West, Foucault suggests, affirms a discourse in which the surface is invented and read while its secret remains hidden. But the secret always gives itself away.[13] The Russian has seen what would destroy the mind of a sane man. To cite Foucault, he has been guided by his "master along a path of initiation" through "skill and severity."[14] The mad survivor has moved from words to "things—things," which threaten the practical activity that makes possible a reconstitution of limited meaning.

As he approaches the inner station, Marlow thinks at first that the "round knobs" on stakes that surround Kurtz's hut are ornaments rather than symbols (58):

> There was no enclosure or fence of any kind; but there had been one apparently, for near the house half-a-dozen slim posts remained in a row, roughly trimmed, and with their upper ends ornamented with round carved balls. The rails, or whatever there had been between, had disappeared. (53)

Yet there is a disjunction between his interpretive attempt and an inscrutable mystery which he regulates through irony, for the ornaments are the gift of a wilderness that has patted Kurtz on the head and magically transformed his head into something like "a ball—an ivory ball" (49). Ivory commodity, staked heads, and Kurtz are likened to something hard and inscrutable, the source of greed and the object of art. But what does this nearly antic set of analogies mean?

Upon closer inspection, Marlow decides that what he sees are in fact symbols:

> Then I went carefully from post to post with my glass, and I saw my mistake. These round knobs were not ornamental but symbolic; they were expressive and puzzling, striking and disturbing—food for thought and also for vultures if there had been any looking down from the sky; but at all events for such ants as were industrious enough to ascend the pole. They would have been even more impressive, those heads on the stakes, if their faces had not been turned to the house. (58)

In the very inscrutability of these symbols lies Marlow's (and Conrad's) meanings. Kurtz is infernally effeminate, flabby, and weak-eyed, having gotten himself adored while absent for several months behind the mask of the inscrutable jungle that "loved him, embraced him, got into his veins" (49). Fittingly, he has surrounded himself with human ornaments that disturb Marlow for more than the obvious reason. The jungle breaks down the opposition between masculine and feminine: it *seems* to Marlow to embody the chthonic feminine because, paradoxically, this stabilizes it somewhat. This explains Marlow's odd comparison in describing Kurtz "as beset by as many dangers as though he had been an enchanted princess sleeping in a fabulous castle" (43). In the jungle's embrace, Kurtz is more the passive female than the active male. Marlow becomes his ironic rescuer. In flaunting the ornamental, Kurtz seems to usurp the identity-by-beautiful-appearances that Marlow associates with woman, above all, the Intended. Marlow is anxious about aesthetic judgment: his initial association of Kurtz's knobs with ornamentation illustrates his wish to find a reasonable stable reading. But Kurtz mocks him; hence, the ornaments must be symbols of some deeper (but inscrutable) mystery beyond the understanding of mere women.

Marlow is the product of European positivism. The Russian's parodic childlike "unreflecting audacity" (55) is thus closed to him, and he does not have the physical distance from the jungle of the alienist, who retains autonomy through irony and the avoidance of symbolic conclusion (his subjects never return for a follow-up). But Marlow must survive in a place where the nightmare of his choice, Kurtz, is "hollow at the core" (59). To insist that the heads are symbols is really to evade the final meaning they symbolize and maintain some positivist control over meaning, even if this results in a series of lies. Marlow maintains some linear control and aesthetic (and ironic) distance. Symbols are neither transcendent nor transcendental; they merely muffle, to use Leavis's term. So there really is no need to unwrap Lazarus's cerements, so to speak: just be ironically awestruck and evade the full meaning of death. What Marlow knows, he knows, but this remains relatively superficial, protected from symbolic finality. To continue to acknowledge the decayed heads as ornaments is to accept ornamentation as the unsignifying final reality. To insist that stakes and heads are symbols, on the other hand, is at least to accept a relation between perverted activity and decay that maintains a limited control over meaning. As symbols, the decayed heads domesticate the terrible; as ornaments, they contradict the very possibility of controlled meaning. "Expressive and puzzling, striking and disturbing" (58), these symbols both evoke and evade interpretation, leaving open enough room to analyze, reify, and read without being sucked into unspeakable things and made the ornament of secrets that cannot be symbolized but only are and devour.

Marlow says he cannot stand lies, yet he keeps secret from the others on the riverboat his pursuit of Kurtz into the jungle. He also hides (yet, as storyteller, reveals to his listeners on the *Nellie*) Kurtz's last words. He appropriates those words like saints' bones, concealing them from the Intended, avowedly to spare her. The rest of the crew are left with the manager's boy's mundane "Mistah Kurtz—he dead" (71). Marlow stands over the dying man "as if transfixed," the ironic worshipper receiving secret information from his idol. He claims an experience with darkness and savagery, but his practical English nature saves him from its full force:

> True, he had made that last stride, he had stepped over the edge, while I had been permitted to draw back my hesitating foot. And perhaps in this is the whole difference; perhaps all the wisdom, and all truth, and all sincerity, are

just compressed into that inappreciable moment of time in which we step
over the threshhold of the invisible. (72)

Marlow "had peeped over the edge myself" (72). But the significant
moment that generates wisdom, truth, and sincerity entails stepping back
as much as stepping over.

Embraced too closely, nature will release the "unlawful soul" and
create an "exalted and incredible degradation" (67). Marlow counters the
"sheer blank fright" caused by Kurtz's escape on childish all-fours with a
"moral shock" (65) that parodies the candor, conviction, and "expression
of some sort of belief" (72) that accompanies, he thinks, Kurtz's final
vision of the horror, the inverse of his previous idealism. Belief is
dangerous. In Brussels, a journalist tells Marlow that Kurtz could have
been an extremist politician of any party: "He had faith—don't you see?
He had the faith. He could get himself to believe anything—anything"
(74). Marlow himself had "taken him for a painter who wrote for the
papers" (73). Like Frankenstein (or Hitler, for that matter), he was a
frustrated artist whose failure unleashed demons. Marlow's endeavors to
turn voice into image and narrative arises from his anxiety at having
necessarily evaded the secret sights generated by the jungle and by
Kurtz's voice. The closest he could approach the political Kurtz is the
written (and hence radically delimited) ideas of his seventeen-page report
to the "International Society for the Suppression of Savage Customs." In
it, the belief in the absolute, "noble words," is emended to belief in
nothing, or everything: "Exterminate all the brutes!" (51). There is no
saving extravagant mystery here, as in the annotations to Towson's book.

In addition to his impressionistic stabilizations of flux, Marlow tries to
organize the inscrutable by focusing meaning in actual paintings and in
the tragic vision of the Intended that her portrait engenders.[15] He seems
to want life to imitate art, but art is not fully adequate. In *Laocoön,*
Lessing contends that painting is best suited to embody a significant
moment in a person's life, while poetry—this includes the novel—is
more suited to represent the full complexity of human character. Yet in
Heart of Darkness, reality is so importunate that prose must be deployed
in symbolic delimitations of momentary meaning: realism of the sort
celebrated by George Eliot has broken down.

At the central station, Kurtz's portrait of a blindfolded woman arouses
Marlow's interest in the man and illustrates the tenuousness of
metaphorical stabilization:

> I noticed a small sketch in oils, on a panel, representing a woman, draped and
> blindfolded, carrying a lighted torch. The background was sombre—almost

black. The movement of the woman was stately, and the effect of the torchlight on the face was sinister. (25)

Something like Aeschylus's Athena threatens to give way to Furies, as patriarchal justice dissolves into chthonic passion, the fear, terror, and retribution of Kurtz's savage justice further up the Congo. The woman must have been inspired by Kurtz's fiancée, for he had not encountered his African lover when he painted it; the effect foreshadows what Marlow later sees in her in Brussels. This woman symbolizes Western aesthetic and legal (blindfolded justice) definitions of objectivity. Yet her autonomous ideal dissolves into the "sombre background" from which she tenuously emerges, making the lighted torch seem sinister. Behind stately representation and sinister effect is the darkness Marlow associates with nature and the chthonic feminine.

Hence Marlow organizes the "savage and superb" lover of Kurtz with a statuesque tragic dignity based on European aesthetic ideals. Edmund Burke uses tragic categories to preserve Marie Antoinette from the mob; Marlow uses them to preserve himself. Kurtz was already "getting savage" when he painted his portrait; he forgot what he was supposed to uphold, whatever his private disillusionments. But Marlow transforms the dark woman into statuary, as Smith notes, muting her savage aspect into a European tragic dignity.[16] If she does not acquire the "noble simplicity and quiet grandeur" praised by Winckelmann, her stately movements, her silent expressiveness, and the hand gestures that the Intended later replicates parallel Lessing's assertion that, in great sculpture, physical pain is compatible with nobility only when passion (here, savagery) is softened and dignified:

She was savage and superb, wild-eyed and magnificent; there was something ominous and stately in her deliberate progress. ... She came abreast of the steamer, stood still, and faced us. Her long shadow fell to the water's edge. Her face had a tragic and fierce aspect of wild sorrow and of dumb pain mingled with the fear of some struggling, half-shaped resolve. (62)

As the steamer departs with the dying Kurtz on board, the woman does not flinch. In a tragic gesture, she stretches "her bare arms after us over the sombre and glittering river" (69). The "wild and gorgeous apparition of a woman" (61) stabilizes the jungle's hidden inner truth, the alternative to which is a collapse of all categories. Marlow grasps at verbal oppositions that will take him safely back up the river to Europe. Thus, she enables Marlow to experience—yet not really experience—the "inner truth" that is hidden—"luckily, luckily" (34). To keep his bearings, he needs to believe that "they—the women I mean—are out of it—should be out of it. We must help them to stay in that beautiful world of their own, lest ours gets worse" (49). The alternative to the feminization of the ideal and the chthonic is the collapse of all categories, including gender: this is Kurtz's fate, whose voice finally becomes a degendered "it" who "could speak English to me" (50). Marlow grasps at verbal oppositions that will return him safely to Europe. But the symbolic skull-topped stakes that surround Kurtz's hut are impersonal and asexual: heads are reduced to symbolic round knobs and human features to decayed uniformity. There is also the suggestion of some cosmic joke, of which Marlow had some premonitions in the Brussels waiting room. He cannot shake off their continuous smiling "at some endless and jocose dream" (58) of an eternal slumber, which takes on the dream-like and disbelieved quality of life itself.

In his lie to the Intended, Marlow affirms a feminine ideal he knows is specious. He has told his listeners on the *Nellie* that women "live in a world of their own, and there had never been anything like it, and never can be. It is too beautiful altogether, and if they were to set it up it would go to pieces before the first sunset" (12). To Marlow, she seems "a tragic and familar Shade" (78) whose "pure brow," "ashy halo," and "sorrowful head" (76) disintegrate before his memory of the jungle, which impinges on his mental portrait, much as it did on Kurtz's painting: "With every word spoken the room was growing darker, and only her forehead, smooth and white, remained illumined by the unextinguishable light of belief and love" (76). Is she the embodiment of beauty, or should this "smooth and white" forehead be linked with the "round curved balls" on the stakes, the ivory, and Kurtz's head? Are belief and love likewise merely fictions, at the heart of which are polluted things? It would be "too dark—too dark altogether" (79) to test this by assaulting her mournful silence with Kurtz's actual last words. Hence, Marlow reassures her. Yet his words are laden with an irony of which she is serenely unaware. Out of the dark negations with which he surrounds her comes an assurance of control, as, hearing her own name in Marlow's crowning lie, she emits "an exulting and terrible cry" (79).

Her love ("I knew it—I was sure!" [79]) rested on a doubt that would disappear if contradicted. Marlow leaves, self-assured about women, disillusioned about civilization, and wondering if his lie will cause the house to collapse before he escapes. (But which lie? Is this "eloquent phantom" herself the horror, as Marlow hints?) Either way, he projects the mystery he has glimpsed onto the Intended; though shaken, he can get on with his life. His fictional creation, the tragic shade, gives him a disillusioned meaning, a deliberate belief that provides some closure in a modern Europe without believable fictional escapes, which conserves itself by relegating the feminine to an aesthetic sphere.

10

E. M. Forster and Artistic Fluidity: Romance, Idyll, and Limited Metaphors

In two novels by E. M. Forster, *A Room With a View* and *Howards End*, we see further developments in the struggle to mediate the gaps between vision, language, and text in realism. Vision, we have seen, is essential to the creation of both transcendental and verisimilar belief; it may be transfixed by monstrous or ideal Medusa-gazes that destroy the capacity for lingual fluidity. But Forster resists the collapse that his early novels trace of language's ability to reach beyond brief metaphorical bursts of fluid unity, where language, like society, is in decay. Forster wrote in the afterglow of the late Victorian-aesthetic endeavor to build subjective bulwarks against the dissolution of objective meaning. Moreover, he wrote just prior to World War I, when those objectivities appeared to dissolve altogether. F. R. Leavis, who carried his dog-eared Milton to the trenches, was to be a key player in a Practical Criticism that stabilizes literary works as artifacts, complicated in their ambiguities, but artifacts all the same. By the 1920s, Forster, like Arnold, abandoned fiction for the relative safety of criticism, unable, it would seem, to sustain metaphorical emplotments of tensions arising from the interplays of Self and Other. Realism, we have seen, necessitates a delimitation of infinitude, yet, in the nineteenth century, this is increasingly difficult; Conrad's stripping nearly bare the horror of existence, influenced by the concentration camps of the Boer War and other European depredations in Africa, foreshadows the charnel house of World War I. The precariousness of delimiting vision and emplotting experience is already apparent in Margeret Schlegel's realization that her epiphanic unions with Howards End can work only in the moments before dawn, before she can see the outskirts of London in the harsh light of day. She must avert the gaze to maintain the vision, but it is apparent that the vision is disappearing, that the master-trope that unites London with the sky is but a hopeless (but hoped-for) literary construct in a world where all such unities decay. At the center of the aporias between the ordering consciousness and the Other (India, the sub-Nietzschean lower classes, etc.) is an "ou-boum" like that of the Marabar Caves. It merely sickens and disillusions. It generates no new images of hope. *A Room With A View* concerns the breaking of the monstrous gaze of Victorianism, which has been rendered effete and decadent in Cecil Vyse. It concludes with a sweet romantic vision that unites life and death, mountain and sea, repression and release, illustrating Levine's comment that late-century fiction that confronts its "disenchanted, and dualistic vision must ... take the shape of romance."[1] But in *Howards End*, Forster moves towards the awareness that meaning is a muffled sound in a dark cave, symbolic of a growing inability to achieve social or verisimilar meaning. Forster lives in the sunset of the British Empire, in a world where simple oppositions between Self and Other break down. Yet aporias created by tensions between the constructed self and the external world actually redouble desires for unity and connection. Forster repeatedly attempts to organize and understand the Other (man, woman, India, Italy, the working class), which leads to muddles out of which he hopes to find meaning, despite suspicions that this is finally impossible.

Forster valorizes visual fluidity in *A Room With A View*, in which the British insist on limiting what they see and how. Thus, Lucy carries her Baedeker to Florence, and the Reverend Eager imposes his ossified Ruskinian interpretations on Renaissance art, just as Cecil later tries to transfix her in his parodic-Paterian aesthetic gaze. Lucy has several key encounters with the loosening of what Nietzsche calls the *principium individuationis*, or imprisonment in the self, after each of which she retreats into propriety. But after each such encounter—at Santa Croce, near Alinari's shop, and in the violet fields—she is subtly changed. She is the product of a society that has mistaken words for things, so that Nietzsche himself is but a book in the Emersons' library beside Byron, Housman, and Butler. The fissure between the hard word and emotion is so pronounced that only a violent experience can awaken the feelings against which society and the psyche have erected powerful bulwarks of denial, aestheticism, and irony. Austen establishes a verisimilar idyllic realism in which language is able to delimit yet not entirely deny what lies outside the consciousness: she is skeptical about passion, believes in its subordination to reason and practicality, but acknowledges its relevance all the same, cloaked though it is behind delimiting words like "esteem." In Austen's idyll, the aesthetic and the moral generate a gap between the private and the public that enables a fluid regulation of visual and social controls. Things are much more problematical for Forster, for the restrictions of Edwardian society are far more brittle, and the possibility of a radically delimited, parodic providential order seems fleeting. Even a proposed exchange of rooms creates a minor furor, as if manners, that investiture of social purpose against the external and chaotic for Austen and Burke, have become merely a reactive bulwark against the collapse of self into unregulated impressions. Thus, Edwardian manners are rooted in a fear of linking unregulated words to dangerous visions (in art, violence, or passion: Lucy's three loosenings).

At Santa Croce, Lucy experiences a series of disorientations that lead her from Eager's anal interpretations of Renaissance church art to an intuitive loosening of boundaries centering on George Emerson. As in *Middlemarch*, confusions about reality are essential to breaking the univocal meaning already imposed on art and life: Renaissance art is yoked to a bigoted Protestant interpretation that parodies Ruskin's search for moral (but creative) meaning in art; George, too, is limited by his social gawkiness and petit bourgeois background. The aesthetic impulse has ceased to engage anything essential but merely fixates itself on an impression of what these things ought to be, and since passion is to be feared, it becomes the substitute for the daemonic Other. Thus, the moral and the aesthetic have confused their functions (Emma has to negotiate an equivalent confusion) and are themselves the source of the transfixion incorrectly associated with natural feeling.

Lucy is caught in the disjunction between the art described in guidebooks and the real thing, which threatens to overwhelm her senses. She overhears Eager but is not of his party; she is further disoriented by Emerson's ironic statements and the presence of his attractive son. Indeed, from the moment she enters, she can't tell "which, of all the sepulchral slabs that paved the nave and transepts, was the one that was really beautiful, the one that had been most praised by Mr. Ruskin."[2] Ruskin has become the aesthetic Baedeker, a kind of bulwark against direct experience; in *Howards End,* the sub-Nietzschean Leonard Bast appropriates Ruskin's language to try to organize his life. Watching some Italians mistake a memorial to Machiavelli for a saint (*RV*, 20), Lucy is confronted with the gap between art as experience and art as verbal interpretive closure. When a child is injured on a slab, she sees this as a "punishment" for a Catholic, but she helps the child; Emerson issues some neopagan silliness about the child's going out into the sun ("kiss your hand to the sun"), a wonderful poetic flourish, yet bound, like Eager's art criticism, to a frozen form that mistakes itself for insight. Yet (and here lies the difficult relation between words and things), Emerson's invocation works a strange alchemy in Lucy, preparing her, like her other interpretive confusions, to be aroused by George. Words are powerful, but not necessarily in the ways people intend them to be, especially when they are set against visual moments with which those words are not intentionally connected.

What I suggest, then, is that Forster delineates a society so limited in its obsession with hard words and attitudes that, at least for Lucy, the aporia that is generative of fluid images that connect with something deeper only comes when untranslatable or inappropriate language combines with defamiliarized perspectives. Perhaps here is the problem with the Other that Forster articulated throughout his literary career, above all in *A Passage To India*: conscious connection is not possible, for the Other and his language are always inappropriate; nevertheless, proximity to what is not understood may be essential to the creative interplay of experience and its emplotment, given the fact that, certainly among the English, too much is known, at least in a superficially rational sense, to encourage a creative interplay between conceptualization and image-making within the confines of traditional English realism.

When Lucy sees George at Santa Croce he seems to hover somewhere between art and life, hardness and tenderness, pagan and Christian cultures. Barriers break down without propelling her into either an abyss or the sort of loss of boundaries experienced by Heathcliff or Kurtz at life's peripheries. Forster, it may be said, evades fixities nearly as successfully as Austen does, while embracing the need to melt the frozen forms of gender, art, and morality:

> She watched the singular creature pace up and down the chapel. For a young man his face was rugged, and—until the shadows fell upon it—hard. Enshadowed, it sprang into tenderness. She saw him once again at Rome, on the ceiling of the Sistine Chapel, carrying a burden of acorns. Healthy and muscular, he yet gave her the feeling of greyness, of tragedy that might only find solution in the night. (*RV*, 24)

She participates (but passively) in what Hayden White, discussing Nietzsche, terms an "image-making" in the "perceptual field," carried out in such a way that mere conceptualization is superseded.[3] As unsettling as this brief experience is, it reflects Forster's hope that the loss of brittle form will not impel one into chaos but renew the possibility of fluidity, so that, through the metaphorical investiture of the distance between language and experience, provisional meaning can be affirmed. In Lucy's vision of George, which the narrator tricks out in mythic metaphor, George emerges from behind infertile dialectics: life comes to art in a way that makes life and art shifting, malleable, and open. The Christian, the pagan, and the skeptic are humanized so that none seems repressive or grossly sensual in this Keatsian feeling "born of silence and of unknown emotion" (*RV*, 24).

The moment, like all Lucy's epiphanies, is visual, but it is given stability not by her but by a narrator who applies mythic and literary registers to give it texture and depth. Lucy's dimness implicitly becomes her saving grace, for she does not have the tenacity to hold on to old strictures, like Miss Lavish; protected as it were by Forster's bulwark, she is saved from the implications of letting loose, which we have encountered in other novels and see in Bast's fall towards a purposeless but domesticated abyss in *Howards End*. For all his emphasis on the need to move from words to things, Forster's things are strangely conceptual, his epiphanies so wrapped in myth and literary allusion that one wonders if there is anything behind it all save a pallid abyss indeed. Forster recognizes the limitations of language, as we see in his ironic distancings of Emerson's neo-Arnoldian and neo-Carlylean aphorisms (*RV*, 27), which nevertheless effect an odd alchemy on Lucy, even if he really cannot accomplish anything with them himself. Salvation is possible through connection with the Other, but preparatory to this is the secretive effect of language—even frozen language, or inept language, as with Miss Lavish's potboiler—as a catalyst in unintended ways. Language becomes the generator of grace in its displaced effects, and the result is a questionable romance.

Lucy's encounter with violence in chapter 4 creates an even greater disorientation, in which the melting of barriers becomes more violently erotic:

> She fixed her eyes wistfully on the tower of the palace, which rose out of the lower darkness like a pillar of roughened gold. It seemed no longer a tower, no longer supported by earth, but some unattainable treasure throbbing in the tranquil sky. (*RV*, 41)

Art and architecture melt once more as the barriers between experience and form momentarily disappear. The photograph of Botticelli's *Birth of Venus* is merely an artifact until bespattered with a man's blood, as lifeless in its sensual representation as the Leaning Tower of Pisa model Miss Bartlett fingers a bit later (*RV*, 52). Old ways of ordering experience dissolve, as Lucy, witness to a murder, loses her bearings and, awakening from a swoon, finds herself in George's arms. Even more radically now, she loses her *principium individuationis* in a confluence of pain and desire from which she retreats into guilt. Lucy's throbbing "unattainable treasure" is masculine yet beyond fixities, for the palace's tower seems "no longer a tower" and is not supported by the earth. Under the impress of passion, what seemed like a pillar is still masculine, yet not threateningly so. But there is also the murder, after which Lucy discovers a world "pale and void of its original meaning" (*RV*, 42). She thinks she has "crossed some spiritual boundary" (*RV*, 43) only to return to a safer but less interesting world. George represents Forster's desire that passion be extricated from violence, much as the pillar is from an earth that produces social and gender fixities and turns the "Eternal Woman" into a social fiction of moral conduct and divine form, or her decadent inverse.

In chapter 6, Lucy's encounter in the violet field with George, following a series of verbal disputes and misunderstandings, leads her to a combining of visual and lingual fields that, once more, underscores Forster's wish to retrieve verisimilar purpose. Words are brittle and untrustworthy, yet they are necessary to fiction and must somehow be essential to its generation. Yet the world insists, like Eager, that the driver cannot be Phaeton, or his girlfriend Persephone; it insists, like Eager, that Emerson should translate the Italian original of don't "go fighting against the spring" (*RV*, 62) correctly, for if we live in an age when fluid images are needed more than ever, language itself has been hijacked by empiricism and science, Huxley and Spencer, and must therefore be subverted in turn, retrieved for myth, metaphor, and image, wrapped, if need be, in a prophylactic narrative irony that insists on a romance ending even in the face of an insistent reality that no longer affirms a transcendence that generates viable delimitations. The danger is that, stripped of narrative verbal desire, Lucy is merely what she seems— if not the human equivalent of "ou-boum," then something perhaps more depressing: a rather dull person. Yet the desire to make her something more is insistent. Misunderstood language, I suggest, becomes the equivalent of the "strange" epiphanic transcendence that used to be placed outside the bounds of the text or in Austen's circumambient history and chaos or in Eliot's hope for a scientic master-trope that perhaps shouldn't be inquired into too closely. Forster is drawn to transcendental significances (London as the symbol of infinity, or the beliefs of Aziz and Godbole), but there really seems to be nothing out there as interesting as an abyss, a God, or a horror: merely a void, an "ou-boum," which has the power to sicken and kill, but not really to terrify in any Medusan sense. But substitutions for oneness are still possible, things in themselves at the wellsprings of experience that language sometimes unintentionally can awaken, as is the case for Freddy, Mr. Beebe, and George at the Sacred Lake, which functions like Susannah's wellspring in Wallace Stevens's "Peter Quince at the Clavier."

The driver's mistaken belief that Lucy's "Dove buoni uomini" (*RV*, 66) refers to George, not Mr. Beebe, is the mistake that precedes Lucy's crossing a "spiritual boundary," as she falls into a violet field and George's arms:

> From her feet the ground sloped sharply into view, and violets ran down in rivulets and streams and cataracts, irrigating the hillside with blue, eddying round the tree stems, collecting into pools in the hollows, covering the grass with spots of azure foam. But never again were they in such profusion; this terrace was the well-head, the primal source whence beauty gushed out to water the earth.

> Standing at its brink, like a swimmer who prepares, was the good man. But he was not the good man that she had expected, and he was alone. (*RV*, 67–68)

Amidst the "spots of azure foam," Lucy experiences what Botticelli's *Birth of Venus* was meant to communicate, the freedom of the "Eternal Woman" from the constraints which limit her field of action and vision. George, too, seems to transcend his constraints once more. Though like "one who had fallen out of heaven," he does not bear the taint of rebellion that makes him seem dangerous at the *Pension Bertolini*. The water imagery symbolizes the intuitive loss of definition. As with D. G. Rossetti's "tide of dreams" in "Sensual Sleep," it symbolizes the mysterious subconscious, the source of unknown being into which the desire for the transcendental has retreated, repressed morally and through psychoanalytical and scientific definitions. Vision and metaphor rescue momentarily what language threatens merely to reduce; indeed, language is the stepchild of the visual moment, its utility in awakening these epiphanies connected, as I suggested, to inappropriate, misunderstood, or simply bad language. Thus, the moment is inadvertently retrieved back in England by the bad narrative of it incorporated into Miss Lavish's potboiler. Within the novel's field, language is inept; it is the reader's task to retrieve meaning from the confluence of brittle language and the epiphanies that occasionally result from the loosening of social and perceptual oppressions of the psyche.

Cecil Vyse, described like St. John Rivers as statuary, similarly tries to reduce women to stable artifacts through control of the visual field: "He was medieval. Like a Gothic statue. . . . [H]e resembled those fastidious saints who guard the portals of a French cathedral (*RV*, 85)." Yet this ironic description contains little of the fear we associate with Victorian characters whose desires for control merely mask the Medusa-gaze. In his desire for a romantic ending to many of the tensions and terrors we have seen in the nineteenth-century novel, Forster depicts a potential monstrosity of frozen form and gaze who is partially redeemed by the effects of weirdly strange language disconnected from its original intention. A parodic artist, Vyse reduces experience to conceptualization and attractive women to an "admirable simplicity" that places them safely within the Romantic naive. He sports with the Emersons at the National Gallery after Mr. Emerson's mispronunciation of some painters' names. He views people, above all Lucy, as *objets d'art*, manipulable at will within an ironic visual space from which inept language must be excluded or foregrounded within an artistry of ridicule. His view of language is, therefore, rather like Cuthbert Eager's, though his register is aesthetic and ironic, not moral and theological.

Moreover, he expects meaning from this aesthetic artifact; thus he asks that Lucy provide him the thrill of passion without decentering his self-control or impelling him into a fluid, hence unstable, vision of life. A model of "Medieval" (read Victorian) rigidity in a time of impressionism, he comically adumbrates the feckless drive to stabilize visually and verbally an existence which, outside his limited gaze, is becoming inchoate, incoherent, and modern, like the aristocrat-realtor's tacky faux-Gothic cottages Vyse scorns yet acquires for the Emersons as part of his sport. Thus the need to turn the subjective into the apparently objective to describe his "Leonardesque" fiancée. Ironically, Forster deploys the language Pater uses to depict *La Gioconda*: "Her sunburnt features were shadowed by fantastic rock; at his words she had turned and stood between him and the light with immeasurable plains behind her" (*RV*, 89). The spell is broken only when, rejected, he sees the living woman behind the impression: "From a Leonardo she had become a living woman, with mysteries and forces of her own, with qualities that even eluded art" (*RV*, 171). Behind his self-control, of course, Vyse is a decadent. He belongs, he suspects, in a room with "no view" (*RV*, 106), in effect as closeted as Dorian Gray's essential self.

At the Sacred Lake, the failed kiss illustrates his inability to feel anything or to act, which generates a sense of absurdity:

> At that supreme moment he was conscious of nothing but absurdities. ... As he approached her he found time to wish that he could recoil. As he touched her, his gold pince-nez became dislodged and was flattened between them. (*RV*, 108)

He mentally recasts the scene, separating it from the event itself and imagining Lucy standing "flower-like" by the water: at first she rebukes him, then permits him and reveres "him ever after for his manliness" (*RV*, 108). This mental recreation, unlike even Miss Lavish's bad novel, is unconnected to feeling, and it imagines the emotions (anger, sub-servient reverence, not the esteem Austen posits as an ideal subordination of passion to reason) he can awaken through visual and verbal powers disconnected from communication. He intellectually knows that he is disconnected from nature and passion, but he can do nothing about it himself and hence seeks in Lucy the magical catalyst for passion that, nevertheless, he must keep up on a pedestal. Thus, just prior to his failed kiss, he envisions Lucy as some "brilliant flower that has no leaves of its own, but blooms abruptly out of a world of green" (*RV*, 107). This has superficial affinities with the Florentine tower that seems poised between sensuality and ineffability, above the earth but also of it. Yet, again, Cecil Vyse merely creates a simulacrum of release, an artificial nature in which Lucy is at once autonomous ("no leaves of its own") and mysterious. This is preciously aesthetic and at variance with the exuberant freedom of the field of violets. In kissing George, Lucy experiences passion and movement yet remains herself. Far from reducing Lucy mentally to a flower, George saw "the flowers beat against her dress in blue waves" (*RV*, 68). She was in nature, but not reduced to artificial nature. Lucy's autonomy, like the "day by day" (*RV*, 88) development Vyse finds so wonderful in her, is a mere semblance of realistic change in which devel-opment is constricted to compartmentalized stages whose temporal sta-bility is anything but a merging of boundaries. On a more pallid level, it would seem, he repeats Naumann's mistake of projecting masculine desire onto the feminine object and calling it perfection.

Cecil's "day by day" parodies the effects of poetic representation as described by Lessing, whose follower in *Middlemarch*, Will Ladislaw, insists that women should change "from moment to moment" and be represented accordingly. But time is the enemy of romance and the necessary vessel of novelistic realism: Cecil is ironically placed as a fool in visualizing Lucy this way, yet she is also, I have suggested, the narrator's object, and her epiphanies are stoppings of time's flux amidst the breakage, violence, and change that threaten to decenter the romance towards which narrative desire tends. The problem is to reach an equipoise between frozen form and a too fluid change, to emplot experience to create a *Nullpunkt* that both cancels and affirms temporality. Forster is aware of the two-edged function of time, including Keats's interest in the equipoise between time and eternity where romance is possible, but we are reminded of the passing away of all things. Yet Forster's reminder at the novel's conclusion is reassuring, for life has been reaffirmed even in its transitory state, and death is no horror but rather a metaphorical melting of "snows of winter into the Mediterranean" (*RV*, 204). Like the monster's final, exquisitely poetic meditation on life and death in *Frankenstein*, this replaces the desire for final meanings, or the awareness of our mutilated reductions vis-à-vis a lost transcendence, with a metaphorical consciousness of the passion (or the thing) in itself, which, I have suggested, the Sacred Lake can symbolize, depending on who is doing the gazing. For Forster it is in metaphorical, not metonymical, perception that the only possibility for meaning exists, and it must be protected by the narrator's ironic, yet limited, perspective. Metonymy, on the other hand, like awareness of the radical disjunctions of time, is central to realism. Forster essentially is writing an elegy to the form he ostensibly adopts.

In the closing chapters, Lucy lies about herself to Cecil, her mother, Mr. Beebe, and Mr. Emerson; only by ceasing to view language as univocal is change possible, which brings us back to the question of inappropriate or inept language as necessary to effect change and unfreeze form. Indeed, all fiction partakes of lying, as Carlyle suggests; but realism rests on the assumption that artistic cunning can create verisimilar representations of experience, which may simply be, as David Lodge suggests, approximations to other prose forms of the day, not to life itself, whatever that is. Not only does Lucy lie, she appropriates George's belief that Cecil should "know no one intimately, least of all a woman" (*RV*, 165) in order to use it against Cecil. She is caught in an absurd gap between wanting to be free to decide for herself, and, despite herself, allowing George to articulate her thoughts. Like Emerson, she becomes aware of a connection between accepting inconsistency and breaking the power of language to constrict—ironically, in this case, by voluntarily submitting herself to another's word: "What nonsense do I talk! but that is the kind of thing" (*RV*, 182). Indeed, this adumbrates the saving possibility of fiction, its ability to break the bond between language and thing, allowing the thing to retrieve the language for a new purpose. Through repetition of a language not her own, Lucy begins to see the difference between language and essence necessary to provisional insight and successful human connections. Similarly, Mr. Emerson realizes the "abstract and remote" nonsense of much of his discourse about souls, darkness, and hell (*RV*, 202) when, at the rectory, he tries once more to exhort Lucy to grasp her chance for happiness and accept George. Life is generally a muddle. But Lucy's growing awareness of the instability of language intermittently enables her to see (shades of Matthew Arnold) "the whole of everything at once" (*RV*, 204).

In George's and Lucy's honeymoon in Florence, George asserts that Miss Bartlett was not "withered up all through." Instead, the sight of them kissing in the field of violets "haunted her" and led her to create bad art, but art all the same, out of something she did not experience directly. "It is impossible," Lucy replies, that Miss Bartlett is "glad." But remembering the "experiences of her own heart," she reverses herself and declares, "No—it is just possible" (*RV*, 209). In reading Miss Lavish's novel George discovered details that "burnt" and inspired his second impetuous kiss of Lucy. Miss Lavish's novel cheapened a glorious experience yet its inadequate language enabled him to recall his earlier experience and repeat it. George acknowledges that they can never "make friends with her or thank her." But in recreating Miss Bartlett as glad, they have affirmed a fluid, mysterious reading of life. Like Mrs. Wilcox in *Howards End* and Mrs. Moore in *A Passage to India*, Miss Bartlett has achieved a significance above and behind the facts of her life. Herein lies the possibility of art, inadequate though the author's experience or language may be. Other writers in this study have affirmed language's capacity to represent experience, or its decay or collapse given the caesuras at the center of experience that enable the recreation of images, or present Medusa-stares from the abyss or the ideal. But Forster seems less hopeful that language can communicate very much beyond a limited metaphorical field, though he hopes that through its very inadequacy a sort of talismanic reawakening of fluid meaning is possible. Still, we are aware that Miss Bartlett can never be glad.

When she first visits Howards End in Forster's 1910 novel, Margaret Schlegel is unable to recreate it as an overarching symbol and so must limit its reach:

> She recaptured the sense of space, which is the basis of all earthly beauty, and, starting from Howards End, she attempted to realize England. She failed—visions do not come when we try, though they may come through trying.[4]

The capacity, like Austen's, to create delimited idyllic spaces has become nearly impossible for Forster, for the world's importunities beckon from without: commerce and colonialism, exemplified by Mr. Wilcox, the inexorable march of the London suburbs towards Windy Corners and Howards End, perhaps most of all the emergence of the masses in Leonard Bast: such forces make it nearly impossible to delimit and exclude, as Jane Austen does in *Emma,* for what impinges is not the apparent Other represented by monstrosity, but something at once more similar to us, and less tractable than previous domestications of the unnameable. Margaret tries to exclude Leonard Bast from the metaphorical unity she wishes to create at the novel's end, but he is much more insistently present than, say, Harriet Smith at the close of *Emma.* Limited, provisional meaning is possible, at least outside the glare of common day. But the radical fissures that enable the creation of verisimilar meaning are less fruitful because, ironically, while the consciousness of decay is ever-present, memories of the collapse of received meaning represented by the French Revolution are a distant memory, and new abysses are still four years away. It never was possible imaginatively to start out from a single place and "realize" all England in a totalizing vision, though Dickens tried, with his providential orders and metaphors of connection or atomization. The very way that Forster's Margaret tries suggests that the old dialectics between the "real" and the experienced "known" have broken down, and what remains is the very limited construction of bulwarks (romance in *A Room With a View*, the idyllic here) against an oncoming tide of modernity that is resistant to organization, compromise, or distancing. Hence the desire for transcendence is projected onto a blending of boundaries that somehow amplifies the capacity for communication and development, an impractical hope to be sure, and one which the novel's practical events call into question.

The cynosure of Margaret's (and Forster's) desire is, of course, Howards End itself which, with its wych-elm, a gender-transcending version of Arnold's signal elm, represents the metaphorical end of a quest for meaning:[5]

> It was a comrade, bending over the house, strength and adventure in its roots, but in its utmost fingers tenderness, and the girth, that a dozen men could not have spanned, became in the end evanescent, till pale bud clusters seemed to float in the air. It was a comrade. House and tree transcended any simile of sex. (*HE*, 203)

But this is essentially a private symbol, based on Margaret's mythologizing of a place and a person, Mrs. Wilcox, who practically speaking is more querulous and unhappy than the earth-deity into which Margaret transforms her. Fiction is aware of its fictionality, just as language is aware of its ineptitude or inappropriateness, yet out of this tension, based on a more radical mistrust of language than at first seems apparent, limited metaphorical meaning is constructed and enwrapped within an irony that both undercuts and affirms meaning. This ironic vision is the only honest one possible in a disillusioned and disillusioning era. Margaret's epiphanies are not necessarily open to others. Indeed, only the addled Miss Avery, mistaking her for Ruth Wilcox, participates at all in Margaret's investiture of analogy between Howards End, a mythical Mrs. Wilcox, and a disappearing England. In other words, the possibilities for emplotment of the circumambient flux have become private and tenuous, and Dickens's hope that all England could be providentially united has disappeared. The novel is perilously close to retreating from representing the broad canvas of external life through an objective or providential vision, however ironically undercut it may be. Instead, only a private, interior vision of connection seems possible, and the best the novel can do is represent that. Or, to shift forward to *A Passage To India*, Fielding, Aziz, and Godbole create emplotments within the parodic master-trope of British imperialism, but realism cannot unite them, whether positively or negatively. It cannot step back, as it were, from these emplotments of life's ferment and unite them in turn, for there is no universal shaping consciousness that makes this possible. So realism tends towards psychological inwardness, though Forster sets his characters within broader, external divisions (England-Italy, London-rural England, England-the Raj-native Indias) as if to await the reemergence of the ironic master-trope that, to return to Margaret's wished-for vision, can unite her private symbol with all of England in all its multiplicities.

Margaret's recognition that life is chaotic and quite different "from the orderly sequence that has been fabricated by historians" (*HE*, 104) points, of course, to a major theme of this study. But, like her wish to unite Howards End with all England in a private metaphorical vision, any attempt to organize chaos must start with the recognition of language's limitations, coupled with the desire to so organize it so that provisional metaphorical unities are possible. Margaret attempts to cover all England with her metaphor, yet she realizes that this will not become a socially attainable goal in her lifetime. The only hope is in the future, not in the retrieval of the past through verisimilar emplotment. This represents a central dilemma of realism, at least Forster's realism, for to direct the gaze to the future is to valorize the hoped-for over the actual, which resists overarching organization, even with the aid of structural ironies. Thus, Margaret's little metaphor is directed towards a "great mythology" (*HE*, 264) of the future, while the narrator hopes for a new sort of literature that transcends gender, and a higher realism that reconciles emplotment with experience, so that the opposition between poetic "voice" and "common talk," voice and unorganized speech—the real and the ideal, in other words—finally dissipates without collapse into meaninglessness or monstrosity:

> England still waits for the supreme moment of her literature—for the great poet who shall voice her, or, better still, for the thousand little poets whose voices shall pass into our common talk. (*HE*, 264)

Ruth Wilcox's mind is, for Margaret, a metaphorical master-trope in which we are "only fragments."

Margaret Schlegel finally glimpses the "diviner wheels" from the "turmoil and horror of those days" (*HE*, 327). But the metaphorical vessels of unity are precarious, and Howards End, where city and country have existed in equipoise, is doomed to become a suburb. She learns that in the notion of "through," the trembling of the mind "towards a conclusion which only the unwise have put into words" (202), there is hope. But this itself entails a metaphorical construction based on an awareness that verisimilitude is no longer possible, that we can only hope for a valorizing master-trope sometime in the future. In a limited way, Margaret can realize this, if she limits her field of vision and affirms illusion even as she acknowledges the difficulty of generating or forgetting it (thus her wish to forget Bast and look towards the future, symbolized by his son). We can experience only moments of unity. It is hoped, however, that all of these experiences may amount to something:

> The present flowed by them like a stream. The tree rustled. It had made music before they were born, and would continue after their deaths, but its song was of the moment. The moment had passed. The tree rustled again. Their senses were sharpened, and they seemed to apprehend life. Life passed. The tree rustled again. (*HE*, 312)

But Margaret can only hope for a cessation of conflict "early in the morning in the garden" (*HE*, 337), while the "melting-pot" London seems almost invisible. What she sees is an idyllic higher realism, like Schiller's concept in *Naive and Sentimental Poetry*, which would reconcile her debate with Tibby over whether we should have activity without civilization, or the reverse:

> "Because a thing is going strong now, it need not go strong forever," she said. "This craze for motion has only set in during the last hundred years. It may be followed by a civilization that won't be a movement, because it will rest on the earth. All the signs are against it now, but I can't help hoping, and very early in the morning in the garden I feel that our house is the future as well as the past." (*HE*, 337)

The novel's conclusion teeters on allegorical closure, as if paradoxically to solidify the desire for idyllic fluidity.[6] Helen exclaims that "the big meadow" is cut and "we've seen to the very end" (*HE*, 340). Yet her exuberance is modified by Margaret's knowledge that Henry concealed Mrs. Wilcox's bequest of Howards End to her (*HE*, 340). Margaret's hope that London's ascendance may in fact lead to a reunification of civilization (emplotment) with the earth (nature, the real) is like Schiller's "calm of perfection, not of inertia."[7] This attitude, it should be recalled, was a desire generated by the French Terror, which seemed to threaten the middle space claimed by the realists yet also made the novel's tropal dynamism possible. Margaret realizes that her desire that the house unite "the future as well as the past" (*HE*, 337) is symbolic rather than real. Moreover, provisional meaning comes from cutting and breaking, not from mysterious unities that arise from nowhere. But how can such cutting lead to unity? Her father was the product of an idealism (a "countryman of Hegel and Kant") or "Imperialism of the air" that soon generated its brutal counterpart in "smashed windows of the Tuileries" (*HE*, 26), that is, a return to the systole-diastole between absolute idea and monstrosity against which realism builds bulwarks even as it represents instability. "The ideal is the monstrous," Levine suggests.[8] For Forster, the problem of unity entails breaking the dialectic of ideal and real, given realism's growing inability to effect this metaphorically, at least in its present forms. The complex vision with which the novel ends requires Charles's imprisonment and Henry Wilcox's consequent breaking (he is "broken," "ended," and "petulant" [*HE*, 331, 325]), a neutering of the masculine that brings to mind the conclusion of *Jane Eyre*.[9] Onto the men is projected the finality associated with desires for closure and control. We must embrace fragmentariness, Friedrich Schlegel writes, if we wish to glimpse the transcendental. In Forster's world, this is possible only if we recognize that what we glimpse is a metaphor that can only be sustained in an ironic vision, not an external reality.

Yet, as I have suggested, Forster already suspects that there may be a nongenerative "ou-boum" behind phenomena, that all such hopes for meaning are purely personal. Leonard Bast, for instance, can experience only "panic and emptiness," not the aesthetic structures that Margaret (with her appreciation of pure music) or Helen (with her narrative word pictures of goblins and reassurance) are able to build. He is incapable of metaphorical transcendences, try as he may to appropriate Ruskin's prose to mediate emptiness. When Helen thinks he must have had a wonderful dawn experience during his aimless ramble through the North Downs, his reply, that the "dawn was only grey, it was nothing to mention" (*HE*, 117), points to his inability to generate myths of transcendence. On another morning, the one when Charles kills him, Leonard fails to attain the epiphanic moment towards which, he hopes, his life is tending in apologetic union. As he dies, struck by Charles's sword and crushed by a bookcase, nothing makes sense and he is confused by "contradictory notions" (*HE*, 321). Yet his voice must somehow be incorporated into Margaret's metaphorical vision of England, even if he is excluded: she asks Helen, the mother of their child, to forget him. Literature (Ruskin,

Stevenson, Moore) can't save him; perhaps his child will be uplifted into a higher aristocracy of talent, or so Forster suggests. But this is an awfully thin reed on which to build a new poetry. Forster again is really at a loss, and his decision to give up longer fiction a decade later seems reasonable in light of this.

Bast's fate suggests a decaying capacity to generate beneficent illusions, as the democratization of aspiration impinges on *rentier* and aesthetic autonomy. Schiller's idyll was predicated on the possibility of an as yet unrealized, autonomous sphere that reconciled irony and meaning; Nietzsche tried to rescue meaning from a flux that could not be ignored, even in art. Forster grasps irony and illusion alike but seeks a rosy afterglow after verbal struggle in romance and idyllic delimitations that create metaphorical stability. Yet the awareness that these metaphorical oases are transitory, and in effect ironically elegaic, is always apparent. Still, while art subverts its own illusions, irony can also be prophylactic; skepticism towards words need not preclude their talismanic utility, if the matrix in which they are used is itself ironic.

Notes

Introduction

1. Michel de Certeau, *The Writing of History*, trans. Tom Conley (New York: Columbia University Press, 1988), 37.

2. Hayden White, *Metahistory: The Historical Imagination in Nineteenth-Century Europe* (Baltimore, Md.: Johns Hopkins University Press, 1973), 37.

3. de Certeau, *The Writing of History*, 46.

4. Hans Kellner, "A Bedrock of Order: Hayden White's Linguistic Humanism," *History and Theory: Studies in the Philosophy of History Beiheft* 19 (1980): 7.

5. de Certeau, *The Writing of History*, 292.

6. White, *Metahistory*, 332.

7. George Levine, *The Realistic Imagination* (Chicago: University of Chicago Press, 1981), 33.

8. Thus, I am skeptical about interpreters who discount ironic subversions and countervoices, which are essential to the creation of meaning. It is true that irony at some point ossifies into self-contained verbal play, a (naively) parodic counterpart of idyllic univocality; and it is true that commentators often find irony where it does not exist.

In *Romantic Vision and the Novel* (Cambridge: Cambridge University Press, 1987), Jay Clayton argues that transcendence is a disruptive "defense against otherness," but what he terms the "visionary experience" (16) is more problematical in the nineteenth-century novel than he asserts.

In *The Providential Aesthetic in Victorian Fiction* (Charlottesville: University of Virginia Press, 1985), Thomas Vargish, analyzing the "providential worldview," writes that "Brontë and Dickens provide in their early novels a splendid celebration of its powers as a structuring principle and in their later work increasingly radical and brilliant defenses against what proved in the end to be its 'extirpation' as a general cultural and aesthetic premise" (6). But there is much more ambivalence about providence in Brontë, and especially in Dickens, than Vargish allows.

9. Friedrich Nietzsche, *Basic Writings of Nietzsche*, trans. Walter Kaufmann (New York: Modern Library, 1968), 239.

10. White, *Metahistory*, 261.

11. Gotthold Ephraim Lessing, *Laocoön: An Essay on the Limits of Painting and Poetry*, trans. Edward Allen McCormick (Baltimore, Md.: Johns Hopkins University Press, 1984).

12. Friedrich Schiller, *Naive and Sentimental Poetry and on the Sublime*, trans. Julias A. Elias (New York: Fredrich Ungar, 1980).

13. Lionel Trilling, introduction to *Emma* by Jane Austen (Boston: Houghton Mifflin, 1957), xxi.

14. Nietzsche, *Basic Writings*, 104.

1: Edmund Burke: *Reflections on the Revolution in France*

1. Nietzsche, *Basic Writings*, 239.

2. In this chapter, all parenthetical citations refer to Edmund Burke, *Reflections on the Revolution in France*, ed. Conor Cruise O'Brien (Harmondsworth: Penguin, 1968).

3. O'Brien defines Burke's "Jacobite" style as "Gothic and pathetic." In Burke, "the friction between outer Whig and inner 'Jacobite' was both ironic itself, and productive of that oblique aggressiveness which is the driving force of irony." Conor Cruise O'Brien, Introduction to *Reflections on the Revolution in France* (Harmondsworth: Penguin, 1986), 43.

Similarly, linking him with Alexander Pope, Frans de Bruyn writes that "the visionary force that fires them both and energizes their writing paradoxically draws its power from precisely those subterraneous elements that their impassioned discourse seeks to exorcise and exclude." "Theater and Countertheater in Burke's *Reflections on the Revolution in France*," in *Burke and the French Revolution: Bicentennial Essays*, ed. Steven Blakemore (Athens: University of Georgia Press, 1992), 32.

4. "And if somebody asked, 'but to a fiction there surely belongs an author?'— couldn't one answer simply: *why*? Doesn't this 'belongs' perhaps belong to the fiction, too? Is it not permitted to be a bit ironical about the subject no less than the predicate and object?" Nietzsche, *Basic Writings*, 237.

5. Nietzsche, *Basic Writings*, 237.

6. O'Brien, Introduction to *Reflections on the Revolution in France*, 34.

7. Punter writes that "within his resonant imagery, what he is holding for the 'literati' is the fear that contamination by reality might expose and destroy the fantasies on which the myth of Englishness was based." David Punter, "1789: The Sex of Revolution," *Criticism* 24 (Summer 1982): 217. Yet Burke's irony was aimed, like Nietzsche's philosophy, at an insightful few. The modern reader is drawn to Burke's stripping of illusions just as many of his contemporaries were to the assertion of a tradition in whose language and "gallery" they found common consent.

8. Burke stated this particularly strongly in 1796. Since the states are "moral essences ... and, in their proximate efficient cause, the arbitrary productions of the human mind," property rights must be grasped as the tangible sign of the worth of what cannot be defined." *Edmund Burke on Revolution*, ed. Robert A. Smith (New York: Harper Torchbooks, 1968), 250.

9. Friedrich Schiller, *On the Aesthetic Education of Man*, trans. Elizabeth M. Wilkerson and L. A. Willoughby (Oxford: Clarendon Press, 1967), 47.

10. Nietzsche, *Basic Writings*, 142.

11. Friedrich Schlegel, *Dialogue on Poetry and Literary Aphorisms*, trans. Ernst Behler and Roman Struc (University Park: The Pennsylvania State University Press, 1968), 131.

12. Ibid., 136.

13. Ibid., 137–38.

14. Ibid., 143. The novel "permeates all modern poetry." Thus, the most characteristic modern poetry is the novel, whose fragmentary voices at once mirror modern life and offer the ironic tensions that facilitate provisional meaning. Like Jean Paul, he argues that something like what Bakhtin calls the "carnivalesque," a "real transcendental buffoonery," is appropriate to the "divine breath of irony" (*Dialogue on Poetry,* 126). This "progressive universal poetry" is nimble: "It can lose itself in what it represents to such a degree that one might think its one and only goal were the characterization of poetic individuals of every type. ... Romantic poetry alone can, like the epic, become a mirror of the entire surrounding world, a picture of its age. ... It cannot be exhausted by any theory, and only a divinatory criticism might dare to characterize its ideal" (140–41).

15. Ibid., 136.

16. Ibid., 140–41.

17. Ibid., 136.

18. Nietzsche, *Basic Writings*, 143.

19. Julia Kristeva, *Desire in Language: A Semiotic Approach to Literature and Art*, trans. Thomas Cora et al. (New York: Columbia University Press, 1980), 93.

20. In "On a Regicide Peace" (1796), Burke sees an even greater confusion in the National Assembly. It is "a lewd tavern for the revels and debauches of banditii, assassins, bravoes, smugglers, and their more desperate paramours, mixed with bombastic players, the refuse and offal of strolling theatres." *Edmund Burke on Revolution*, 273. To the association of bad theater with sexual licentiousness is added a Swiftian excremental disgust.

21. Furniss writes that "Burke's exploitation of the emotive possibilities of rape is perhaps symptomatic of an implicit aggression toward (aristocratic) women operating within his 'chivalric' text. After all, it is Burke's text, rather than the revolutionary 'mob,' which exposes the queen to 'the last disgrace.'" "Stripping the Queen: Edmund Burke's Magic Lantern Show," in *Burke and the French Revolution: Bicentennial Essays*, ed. Steven Blakemore (Athens: University of Georgia Press, 1992), 83.

22. Christopher Reid writes that Burke was influenced in his presentation of Marie Antoinette's assault by the celebrated actress Sarah Siddons, whose roles typically combined vulnerability with fortitude. "Burke's Tragic Muse: Sarah Siddons and the 'Feminization' of Politics," in *Burke and the French Revolution: Bicentennial Essays*, ed. Steven Blakemore (Athens: University of Georgia Press, 1992), 2.

23. See de Bruyn, "Theater and Countertheater," 28–68.

24. Louis XVI is a nonentity, the metonymic "feet" at which the Queen seeks refuge, after which "no more" is said of him. He is passive and effeminate; the Queen is tragically sublime and feminine. But both are passive. This is the same pattern followed by Thomas Carlyle in his 1837 history, in which Louis is a "living passivity only." Marie, in contrast, displays "energy." *The Centenary Edition of the Works of Thomas Carlyle*, ed. H. D. Traill (London: Chapman and Hall, 1897), 4: 235, 238.

25. J. Hillis Miller, *Thomas Hardy: Distance and Desire* (Cambridge: Harvard University Press, 1970), 38.

26. In his *The Ethics of Reading* (New York: Columbia University Press, 1987), J. Hillis Miller writes on chapter 17 of Eliot's *Adam Bede* that Eliot uses "catachresis," or "terms borrowed from another realm to name what has no literal language of its own." This makes

a break in the remorseless chain of cause and effect which ordinarily operates, for Eliot, both in the physical or social worlds and in the internal world of the self. Only such a break, a fissure dividing before and after, can effect a redirection of the power of feeling in the self. This produces a consequent redirection of the power of doing in the outer world of the neighbors of that self. (73–74)

Miller's use of "catachresis" is similar to Nietzsche's revaluation. Burke, I have noted, attempts a revaluation to counter those of the revolutionaries. When finally he is unable to "play" with the fissure of before and after, old meaning and new, he is instead obliged to insist on the value of the idea he has already deconstructed and relegated to the past no less successfully than any philosophe. His essential appeal is to class solidarity.

27. Nietzsche, *Basic Writings*, 140.

28. F. R. Leavis, *The Great Tradition* (Harmondsworth: Penguin, 1974), 13, 10.

2: Jane Austen's *Emma*: Realism and Delimitation

1. White, *Metahistory*, 39.

2. Levine, *The Realistic Imagination*, 4.

3. Thus I question Susan Morgan's conclusion that "we learn that there is no escape into imagination" and that "reality, or the truth Emma comes to know, is not in conflict with imagination." "*Emma* and the Charms of Imagination," in *Modern Critical Views: Jane Austen's "Emma,"* ed. Harold Bloom (New York: Chelsea House, 1987), 78, 79. Instead, Emma learns that there should be no *public* escape into the aesthetic.

4. Vargish, *The Providential Aesthetic*, 48.

5. Trilling, introduction to *Emma*, xxi.

Trilling's assertion that Austen creates a Schillerian idyll (xxi) in which "the England of her novels was not the real England" (xxiii) has been questioned by more recent readings that see instability and historicity at *Emma*'s heart. For instance, Beatrice Marie sees an "illusion of Burkean stability" disappearing "before a picture of a traditional society in rapid, almost chaotic, flux." "Emma and the Democracy of Desire," *Studies in the Novel* 17 (Spring 1985): 10.

Closer to my own reading is Nicola Watson's assertion that Austen seems "peculiarly alive to the scandal of signs cut loose from their supposedly proper destinations, but to 'rehabilitate' her as a champion of anarchic free play by misreading or deliberately suppressing her own ideological choices seems both patronizing and dishonest." *Revolution and the Form of the British Novel 1790-1825* (Oxford: Clarendon Press, 1994), 95 n.

6. Jane Austen, *Emma*, ed. Stephen M. Parrish (New York: W. W. Norton & Co., 1993), 4. All parenthetical references in this chapter refer to *Emma*.

7. de Certeau, *The Writing of History*, 37.

8. *Emma* has inspired much commentary as a novel about novel production and reading. Adena Rosmarin notes the superseding of "passive reading" by a "hemeneutic

dance." "'Misreading' *Emma*: The Powers and Perfidies of Interpretive History," in *Jane Austen: Emma, a Casebook*, ed. David Lodge (London: Macmillan, 1991), 222.

J. M. Q. Davies, focusing on the charades episode, interprets it as a reader-response exercise that provides "the key to, and models in miniature for, the relationships between text and reader Jane Austen intended to establish." *"Emma* as Charade and the Education of the Reader," *Philological Quarterly* 65 (Spring 1986): 232.

Darrell Mansell notes that, in *Emma*, "the ironies seem to stop at the edges of the novel, rather than to reach out with much moral significance that would directly apply in the world of our own experience." *The Novels of Jane Austen: An Interpretation* (New York: Macmillan, 1973), 150. This suggests a complex relationship between the novel and the "real" world outside its bounds.

9. In this respect, Emma has much in common with other literary characters who confuse fiction and life. Beatrice Marie notes her affinities with Julien Sorel in *The Red and the Black*. "Emma and the Democracy of Desire," 5.

But a better comparison, as Douglas Bush suggests, is with Emma Bovary. *Jane Austen* (New York: Macmillan, 1975), 162.

10. Knightley accuses Emma of being unable to distinguish between English "amiable" and French "aimable" behavior in evaluating Frank Churchill. He is, of course, correct about Emma's difficulty in linking the "real" with aesthetic reformulation. In fact, Austen subverts Knightley's "amiability" even as she upholds it, much as she does with "likeness" and other univocal formulations. Even as she affirms conservative structures, Jane Austen uses uniform descriptions to point out the limitations of official discourse. The word is so promiscuously applied to characters that, like "likeness," it is at once affirmed and ironically undercut. Austen points to unities of character, yet, applied so often to inappropriate characters, "amiability" both affirms and parodies itself. In fact, the word applies to every major character. Miss Bates calls Mr. Dixon a "most amiable, charming young man" (106), Harriet calls Robert Martin "amiable" (35), and Isabella applies the term to both Jane Fairfax (71) and (sight unseen) Frank Churchill. Emma sarcastically applies the term to Jane (165) when her resentment at Jane's perfection leads her to take some delight in Frank's tormenting her. Even the often apoplectic John Knightley is capable of intermittent "amiableness" (95) during his stay at Hartfield. And Miss Bates, with her "guileless simplicity and warmth" is "the most amiable, affable, delightful woman" (193).

11. See Joseph Litvak's argument that in Jane Fairfax's trips to the post office we can detect a "synecdoche for the much larger system of communication on which the novel centers." "Reading Characters: Self, Society, and Text in *Emma*," *PMLA* 100 (October 1985): 766.

12. Samuel Johnson, *The History of Rasselas Prince of Abissinia*, ed. J. P. Hardy (New York: Oxford University Press, 1988), 26.

13. Rosmarin, "'Misreading' *Emma*, 228.

14. See Marvin Mudrick's discussion of Emma's skill in "absolving" herself of the past whenever it suits her, as is the case with Harriet. It is significant that, for all her admiration of Donwell Abbey, Emma stays at Hartfield after marrying Knightley, the result of her manipulation of his real solicitude for her father's well-being. *Jane Austen: Irony as Defense and Discovery* (Berkeley: University of California Press, 1968).

15. Ralph Rader, "Literary Permanence and Critical Change," *Works-And-Days* 4 (Spring 1986): 14.

16. Darrell Mansell's statement that here "Emma is seen ... whispering with him as if

she were actually communing with her innermost soul" reinforces the sense that Churchill is the mirror of Emma's aesthetic desire. *The Novels of Jane Austen*, 162.

17. The potential success of Emma's marriage has been debated for years. Anne K. Mellor writes that Austen was "a moderate feminist" who, while desiring "a marriage of genuine equality between husband and wife ... is honest enough to remind us that such marriages may not yet exist in England." *Romanticism and Gender* (New York: Routledge, 1993), 57.

This parallels my reading, which stands between relative skeptics like Mudrick and critics like Ralph Rader and Laura G. Mooneyham. The last writes that "Emma's marriage to Mr. Knightley is among the most mature and satisfying matches in Austen's work." *Romance, Language and Education in Jane Austen's Novels* (New York: St. Martin's Press, 1988), 143.

3: *Frankenstein* and Aesthetic Decay

1. Mary Shelley, *Frankenstein*, ed. Maurice Hindle (Harmondsworth: Penguin, 1988), 256, 257. All parenthetical references in this chapter refer to *Frankenstein*.

2. William Veeder argues that Victor seeks to abolish the alpha-father, Alphonse, by discovering life's secret. He notes that the monster's murders move in reverse order down the alphabet. "The Negative Oedipus: Father, *Frankenstein*, and the Shelleys," *Critical Inquiry* 12 (Winter 1986): 380, 385.

3. Nietzsche, *Basic Writings*, 42.

4. George Levine, *The Realistic Imagination*, 32.

5. Dante, *The Divine Comedy: Inferno*, trans. Charles S. Singleton (Princeton: Princeton University Press, 1970), 93.

John Freccero writes of Dante's Medusa that "despair, like death, is a sign emptied of its significance and is therefore mute." "Infernal Irony: The Gates of Hell," *Modern Language Notes* 99 (September 1984): 777.

6. Levine, *The Realistic Imagination*, 29.

7. Paul Sherwin, "*Frankenstein*: Creation as Catastrophe," *PMLA* 96 (October 1981): 888.

8. Virgil, *The Aeneid*, trans. Robert Fitzgerald (New York: Vintage Books, 1990), 4.677.

Loury Nelson writes that "the plunge into the depths of the mind, so fateful for the age, seems to have revealed both a yearning for the utopian, simplistic solution and an indulging of irrational impulses." "Night Thoughts on the Gothic Novel," in *Modern Critical Views: Frankenstein*, ed. Harold Bloom (New York: Chelsea House, 1985), 42. When Victor's attempt to find his solution through science fails, he finds himself at the mercy of the irrational.

Victor's nightmare in chapter 5 has generated all manner of interpretations. Paul Sherwin thinks that "in embracing this cousin-sister-bride Frankenstein reaches through her to take hold of the maternal body he intends to possess." "*Frankenstein*: Creation as Catastrophe," 887.

Veeder argues that the nightmare "is manifestly *not* oedipal": Victor wants to "reduce Elizabeth to Caroline's moribund state" and is then free "to move beyond woman to father." "The Negative Oedipus," 379.

Sandra M. Gilbert and Susan Gubar write that Victor's "self-defining procreation" links him to Eve. *The Madwoman in the Attic: The Woman Writer and the Nineteenth Century Literary Imagination* (New Haven: Yale University Press, 1979), 233.

Paul Youngquist views the dream, like the rest of the novel, as Shelley's "fantasy of female independence from biological constraints." *"Frankenstein*: The Mother, the Daughter, and the Monster," *Philological Quarterly* 70 (Summer 1991): 355–56.

Anne K. Mellor's discussions of the novel have been especially influential, above all her criticisms of the 1831 edition. She emphasizes the monster's imprisonment in appearances as an indication of his barely hidden feminine nature. *Mary Shelley: Her Life, Her Fiction, Her Monsters* (New York: Methuen, 1988).

Mellor has been criticized by Bette London, who sees in *Frankenstein* a "fixation on masculine spectacle." She accuses Mellor, like Rieger, of assuming "the author's stabilizing and authenticating signature" and of sustaining "authorship as an exclusive institution—one whose configurations best serve male members." "Mary Shelley, *Frankenstein*, and the Spectacle of Masculinity," *PMLA* 108 (March 1993): 264, 260.

9. Jean Paul Friedrich Richter, *School for Aesthetics*, trans. Margaret H. Hale, vol. 21 of *German Romantic Criticism*, ed. Leslie Willson (New York: Continuum, 1982), 32.

10. The nameless evades classification; indeed, it cancels volition and language. Anxiety towards the feminine leads Victor to create fictive unities that break down. The vision of unspeakable pollution accelerates the disintegration of meaning which, in desperation, he repeatedly tries to reconstruct. This process generates rage until life ends.

11. Nietzsche, *Basic Writings*.

4: *Jane Eyre*: Vision and Aesthetic Control

1. White, *Metahistory*, 332.

2. Mark M. Hennelly, Jr., writes that *Jane Eyre* is preoccupied "with the phenomenology of reading." "Jane Eyre's Reading Lesson," *ELH* 51 (Winter 1984): 694.

3. de Certeau, *The Writing of History*, 320.

4. Rosemary Bodenheimer, "Jane Eyre in Search of Her Story," in *Charlotte Brontë's "Jane Eyre": Modern Critical Interpretations*, ed. Harold Bloom (New York: Chelsea House, 1987), 97–112.

For a different perspective, see Janet Gezari, who writes that in the end Jane redefines her rebellion as "accomodation," which undermines the novel's "powerful defense against the exclusion of women from visual pleasure and authority." *Charlotte Brontë and Defensive Conduct: The Author and the Body at Risk* (Philadelphia: University of Pennsylvania Press, 1992), 89.

5. de Certeau, *The Writing of History*, 321.

Terry Eagleton writes that Burke and Schiller exclude women from "the domain of truth and morality." A double standard is at work in that "the form-giving potency of male reason penetrates and subdues the inchoate sensual female, but as 'feeling' she has no reciprocal voice in the sphere of truth and morality." *The Ideology of the Aesthetic* (Oxford: Basil Blackwood, 1990), 59, 117.

As informative as Eagleton's study of (mostly) German aesthetics is, he neglects discussion of Schiller's ideas about plastic art, whose political and educational ramifications are overt. Even more curiously, he altogether neglects any discussion of the

Winckelmann-Lessing-Goethe debate about the relationship between visual and poetic art forms, which likewise had important political implications.

6. Levine, *The Realistic Imagination*, 42.

7. White, *Metahistory*, 332.

8. John S. Nelson, "Tropal History and the Social Sciences," *History and Theory: Studies in the Philosophy of History Beiheft* 19 (1980): 92.

9. Charlotte Brontë, *Jane Eyre*, ed. Q. D. Leavis (Harmondsworth: Penguin, 1986), 47. All parenthetical references in this chapter refer to *Jane Eyre*.

10. According to Gilbert and Gubar, Bertha enacts Jane's secret desire to punish Rochester by destroying herself and Thornfield. *The Madwoman in the Attic*, 481.

11. Virginia Woolf, *A Room of One's Own* (New York: Harbrace, 1989).

12. Nietzsche, *Basic Writings*, 353, 358–59.

13. de Certeau, *The Writing of History*, 316.

14. Wolfgang Iser, *The Fictive and the Imaginary: Charting Literary Anthropology* (Baltimore, Md.: The Johns Hopkins University Press, 1993), 88, 109.

15. Terry Eagleton, *Myths of Power: A Marxist Study of the Brontës* (London: Macmillan Press, 1975), 15.

16. White, *Metahistory*, 332.

17. George L. Mosse argues that the German mania for Greece valorized eugenics, which combined aesthetics with pseudoscience. *Toward the Final Solution: A History of European Racism* (New York: Howard Fertig, 1978).

18. Helene Moglen, *Charlotte Brontë: The Self Conceived* (Madison: University of Wisconsin Press, 1984), 487.

19. Friedrich Schiller, *Die Räuber*, vol. 1 of *Sämtliche Werke* (Munich: Winkler Verlag, 1968), 899–900; translation mine. Here is the portion of the original in the 1781 edition that Jane overhears:

Da trat einer hervor, anzusehen wie die Sternennacht. ... Ich wäge dies Gedanken in der Schale meines Zornes und die Werke mit dem Gewichte meines Grimms.

20. There are similarities with Johann Joachim Winckelmann's celebrated description of the Laocoön statue, though there is no evidence that Brontë read his *Nachahmung*. In describing the "noble simplicity" and "quiet greatness" of Laocoön's calmness in suffering, Winckelmann writes, "Just as the sea's depths always remain quiet, no matter how much the surface may rage, just so amid all sufferings a great and calm soul is evident in the Greek figures" (my translation. Winckelmann, *Gedanken über die Nachahmung der griechischen Werke in der Malerei und Bildhauerkunst* (Stuttgart: Reclam, 1977), 20.

The metaphor Rivers chooses for his self-control is not the sea's depths but a rock "in the depths" of a sea that is restless at every depth. He does not reconcile passion with reason but uses one to repress the other.

21. Brontë's narrative technique and Jane Eyre's realism and rejection of "classical" aesthetics are connected. Q. D. Leavis writes of the Brontë sisters, "In order to be great art their novels, these girls realized, must include 'poetry,' necessarily employing a poetic method and evolving new prose techniques." Q. D. Leavis, introduction to *Jane Eyre* by Charlotte Brontë (Harmondsworth: Penguin, 1986), 11.

Jane Austen and Charlotte Brontë both probe specious aesthetic and social structures, but Austen does so as a subversive insider, Brontë as an outsider who, as outsider, can more overtly acknowledge her rebellion even as she (like Jane Eyre) develops a means to express that passion.

22. Gezari, *Charlotte Brontë and Defensive Conduct*, 67.

5: Aesthetic Escapes in Four Novels by Charles Dickens

1. White, *Metahistory*, 332.

2. Charles Dickens, *Oliver Twist*, ed. Kathleen Tillotson (New York: Oxford University Press, 1990), 32. All further citations to this work in this chapter are indicated parenthetically as *OT* in the text. By permission of Oxford University Press.

3. J. Hillis Miller calls London a "dream or poetic symbol of an infernal labyrinth, inhabited by the devil himself." *Charles Dickens: The World of His Novels* (Bloomington: Indiana University Press, 1958), 58.

4. D. A. Miller writes that the police "simultaneously produce and permeate (produce as permeable) the space they leave to be 'free.'" In this reading, it seems that everything (including opposition) is part of a "perpetual grid." *The Novel and the Police* (Berkeley: University of California Press, 1988), 212, 200.

5. Burke, *Reflections on the Revolution*, 161.

6. F. R. Leavis extolled *Hard Times* as Dickens's one completely serious, "moral" novel with distinctly "Jonsonian affinities." *The Great Tradition*, 258, 269.

David M. Hirsch dismisses the "embarrassingly obvious" nature of its general symbolic structure. "*Hard Times* and Dr. Leavis," *Criticism* 6 (Winter 1964): 5.

John Holloway also finds *Hard Times* psychologically shallow; Dickens's outlook "partook a little of the shallowness of the merely topical, and the defects of the bourgeois." "*Hard Times*: A History and a Criticism," in *Dickens and the Twentieth Century*, ed. John Gross and Gabriel Pearson (London: Routledge and Kegan Paul, 1962), 160–70.

For the philosophical ideas behind *Hard Times*, see William Oddie, *Dickens and Carlyle: The Question of Influence* (London: Centenary, 1972); and Michael Goldberg, who writes that Dickens "enters a romantically charged plea for the sense of wonder and imagination." *Carlyle and Dickens* (Athens: University of Georgia Press, 1973), 79. Yet the novel, as I suggest, is about the failure of the realistic vision.

7. Stephen J. Spector notes Dickens's "metonymic character creation." "Monsters of Metonymy: *Hard Times* and Knowing the Working Class," *ELH* 51 (Summer 1984): 373.

Schiller contrasts a fragmented modern humanity with the ancient Greeks, among whom "every individual enjoyed an independent existence but could, when need arose, grow into the whole organism." *On the Aesthetic Education of Man*, 25.

8. Charles Dickens, *Hard Times*, ed. George Ford and Sylvère Monod (New York: W. W. Norton & Co., 1966), 6. All further citations to this work in this chapter are indicated parenthetically as *HT* in the text.

9. White, *Metahistory*, 31n.

10. See David M. Craig's discussion of passages that illustrate how "the anarchic world overcomes the order principles of the interpretive mind." "The Interplay of City and Self in *Oliver Twist*, *David Copperfield*, and *Great Expectations*," *Dickens Studies Annual* 16 (1987): 21.

Robert Tracy suggests that Fagin's "efforts to shape Oliver's story" betray Dickens's "uneasiness." When we last see Fagin, "in the condemned cell, he has lost control of

Oliver's story and, despite his effort to contrive a Newgate novel escape, of his own." "'The Old Story' and Inside Stories: Modish Fiction and Fictional Modes in *Oliver Twist*," *Dickens Studies Annual* 17 (1988): 25.

11. Brownlow represents a nurturing alternative to Fagin's demonic and Rose's idyllic-maternal extremes. At the novel's end, he links together for Oliver "a little society, whose condition approached as nearly to one of perfect happiness as can ever be known in this changing world" (*OT,* 348). The pattern is intriguing: Dickens establishes an unrealistic maternal ideal in a Rose Maylie and places his maternal hope in an elderly gentleman, Brownlow, who is free of sexual danger.

Fagin confuses parental roles in a way Brownlow does not. Steven Marcus discerns a "treacherous maternal care" arising from Dickens's own resistance to "a companionship or affection which is at once needed and intolerable." "Who is Fagin," in *Oliver Twist*, ed. Fred Kaplan (New York: W. W. Norton, 1993), 486.

James Kincaid similarly notes that "there is something maternal ... about the recurring image of Fagin bending over the fire and about his favorite phrase, 'my dear.'" *Dickens and the Rhetoric of Laughter* (Oxford: Oxford University Press, 1971), 72.

In *Great Expectations,* Dickens contrasts cruel feminine sexuality with a maternal-paternal ideal, Joe Gargery, with whom Pip cannot be united. Many have pointed out a biographical connection with this desire for the effacement of gender functions in a sort of paternal-maternal apocalypse. Tracy argues that Fagin represents "Dickens's uneasiness with the act of fiction." "The Old Story," 8.

12. Charles Dickens, *Great Expectations*, ed. Angus Calder (Harmondsworth: Penguin, 1985), 145. All further references to this work in this chapter are indicated parenthetically as *GE* in the text.

13. Charles Dickens, *Bleak House*, ed. Norman Page (Harmondsworth: Penguin, 1985), 935. All further references to this work in this chapter are indicated parenthetically as *BH* in the text.

14. Esther's diminutives, Q. D. Leavis notes, ironically point to an "excessive maturity"; they also reflect her need for assurance. F. R Leavis and Q. D. Leavis, *Dickens the Novelist* (New Brunswick, N.J.: Rutgers University Press, 1979), 154.

Themes of language and naming have attracted much attention, particularly by the Lacanians. Chiara Briganti argues that Esther deconstructs patriarchal discourse to "become the subject of her text," rather like Jane Eyre. "The Monstrous Actress: Esther Summerson's Spectral Name," *Dickens Studies Annual* 19 (1990): 206.

Michael Ragussis regards *Bleak House* as a novel "whose mysteries are linguistic," where names function as "ironic commentaries" or "deliberate masks." "The Ghostly Signs of *Bleak House*," in *Critical Essays on Charles Dickens's Bleak House*, ed. Elliot L. Gilbert (Boston: G. K. Hall & Co., 1989), 143, 144.

Robert Newsom reflects a less skeptical approach in writing that "to say that characters exist *only* in language demystifies of course a good deal more than the authority of 'documents.'" "*Bleak House*, I: Suspended Animation," in *Critical Essays on Charles Dickens's Bleak House*, 123.

15. The dual voices of *Bleak House* represent a chasm between objective and subjective voices that occasionally interpenetrate yet finally offer no unitary vision. Q. D. Leavis's statement that Esther is "Dickens's first successful attempt at creating a girl from the inside" underestimates the unresolved conflicts in her personality. *Dickens the Novelist*, 156.

Virginia Blain sees "a submerged dialectic between male and female viewpoints." "Double Vision and the Double Standard in *Bleak House*: A Feminist Perspective," in

Charles Dickens's "Bleak House": Modern Critical Interpretations, ed. Harold Bloom (New York: Chelsea House, 1987), 139.

Janet L. Larson, drawing on Bakhtin, sees "dialogical tensions" in *Bleak House*. *Dickens and the Broken Scripture* (Athens: University of Georgia Press, 1985), 126.

Joseph Gold notes a contrast between the "objective" society and a "subjective quest of the 'I' for an existential redemption." *Charles Dickens: Radical Moralist* (Minneapolis: University of Minnesota Press, 1972), 186.

Marcia Renee Goodman, in a feminist analysis, sees Esther's first-person narrative as reflecting Dickens's "particularly male wish for and fear of merging." "'I'll Follow the Other': Tracing the (M)other in *Bleak House*," *Dickens Studies Annual* 19 (1990): 150. While Goodman's definition of male discourse is questionable, she identifies a desire that is also apparent in *Great Expectations*.

See also Barbara Gottfried's analysis of Esther's wish to "empower herself." "Fathers and Suitors: Narratives of Desire in *Bleak House*," *Dickens Studies Annual* 19 (1990): 170.

16. William Wordsworth, *The Prelude*, in *Poetical Works*, ed. Thomas Hutchinson and Ernest de Selincourt (New York: Oxford University Press, 1984), 12: 210, 224–25, 207.

17. J. Hillis Miller writes that, for Dickens, "any attempt to find an intelligible order in the universe is doomed to failure." *Charles Dickens: The World of His Novels*, 167. Yet Dickens's optimistic countervoice wishes otherwise, especially in the earlier stages of his career, when it denies what the text suggests about the practicality of idyllic escapes. The need to affirm the idyllic suggests that it does not exist.

18. Krook's spontaneous combustion into soot and a greasy residue offers a contrast with Esther's physical loss and reinvention. She gains strength through her reinvention, while Krook, like Lady Dedlock, simply disappears.

19. Iain Crawford makes a convincing argument that *Frankenstein* influenced Dickens's portrayal of Pip. Yet he overemphasizes Dickens's belief in his own morality: "Where Shelley's work posits an ideology of assertive individual self-reliance in a godless world, Dickens's text emphasizes the values of human community and, especially, of submission to divine grace." "Pip and the Monster: The Joys of Bondage," *SEL* 28 (Autumn 1988): 625.

20. Naturally, the Lacanians—and their opponents—have made much of writing and counterfeiting in *Great Expectations*. Murray Baumgarten focuses on the capacity of reading and writing to "distort the world." Pip uses words "to SEE through time to the subjects that acted in it ... rather than treating language as an enclosed symbol system with its own rules and values." "Calligraphy and Code: Writing in *Great Expectations*, *Dickens Studies Annual* 11 (1983): 62.

Steven Connor applies Lacan directly to the novel as he discusses "questions about the relationship of consciousness and language." *Charles Dickens* (Oxford: Basil Blackwell, 1965), 111.

Such interpretive positions center on assumptions about spiritual presence or absence.

21. Dante, *The Divine Comedy: Inferno*, 319.

22. Connor writes that "however attractive they may be, the worlds of the forge and of Wemmick's castle represent an "untenable illusion." *Charles Dickens*, 143.

23. The endings have received all manner of critical attention, and again the interpretive poles I have identified (as well as everything in between) are evident.

Douglass Thomson sees more than two endings. "The Passing of Another Shadow: A Third Ending to *Great Expectations*," *Dickens Quarterly* 1 (September 1984): 94–96.

John Kuchich thinks the novel ends "on a note of rejustified aspiration." *Excess and Restraint in the Novels of Charles Dickens* (Athens: University of Georgia Press, 1981), 156.

Susan Schoenbauer Thurin, interpreting the novel as a "moral fable" in which Pip supersedes embodiments of the seven deadly sins, argues that "Pip learns finally that self-improvement cannot be gained by defying traditional morality." "The Seven Deadly Sins in *Great Expectations*," *Dickens Studies Annual* 15 (1986): 210.

24. Though able to define a horse in the classroom, Bitzer is unable to handle the animal itself in the trick devised by Sleary to facilitate Tom's flight from England (*HT*, 220). Bitzer rejects Gradgrind's plea for mercy for Tom, declaring that the heart is just an organ (*HT*, 217).

25. Levine, *The Realistic Imagination*, 20.

26. Keith Hollingsworth writes that "Rose and other innocent young girls in Dickens are astral bodies emanating from Mary Hogarth." *The Newgate Novel, 1830-1847* (Detroit: Wayne State University Press, 1963), 123.

John Bayley argues that the worlds of Rose and Nancy "are twin sides of the same coin of fantasy." "*Oliver Twist*: 'Things as They Really Are,'" in *Dickens and the Twentieth Century*, ed. John Gross and Gabriel Pearson (London: Routledge and Kegan Paul, 1962), 51.

27. Nietzsche, *Basic Writings*, 348.

28. White, *Metahistory*, 25.

29. As is so often the case with Dickens, the essential critical debate centers on the degree to which he faces, recognizes, or flees from an abyss at the center of identity. Thomas Vargish writes that "Dickens's characters stick their fingers into existence all right, but they don't usually complain that it smells of nothing." *The Providential Aesthetic*, 54. But this understates the fear of nothingness at the center of Dickens's art.

30. The ending of *Bleak House* has been debated for years; its ambiguity rests in part on the degree of irreconcilability of the novel's narrative voices, and the question of providential order (parodic or real) for Dickens.

Joseph Gold insists that Esther embodies a love that brings "meaning and order out of chaos." Like Vargish, he believes that, despite the growing gloom, a "sense of universal Divine order is wrought into the very fabric, structure, and diction of the later novels." *Charles Dickens: Radical Moralist*, 188, 186.

Reflecting a different view, Chiara Briganti sees a "fragmentary" ending (despite which, through "duplicity and evasions," Esther asserts her "Otherness"). "The Monstrous Actress," 224.

Virginia Blain writes that the conclusion "deconstructs" itself. "Double Vision and the Double Standard," 156.

Similarly, D. A. Miller writes of the novel's "imposing refusal of rest and enjoyment" and its closure that "missed the essence of what it aspired to grasp." *The Novel and the Police*, 228, 222.

Placing myself between these positions, I argue that Dickens has more control over his questionings than some give him credit for. At the same time, he by no means mounts a "defense" of providential order.

31. Blain writes that "hidden sexual hostilities" are at the core of the social dislocations in *Bleak House*. "Double Vision and the Double Standard," 151, 155. Bucket

codifies "the tough masculine ethic of law, which has its face of vengeance hidden under rationalisation" (151), while Esther kills the mother within herself "to escape her contagion" (155).

32. Esther reflects Dickens's disillusioned desire that, translated from Jarndyce's dubious Bleak House to a smaller idyllic copy, she can escape the taints embodied in Lady Dedlock. Briganti argues that Esther "feels the urgency to abandon it to go back to a grievous past to tell her story." "The Monstrous Actress," 212.

6: George Eliot's Visions: Idealism and Realism

1. White, *Metahistory*, 372.

2. Levine, *The Realistic Imagination*, 205.

3. Susan E. Gustafson, "Beautiful Statues, Beautiful Men: The Abjection of the Feminine Imagination in Lessing's *Laokoon*," *PMLA* 108 (October 1993): 1088, 1083.

4. George Eliot, *Silas Marner*, ed. Q. D. Leavis (Harmondsworth: Penguin, 1985), 167. All further citations to this work in this chapter are indicated parenthetically as *SM* in the text.

5. Silas is shortsighted, but after his adoption of Eppie, "his large brown eyes seem to have gathered a longer vision" (*SM*, 137). Shortsightedness is also Dorothea Brooke's mental and physical handicap prior to the deepening of her sympathetic double vision. Hence her youthful reinvention of Dagley's home (which is squalid; Dagley is drunkenly abusive) as a picturesque dwelling with its "mossy thatch," etc.

6. Eliot's imposition of a Wordsworthian register on Eppie (above all, that of the naive child in unison with nature) is a univocality associated with a moral meaning that F. R. Leavis sees "realized in terms of a substantial real world." *The Great Tradition*, 60. The novel's hard moral content works only because of a dense fictive texture in which meanings are open-ended. The Romantic register is in tension with novelistic realism. Eppie offers the possibility of idyllic experience in a Midlands world soon to be overwhelmed by industrialism. Her world has passed away, but her power is valorized. Her influence on Marner is like that of the naive child in Schiller's *Naive and Sentimental Poetry*: "They are what we were; they are what we should once again become. We were nature just as they, and our culture, by means of reason and freedom, should lead us back to nature." *Naive and Sentimental Poetry*, 85. The narrator's formulation places her as a philosophical type, hence as an ideal.

7. Like Homer, Eliot employs weaving imagery to indicate social connection as well as egoistic imprisonment. Penelope, Circe, and Calypso all weave, but for different ends. Eliot's webs signal the paradox between alienation and entrapment (e.g., Rosamond's "gossamer web" and siren song in *Middlemarch*), and the limited possibilities of social participation.

8. Kellner, "A Bedrock of Order," 7.

9. Susan Cohen writes, "The register is a piece of writing accepted as authoritative, the wedding a fiction made fact by social, legal, and religious convention. The register is a model within the novel of the novel itself." "'A History and a Metamorphosis': Continuity and Discontinuity in *Silas Marner*," *Texas Studies in Literature and Language* 25 (Fall 1983): 411.

10. In *Adam Bede,* Eliot suggests a middle way between "a life of pomp or of absolute indigence, of tragic suffering or of world-stirring actions." This is found in the sympathy with which the artist describes "monotonous homely existence." George Eliot, *Adam Bede*, ed. Stephen Gill (Harmondsworth: Penguin, 1985), 223. To insist on extremes of absolute idealism or realism is to give up the search for meaningful unity between matter and form. Hence Eliot rejects the abstract formulations offered by Naumann in favor of pragmatic encounters with life that test the social web.

11. Kellner, *A Bedrock of Order,* 16.

12. George Eliot, *Middlemarch*, ed. David Carroll (Oxford: Clarendon Press, 1986), 110. All further citations to this work in this chapter are indicated parenthetically as *MM* in the text. By permission of Oxford University Press.

13. George Levine, *The Realistic Imagination,* 256.

14. Dante, *The Divine Comedy: Purgatorio*, trans. Charles S, Singleton (Princeton: Princeton University Press, 1973), 73.

15. Ibid., 67.

16. Ibid., 73.

17. Ibid., 71.

18. See Gilbert and Gubar, who discuss the "deathliness of nonbeing" that Dorothea faces: she seeks unity in a society increasingly given to fragmentary interpretations. *The Madwoman in the Attic*, 510. Andres writes that Eliot "doubts the possibility of harmonious Romantic fusions" yet "seems to long for them, and thus resists acquiescing in the modern fragmentary, disorderly vision." "The Germ and the Picture in *Middlemarch*," *ELH* 55 (Winter 1988): 857.

If her marriage to Will Ladislaw is, as Barbara Hardy suggests, a consoling lie, its humanity substitutes for the loss of providential meaning. *The Novels of George Eliot: A Study in Form* (New York: Oxford University Press, 1959). This is the best a world shorn of religious transcendence can offer.

As an author, Eliot, too, fills blankness; hence her preference for a realism contrary to what the narrator of *Adam Bede* calls "divine beauty of form" that teeters on blankness. Allen suggests that Eliot's narrator in *Middlemarch* is God-like. K. M. Newton writes that "the narrator's 'omniscience' . . . is an imaginative reconstruction and does not imply God-like knowledge." *George Eliot: Romantic Humanist* (Towota, N.J.: Barnes and Noble, 1981), 165.

Gilbert and Gubar argue that "Eliot becomes entangled in contradictions that she can only resolve through acts of vengeance against her own characters." *The Madwoman in the Attic*, 479.

Eliot favors realism, yet, J. Hillis Miller writes, the novel is a fiction twice removed from actuality because "objective things" have "already made a detour into necessarily distorted subjective reflections" prior to their artistic representation. Yet this creates a possibility of imaginative freedom arising from a break in the "remorseless chain of cause and effect which ordinarily operates." *The Ethics of Reading*, 65, 73.

19. Lessing, *Laocoön,* 77.

20. Ibid., 63, 85.

21. Ibid., 87.

22. Ibid., 90.

23. To remind the reader once more of the "doubleness" with which life should be approached, Eliot describes Dorothea dreamily staring at a "streak of sunlight" (*MM*,

184) rather than at the "Ariadne, then called Cleopatra" (*MM*, 183). Another statue has been misidentified, this time the representation of the goddess who, like Dorothea, had to negotiate a labyrinth. Dorothea, however, stares not at "Cleopatra," emblem of sexuality and suicidal despair, but at the sun, the mythic phallic-creative antitype to the barren, disillusioning marriage into which she has entered.

24. Schiller, *Naive and Sentimental Poetry*, 182.

25. Schiller, *Naive and Sentimental Poetry*, 179.

26. Gilbert and Gubar, *The Madwoman in the Attic*, 513.

27. Schiller, *Naive and Sentimental Poetry*, 182, 181.

28. Robert Caserio, *Plot, Story, and the Novel: From Dickens to Poe to the Modern Period* (Princeton: Princeton University Press, 1979), 132.

7: Hardy's *Tess of the D'Urbervilles*: Realism As a Form of Idealism

1. de Certeau, *The Writing of History*, 46.

2. Thomas Hardy, *Tess of the D'Urbervilles*, ed. David Skilton (Harmondsworth: Penguin, 1986), 227. All parenthetical references in this chapter refer to *Tess*.

3. White, *Metahistory*, 37.

4. See Kathleen Blake, "Pure Tess: Hardy on Knowing a Woman," *SEL* 22 (Autumn 1982): 692–93.

5. Hayden White, *Metahistory*, 56.

6. Schiller, *Naive and Sentimental Poetry*, 181.

7. J. Hillis Miller, *Fiction and Repetition: Seven English Novels* (Cambridge: Harvard University Press, 1982), 127.

8. Rosemary Morgan regards the scene as a parody of Eden. *Women and Sexuality in the Novels of Thomas Hardy* (New York: Routledge, 1988).

Charlotte Thompson suggests that "reality becomes contorted to fit ancient stereotypes." Mythology "has the power virtually to obliterate reality by systematically replacing a living event with a construct of the past." "Language and the Shape of Reality in *Tess of the D'Urbervilles*," *ELH* 50 (Winter 1983): 742, 743.

Kathleen Blake sees the garden as "fecund yet decaying." "Pure Tess: Hardy on Knowing a Woman, 32.

Yet the issue again is one of blurred perspective: whose *mind* does the garden represent? The narrator's? Hardy's? Morgan thinks that Tess's placement outside the garden keeps her "beyond the boundary of sin-laden archetypes" (87), but others see her as an unconscious participant in what Thompson terms mythology's "disease in language" (743).

Laura Claridge observes that Tess is both serpent and Eve. Even her rape is problematical, for "Hardy shifts perspectives on Tess's real responsibility for her eventual fate as he alternately defines her as an unfallen Eve or an Eve who willingly accepts the serpent." "Tess: A Less Than Pure Woman Ambivalently," *Texas Studies in Literature and Language* 28 (Fall 1986): 331.

9. Sheila Berger sees in Hardy's insistent uses of visual images a means of creating stability so that "visual structures become a continuum along which character, reader, and

writer seek and create meaning." From this process arise substitutes for transcendence. *Thomas Hardy and Visual Structures: Framing, Disruption, Process* (New York: New York University Press, 1990), 18.

10. As can be imagined, Hardy's relation to Tess has received much attention in recent years:

Penny Boumelha discerns an urge in Hardy "towards narrative androgyny." *Thomas Hardy and Women: Sexual Ideology and Narrative Form* (Towota, N.J.: Barnes and Noble, 1982), 120.

More radically, Mary Childers writes that Hardy "offends and affirms feminist sensibility" and, in Tess, creates an object of desire whose "projection does not balk at transvestism." "Thomas Hardy: The Man Who 'Liked' Women," *Criticism* 23 (Fall 1981): 321, 326.

Kathleen Blake's assertion that "Hardy generalizes about Tess and women almost as incautiously as Angel does" is typical of much feminist criticism. "Pure Tess: Hardy on Knowing a Woman," 96.

For instance, Childers writes that "in his desire to devise rules that will permit women to be provocatively unruly—within reason—he asserts the benefits of keeping women trapped between the moral and the romantic." "Thomas Hardy: The Man Who 'Liked' Women," 332.

Charlotte Thompson also focuses on Tess as a prisoner of language, but she distinguishes Hardy from his narrator rather more than I do. "Language and the Shape of Reality," 729–62.

Adrian Poole and Rosemary Morgan are more hesitant than Blake to regard Tess as merely an object of Hardy's will. Poole argues that Tess refuses to keep to a settled or "middle" distance or be "accommodated" by men's words. "'Men's Words' and Hardy's Women," *Essays in Criticism* 31 (October 1981): 333–34. She situates Hardy within a feminism that assumes sexual difference: his women have a "finer sense of the *use* of words" than men have (343).

Morgan's radical-conservative aim, in contrast, is "to resurrect Hardy's originally strong Tess from the blurred stereotype of the sexually passive, fallen woman, as critics and film directors would have it." Her insistence on Tess's "fierce impulse to self-determination" is belied by the novel's events. *Women and Sexuality in the Novels of Thomas Hardy*, 85.

11. John Humma, "Language and Disguise: The Imagery of Nature and Sex in Tess," *South Atlantic Review* 54 (November 1989): 64.

12. Against the tendency of many critics to blur the distances between Hardy, his narrator, and Tess, Tony Tanner and Bruce Johnson accept Hardy's gender inscriptions as natural. Tanner writes that "fully to be human is partly to be heathen, as the figure of Tess on the altar makes clear." "Colour and Movement in Hardy's *Tess of the D'Urbervilles*," in *Thomas Hardy's "Tess of the D'Urbervilles": Modern Critical Interpretations*, ed. Harold Bloom (New York: Chelsea House, 1987), 11.

Bruce Johnson states that Hardy "seems to associate the ability to be in touch with primeval, pagan meanings with the ability to be in touch with the emotional, primitive sources of one's own being." "'The Perfection of the Species' and Hardy's Tess," in *Thomas Hardy's "Tess of the D'Urbervilles": Modern Critical Interpretations*, 27.

Most critics are aware of the suspension of voices between categories of the real and the ideal in *Tess*:

Peter J. Casagrande, for instance, sees "objective" and "moral" narrative voices. *Tess of the D'Urbervilles: Unorthodox Beauty* (New York: Twayne, 1992), 25.

Charlotte Thompson focuses on the narrator's transgressing "the border dividing the factual from the imaginary." "Language and The Shape of Reality," 737.

Kathleen Blake associates the "real" in *Tess* with individuality, the ideal with "group identity." "Pure Tess: Hardy on Knowing a Woman," 91.

The debate is over the degree to which, and by whom (as Thompson puts it), "reality becomes contorted to fit ancient stereotypes," of which "the pagan" is merely one instance. "Language and The Shape of Reality," 742.

Laura Claridge points to a "textual incoherence" in *Tess*, and surely the novel contains unresolved disjunctions. "Tess: A Less Than Pure Woman," 325.

J. Hillis Miller suggests that blank spaces receive meaning as characters invent origins: "For Hardy, as for George Eliot or for Nietzsche there is 'behind each cave a deeper cave.'" *Fiction and Repetition: Seven English Novels*, 136, 37 n. Angel Clare is Hardy's mask: in imbuing Tess with a differentiated personality yet insisting on her association with a nature prior to modern experience, Clare creates her origin and holds her to it.

13. Thomas Hardy, *The Literary Notebooks of Thomas Hardy*, vol. 2, ed. Lennart A. Bjork (New York: New York University Press, 1985), 30–31.

14. Ibid., 139.

15. Schiller, *Naive and Sentimental Poetry*, 176, 177.

16. Ibid., 182.

17. There is no direct evidence that Hardy read *Naive and Sentimental Poetry*. Yet, judging from the *Literary Notebooks* and internal evidence in the novels, he clearly was aware of the philosophical categories of realism and idealism. In 1881, he cites Lange's explanation of the contrast between idealism and materialism (which he confuses with realism), noting that Schiller participates in a "literary reaction in Germany against Materialism." *The Literary Notebooks*, 139–40.

18. Tennyson's relation to lyric 33, which Hardy cites, is palinodic. In its companion piece, lyric 96, doubt and the "jarring lyre" are acknowledged as essential parts of a stronger faith than that possessed by the protected young girl in the earlier poem: "There lives more faith in honest doubt, / Believe me, than in half the creeds" (ll. 11–12). Tennyson, *In Memoriam*, ed. Susan Shatto and Marion Shaw (Oxford: Clarendon Press, 1982).

It is interesting that a counterpart to the "jarring lyre" can be found in chapter 19 in Angel's "second-hand harp," which he does not play very well. In fact, the strumming breaks her synaesthetic moment that makes her feel "close to everything within the horizon": "inanimate objects seemed endowed with two or three senses, if not five" (178). Yet Angel's playing, imperfect only to the narrator and reader (Tess is likened to a "fascinated bird" [178]), raises her into an apparent bliss outside time and space. Behind the epiphany created for Tess by Angel (both are associated with Satan, he in his seduction, she in her stealthy movement and unobserved observation of Angel) is the possibility that nature is brutal and amoral.

8: Oscar Wilde's *The Picture of Dorian Gray*:
The Monstrous Portrait and Realism's Demise

1. White, *Metahistory*, 254.

2. Ibid., 232.

3. Oscar Wilde, *The Writings of Oscar Wilde*, ed. Isobel Murray (Oxford: Oxford University Press, 1989), 65. In this chapter, all parenthetical references refer to *The Writings of Oscar Wilde*. By permission of Oxford University Press.

4. Richard Ellmann, "The Critic as Artist as Wilde," in *Modern Critical Views: Oscar Wilde*, ed. Harold Bloom (New York: Chelsea House, 1985), 105.

5. White, *Metahistory*, 232.

6. Joseph Conrad, *Heart of Darkness*, ed. Robert Kimbrough (New York: W. W. Norton & Co., 1971), 5. For a discussion of this passage, see J. Hillis Miller, "*Heart of Darkness* Revisited," in *Joseph Conrad, Heart of Darkness: A Case Study in Contemporary Criticism*, ed. Ross C. Murfin (New York: St. Martin's Press, 1989), 209–25.

7. White, *Metahistory*, 253.

8. Levine, *The Realistic Imagination*, 4.

9. Rita Felski, "The Counterdiscourse of the Feminine in Three Texts by Wilde, Huysmans, and Sacher-Masoch," *PMLA* 106 (October 1991): 1095.

10. Nietzsche, *Basic Writings*, 419.

11. Ibid., 52.

12. Rita Felski writes that, in *Dorian Gray,* "the parodic subversion of gender norms reinscribes more insistently the divisions that the text ostensibly calls into question." "The Counterdiscourse of the Feminine," 1094.

13. Walter Pater, *Three Major Texts*, ed. William E. Buckler (New York: New York University Press, 1986), 214.

14. Nietzsche, *Basic Writings*, 23.

15. Ibid., 48.

16. Pater, *Walter Pater: Three Major Texts*, 150.

17. Christopher S. Nassaar, *Into the Demon Universe: A Literary Exploration of Oscar Wilde* (New Haven: Yale University Press, 1974), 41.

18. Pater, *Walter Pater: Three Major Texts*, 219, 220.

19. Certain operas, Nietzsche argues in his defense of Richard Wagner in *The Birth of Tragedy*, display an "Alexandrian cheerfulness" and an "idyllic tendency" influenced by the Rousseauan "primitive man" idea. The "virtuous hero of the opera" is "the eternally piping or singing shepherd" who must rediscover the "man-in-himself." *Basic Writings*, 118. He restates Friedrich Schiller's statement in *Naive and Sentimental Poetry* about the relationship between the elegy and the idyll:

> Nature and the ideal, he says, are either objects of grief, when the former is represented as lost, the latter unattained; or both are objects of joy, in that they are represented as real. The first case furnishes the elegy in its narrower signification, the second the idyll in its widest sense. (117)

But this "comfortable delight in an idyllic reality" is "nothing but a fantastically silly dawdling." (118).

20. See Brook Thomas, who writes that a crisis of historicism at the end of the nineteenth century led historians "to see that all beliefs were historically contingent, including the belief in scientific objectivity." Historicism was saved from the vortex of relativism because of a lingering faith in progress. "Preserving and Keeping Order by Killing Time in *Heart of Darkness*," in *Joseph Conrad, Heart of Darkness: A Case Study in Contemporary Criticism*, ed. Ross C. Murfin (New York: St. Martin's Press, 1989), 239.

9: Symbols, Ornaments, and Things in Joseph Conrad's *Heart of Darkness*

1. Conrad, *Heart of Darkness*, 74. In this chapter, all parenthetical references refer to *Heart of Darkness*.

2. As Barbara DeMille notes, the parallels between Nietzsche and Conrad (and Hardy) are compelling, even though both novelists expressed unfavorable opinions about Nietzsche. "Cruel Illusions: Nietzsche, Conrad, Hardy, and the 'Shadowy Ideal,'" *SEL* 30 (Autumn 1990): 699.

3. Bette London writes that this passage grounds "the text in colonial genealogies" and "performs the originary moment of colonial authority." "Reading Race and Gender in Conrad's Dark Continent," *Criticism* 31 (March 1993), 242. We are alone in a world without stable relations, it would seem, and must create them, or supersede them with higher meanings based on sympathy. Yet increasingly, as Conrad (like Hardy) discovers, this is difficult in a world where illusions are continually dissipated and strategies of transcendence merely mock their originators.

4. Carlyle, *Past and Present*, 121.

5. Nietzsche, *Basic Writings*, 113.

6. Brook Thomas writes that "Conrad brings us face to face with the disillusionment that many twentieth-century thinkers continue to confront, although much of the culture operates by trying to forget it." "Preserving and Keeping Order," 240.

7. F. R. Leavis, *The Great Tradition*, 204–5.

8. Carlyle, *Past And Present*, 44.

9. See *The Renaissance*, where Walter Pater writes that significant "moments" of provisional meaning are possible if we gather everything into a "desperate effort to see and touch" that precedes (and cancels the need for) "theories about the things we see and touch." *Walter Pater: Three Major Texts*, 219. Failing this, we may be buried "under a flood of external objects, pressing upon us with a sharp and importunate reality, calling us out of ourselves in a thousand forms of action" (218). We must create impressions, provisional artifacts of objectivity, to evade paralyzing external forces.

10. Wilde, *The Writings of Oscar Wilde*, 138.

11. J. Hillis Miller writes that the typical seaman and Marlow hear the relation of story to meaning differently. For the former, "the meaning is adjacent to the story, contained within it as nut within shell," while for Marlow, the meaning "is outside, not in. It envelops the tale rather than being enveloped by it. The relation of container and thing contained is reversed." "*Heart of Darkness* Revisited," 212.

12. F. R. Leavis, *The Great Tradition*, 206.

13. Michel Foucault, *The History of Sexuality. Volume I: An Introduction* (New York: Random House, 1960), 43.

14. Ibid., 57, 70.

15. The subject of painting and painterly effects in *Heart of Darkness* has gotten relatively little attention, though Wendy B. Faris's analysis of the parallels between Conrad and J. M. W. Turner is instructive: "In Turner we sense the beginnings of non-objective painting, in Conrad the seeds of radical experiments with point of view and self-referentiality in literature." "The 'Dehumanization' of the Arts: J. M. W. Turner, Joseph Conrad, and the Advent of Modernism," *Comparative Literature* 41 (Fall 1984): 325, 673 n. 91.

16. Predictably, much attention has been paid of late to Conrad's depictions of the feminine:

Johanna M. Smith focuses on the accountant's washerwoman in arguing that women are present as absences in *Heart of Darkness*. "'Too Beautiful Altogether': Patriarchal Ideology in *Heart of Darkness*," in *Joseph Conrad, Heart of Darkness: A Case Study in Contemporary Criticism,* ed. Ross C. Murfin (New York: St. Martin's Press, 1989).

Similarly, Bette London argues that "women's absence constitutes a condition of narrative coherence." "Reading Race and Gender," 238.

There is general agreement among critics that Marlow projects something or other onto the Intended and other European women. Marlow usurps Kurtz's place in his interview with her (London, 244), makes her like the rape victim (Smith, 193), inscribes her within Western linear language (Brook Thomas, "Preserving and Keeping Order"), or, according to Peter Hyland, makes her the "good little Victorian woman" ("The Little Woman in *Heart of Darkness*," *Conradiana* 20 [Spring 1988]: 10).

There is less agreement about the chthonic feminine with which Africa is associated, perhaps because here Conrad, like Hardy, is implicated in a narrative desire of which he is not fully aware. Marlow wishes to "colonize" both "savage darkness and women" (Smith, 180), or control the unknown through knowledge (Thomas, 243, 245), or reveal a "fear of the feminine and passive" (Albert J. Guerard's Freudian reading in *Conrad the Novelist* [Cambridge: Harvard University Press, 1969], 47). Yet there is disagreement about whether the feminine body of Africa is a presence or merely Marlow's construct. Conrad intends it to be a presence whose mystery (like the meanings behind the symbolic skulls) transfixes language and volition. Conrad is ironic about Marlow's rather wooden misogyny, yet participates in his fear of this strange manifestation of the feminine.

10: E. M. Forster and Artistic Fluidity: Romance, Idyll, and Limited Metaphors

1. Levine, *The Realistic Imagination*, 53.

2. E. M. Forster, *The Abinger Edition of E. M. Forster*, ed. Oliver Stallybrass, vol. 3: *A Room With a View* (London: Edward Arnold, 1977), 19–20. All further citations to this work are indicated parenthetically in the text as *RV*.

3. White, *Metahistory*, 372. Wilfrid Stone's discussion of Lucy's Dionysian remission from Baedeker and propriety is valuable. *The Cave and the Mountain* (Stanford, Calif.: Stanford University Press, 1966).

4. E. M. Forster, *The Abinger Edition of E. M. Forster*, ed. Oliver Stallybrass, vol. 4: *Howards End* (London: Edward Arnold, 1973), 202. All further citations to this work in this chapter are indicated parenthetically as *HE* in the text.

5. See Bonnie Finkelstein, who argues that Forster's androgynous mind transcends gender. *Forster's Women: Eternal Differences* (New York: Columbia University Press, 1975).

6. Jeane N. Olson sees a "social cross-fertilization between the descendant of yeoman stock (Tom) and the heir (Helen's baby) of an intellectual family consciously making that vital connection with the land as personified by the first Mrs. Wilcox." "E. M. Forster's Prophetic Vision of the Modern Family in *Howards End*," *Texas Studies in Literature and Language* 35 (Fall 1993): 356.

7. Schiller, *Naive and Sentimental Poetry*, 153.

8. Levine, *The Realistic Imagination*, 30.

9. James McConkey discerns in the conclusion "a flow without beginning or end, passing from horizon to horizon, forever rising and falling, yet mysteriously serene, mysteriously ordered." *The Novels of E. M. Forster* (Ithaca: Cornell University Press, 1957), 132.

Alistair M. Duckworth writes that Howards End "suggests a conservative rather than liberal system of values" that is "resistant to the 'improvements' of utilitarian and predatory capitalists." He concludes that "its continuing presence in the landscape" is nonetheless "the consequence of the reparative action of a liberal imperialist." *Howards End: E. M. Forster's House of Fiction* (New York: Twayne, 1992), 73–74.

Bibliography

Primary Sources

Arnold, Matthew. *The Oxford Authors: Matthew Arnold*. Edited by Miriam Abbott and Robert H. Super. New York: Oxford University Press, 1986.

Austen, Jane. *Emma*. Edited by Stephen M. Parrish. New York: W. W. Norton & Co., 1993.

―――. *Pride and Prejudice*. Edited by Tony Tanner. Harmondsworth: Penguin, 1986.

Brontë, Charlotte. *Jane Eyre*. Edited by Q. D. Leavis. Harmondsworth: Penguin, 1986.

Brontë, Emily. *Wuthering Heights*. Edited by David Daiches. Harmondsworth: Penguin, 1986.

Browning, Robert. *The Poems: Volume I*. Edited by John Pettigrew. New Haven: Yale University Press, 1981.

Burke, Edmund. *A Philosophical Enquiry into the Origins of Our Ideas of the Sublime and Beautiful*. Monston, England: The Scholar Press, Ltd., 1970.

―――. *Reflections on the Revolution in France*. Edited by Conor Cruise O'Brien. Harmondsworth: Penguin, 1968.

―――. *Edmund Burke on Revolution*. Edited by Robert A. Smith. New York: Harper Torchbooks, 1968.

Carlyle, Thomas. *The Centenary Edition of the Works of Thomas Carlyle*. Edited by H. D. Traill. Vol. 4, *The French Revolution*. London: Chapman and Hall, 1897.

―――. *The Centenary Edition of the Works of Thomas Carlyle*. Edited by H. D. Traill. Vol. 10, *Past and Present*. London: Chapman and Hall, 1897.

―――. *Sartor Resartus*. Edited by Charles Frederick Harrold. Indianapolis: Odyssey, 1937.

Conrad, Joseph. *Heart of Darkness*. Edited by Robert Kimbrough. New York: W. W. Norton & Co., 1971.

―――. *Lord Jim*. Edited by John Batchelor. Oxford: Oxford University Press, 1983.

Dante. *The Divine Comedy: Inferno*. Translated by Charles S. Singleton. Princeton: Princeton University Press, 1970.

―――. *The Divine Comedy: Purgatorio*. Translated by Charles S. Singleton. Princeton: Princeton University Press, 1973.

Dickens, Charles. *Bleak House*. Edited by Norman Page. Harmondsworth: Penguin, 1985.

―――. *Great Expectations*. Edited by Angus Calder. Harmondsworth: Penguin, 1985.

―――. *Hard Times*. Edited by George Ford and Sylvère Monod. New York: W. W. Norton & Co., 1966.

————. *Oliver Twist*. Edited by Kathleen Tillotson. New York: Oxford University Press, 1990.

Eliot, George. *Adam Bede*. Edited by Stephen Gill. Harmondsworth: Penguin, 1985.

————. *Middlemarch*. Edited by David Carroll. Oxford: Clarendon Press, 1986.

————. *Silas Marner*. Edited by Q. D. Leavis. Harmondsworth: Penguin, 1985.

Forster, E. M. *The Abinger Edition of E. M. Forster*. Edited by Oliver Stallybrass. Vol. 4, *Howards End*. London: Edward Arnold, 1973.

————. *The Abinger Edition of E. M. Forster*. Edited by Oliver Stallybrass. Vol. 3, *A Room With A View*. London: Edward Arnold, 1977.

Goethe, Johann Wolfgang von. *Faust, eine Tragoedie*. Vol. 3 of *Goethes Werke*. Hamburg: Christian Wegner Verlag, 1972.

Hardy, Thomas. *The Literary Notebooks of Thomas Hardy*. Vol. 2. Edited by Lennart A. Bjork. New York: New York University Press, 1985.

————. *Tess of the D'Urbervilles*. Edited by David Skilton. Harmondsworth: Penguin, 1986.

Johnson, Samuel. *The History of Rasselas Prince of Abissinia*. Edited by J. P. Hardy. New York: Oxford University Press, 1988.

Keats, John. *The Letters of John Keats*. 2 vols. Edited by Hyder E. Rollins.

Lessing, Gotthold Ephraim. *Laocoön: An Essay on the Limits of Painting and Poetry*. Translated by Edward Allen McCormick. Baltimore, Md.: Johns Hopkins University Press, 1984.

Nietzsche, Friedrich. *Basic Writings of Nietzsche*. Translated by Walter Kaufmann. New York: Modern Library, 1968.

Pater, Walter. *Walter Pater: Three Major Texts*. Edited by William E. Buckler. New York: New York University Press, 1986.

Plato. *The Republic*. Translated by Benjamin Jowett. New York: Vintage.

Richter, Jean Paul Friedrich. *School for Aesthetics*. Translated by Margaret H. Hale. Vol. 21 of *German Romantic Criticism*, edited by Leslie Willson, 31–61. New York: Continuum, 1982.

Schiller, Friedrich. *Naive and Sentimental Poetry and on the Sublime*. Translated by Julias A. Elias. New York: Frederick Ungar, 1980.

————. *On the Aesthetic Education of Man*. Translated by Elizabeth M. Wilkerson and L. A. Willoughby. Oxford: Clarendon Press, 1967.

————. *Die Raeuber*. Vol. 1 of *Sämtliche Werke*. München: Winkler Verlag, 1968.

————. *Gedichte, Erzählungen, Uberstezungen*. Vol. 3 of *Sämtliche Werke*. München: Winkler Verlag, 1968

Schlegel, Friedrich. *Dialogue on Poetry and Literary Aphorisms*. Translated by Ernst Behler and Roman Struc. University Park: The Pennsylvania State University Press, 1968.

————. *Kritische Schriften*. München: Carl Hanser Verlag, 1970.

Shelley, Mary. *Frankenstein*. Edited by Maurice Hindle. Harmondsworth: Penguin, 1988.

Shelley, Percy. *Poetical Works*. Edited by Thomas Hutchinson and G. M. Matthews. Oxford: Oxford University Press, 1970.

Stevens, Wallace. *The Collected Poems*. New York: Vintage Books, 1982.

Tennyson. *In Memoriam*. Edited by Susan Shatto and Marion Shaw. Oxford: Clarendon Press, 1982.

Virgil. *The Aeneid*. Translated by Robert Fitzgerald. New York: Vintage, 1990.

Voltaire. *Candide, or Optimism*. Translated by John Butt. Harmondsworth: Penguin, 1947.

Wilde, Oscar. *The Writings of Oscar Wilde*. Edited by Isobel Murray. New York: Oxford University Press, 1989.

Winckelmann, Johann Joachim. *Gedanken über die Nachahmung der griechischen Werke in der Malerei und Bildhauerkunst*. Stuttgart: Reclam, 1977.

Woolf, Virginia. *A Room of One's Own*. New York: Harbrace, 1989.

Wordsworth, William. *Poetical Works*. Edited by Thomas Hutchinson and Ernest de Selincourt. New York: Oxford University Press, 1984.

Secondary Sources

Allen, Walter. *The English Novel: A Short Critical History*. Harmondsworth: Penguin, 1975.

Andres, Sophia. "The Germ and the Picture in *Middlemarch*." *ELH* 55 (Winter 1988): 853–68.

Baumgarten, Murray. "Calligraphy and Code: Writing in *Great Expectations*. *Dickens Studies Annual* 11 (1983): 61–72.

Bayley, John. "*Oliver Twist*: 'Things as They Really Are.'" In *Dickens and the Twentieth Century*, edited by John Gross and Gabriel Pearson, 49–64. London: Routledge and Kegan Paul, 1962.

Beckson, Karl, ed. *Aesthetes and Decadents of the 1890's*. Rev. ed. Chicago: Academy Chicago Publishers, 1981.

Beer, Gillian. *George Eliot*. Bloomington: Indiana University Press, 1986.

Berger, Sheila. *Thomas Hardy and Visual Structures: Framing, Disruption, Process*. New York: New York University Press, 1990.

Blain, Virginia. "Double Vision and the Double Standard in *Bleak House*: A Feminist Perspective." In *Charles Dickens's "Bleak House": Modern Critical Interpretations*, edited by Harold Bloom, 139–56. New York: Chelsea House, 1987.

Blake, Kathleen. "Pure Tess: Hardy on Knowing a Woman." *SEL* 22 (Autumn 1982): 689–705.

Bodenheimer, Rosemarie. "Jane Eyre in Search of Her Story." In *Charlotte Brontë's "Jane Eyre": Modern Critical Interpretations*, edited by Harold Bloom, 97–112. New York: Chelsea House, 1987.

Boumelha, Penny. *Thomas Hardy and Women: Sexual Ideology and Narrative Form*. Towota, N.J.: Barnes and Noble, 1982.

Briganti, Chiara. "The Monstrous Actress: Esther Summerson's Spectral Name." *Dickens Studies Annual* 19 (1990): 205–30.

Brown, Tony. "Edward Carpenter, Forster, and the Evolution of *A Room With a View*. *English Literature in Transition, 1880-1920* 30 (1987): 279–300.

de Bruyn, Frans. "Theater and Countertheater in Burke's *Reflections on the Revolution in France*." In *Burke and the French Revolution: Bicentennial Essays*, edited by Steven Blakemore, 28–68. Athens: University of Georgia Press, 1992.

Bush, Douglas. *Jane Austen*. New York: Macmillan, 1975.

Casagrande, Peter J. *Tess of the D'Urbervilles: Unorthodox Beauty*. New York: Twayne, 1992.

Caserio, Robert. *Plot, Story, and the Novel: From Dickens to Poe to the Modern Period*. Princeton: Princeton University Press, 1979.

de Certeau, Michel. *The Writing of History*. Translated by Tom Conley. New York: Columbia University Press, 1988.

Childers, Mary. "Thomas Hardy: The Man Who 'Liked' Women." *Criticism* 23 (Fall 1981): 317–34.

Claridge, Laura. "Tess: A Less Than Pure Woman Ambivalently." *Texas Studies in Literature and Language* 28 (Fall 1986): 324–38.

Clayton, Jay. *Romantic Vision and the Novel*. Cambridge: Cambridge University Press, 1987.

Cohen, Susan. "'A History and a Metamorphosis': Continuity and Discontinuity in *Silas Marner*." *Texas Studies in Literature and Language* 25 (Fall 1983): 410–26.

Connor, Steven. *Charles Dickens*. Oxford: Basil Blackwell, 1985.

Craig, David M. "The Interplay of City and Self in *Oliver Twist, David Copperfield*, and *Great Expectations*. *Dickens Studies Annual* 16 (1987): 17–38.

Crawford, Iain. "Pip and the Monster: The Joys of Bondage." *SEL* 28 (Autumn 1988): 625–48.

Davies, J. M. Q. "*Emma* as Charade and the Education of the Reader." *Philological Quarterly* 65 (Spring 1986): 231–42.

DeMille, Barbara. "Cruel Illusions: Nietzsche, Conrad, Hardy, and the 'Shadowy Ideal.'" *SEL* 30 (Autumn 1990): 697–714.

Deneau, Philip. "The Brother-Sister Relationship in *Hard Times*." In *Hard Times*, edited by George Ford and Sylvère Monod, 372–77. New York: W. W. Norton, 1966.

Duckworth, Alistair M. *Howards End: E. M. Forster's House of Fiction*. New York: Twayne, 1992.

Eagleton, Terry. *The Ideology of the Aesthetic*. Oxford: Basil Blackwood, 1990.

———. *Myths of Power: A Marxist Study of the Brontës*. London: Macmillan Press, 1975.

Ellmann, Richard. "The Critic as Artist as Wilde." In *Modern Critical Views: Oscar Wilde*, edited by Harold Bloom, 91–106. New York: Chelsea House, 1985.

———. *Oscar Wilde*. New York: Random House, 1987.

Faris, Wendy B. "The 'Dehumanization' of the Arts: J. M. W. Turner, Joseph Conrad, and the Advent of Modernism." *Comparative Literature* 41 (Fall 1984): 305–26.

Felski, Rita. "The Counterdiscourse of the Feminine in Three Texts by Wilde, Huysmans, and Sacher-Masoch." *PMLA* 106 (October 1991): 1094–1105.

Ferguson, Jean. "Writing as a Woman: Dickens, *Hard Times*, and Feminine Discourses." *Dickens Studies Annual* 18 (1989): 161–78.

Finkelstein, Bonnie. *Forster's Women: Eternal Differences*. New York: Columbia University Press, 1975.

Foucault, Michel. *The History of Sexuality. Volume I: An Introduction*. New York: Random House, 1960.

Freccero, John. "Infernal Irony: The Gates of Hell." *Modern Language Notes* 99 (September 1984): 769–86.

Furniss, Tom. "Stripping the Queen: Edmund Burke's Magic Lantern Show." In *Burke and the French Revolution: Bicentennial Essays*, edited by Steven Blakemore, 69–96. Athens: University of Georgia Press, 1992.

Gezari, Janet. *Charlotte Brontë and Defensive Conduct: The Author and the Body at Risk*. Philadelphia: University of Pennsylvania Press, 1992.

Gilbert, Sandra M., and Susan Gubar. *The Madwoman in the Attic: The Woman Writer and the Nineteenth Century Literary Imagination*. New Haven: Yale University Press, 1979.

Gold, Joseph. *Charles Dickens: Radical Moralist*. Minneapolis: University of Minnesota Press, 1972.

Goldberg, Michael. *Carlyle and Dickens*. Athens: University of Georgia Press, 1973.

Goodman, Marcia Renee. "'I'll Follow the Other': Tracing the (M)other in *Bleak House*." *Dickens Studies Annual* 19 (1990): 147–67.

Gottfried, Barbara. "Fathers and Suitors: Narratives of Desire in *Bleak House*. *Dickens Studies Annual* 19 (1990): 169–203.

Guerard, Albert J. *Conrad the Novelist*. Cambridge: Harvard University Press, 1969.

Gustafson, Susan E. "Beautiful Statues, Beautiful Men: The Abjection of the Feminine Imagination in Lessing's *Laokoon*." *PMLA* 108 (October 1993): 1083–97.

Hardy, Barbara. *The Novels of George Eliot: A Study in Form*. New York: Oxford University Press, 1959.

———, J. Hillis Miller, and Richard Poirier. "*Middlemarch*, Chapter 85: Three Commentaries." In *George Eliot: Modern Critical Views*, edited by Harold Bloom, 167–85. New York: Chelsea House, 1986.

Hennelly, Mark M., Jr. "Jane Eyre's Reading Lesson." *ELH* 51 (Winter 1984): 693–717.

Hertz, Neil. "Recognizing Casaubon." In *George Eliot: Modern Critical Interpretations*, edited by Harold Bloom, 151–66. New York: Chelsea House, 1966.

Higbie, Robert. "*Hard Times* and Dickens' Concept of the Imagination." *Dickens Studies Annual* 17 (1988): 91–110.

Hirsch, David M. "*Hard Times* and Dr. Leavis." *Criticism* 6 (Winter 1964): 1–16.

Hollingsworth, Keith. *The Newgate Novel, 1830-1847*. Detroit: Wayne State University Press, 1963.

Holloway, John. "*Hard Times*: A History and a Criticism." In *Dickens and the Twentieth Century*, edited by John Gross and Gabriel Pearson, 159–74. London: Routledge and Kegan Paul, 1962.

Huizinga, J. *The Waning of the Middle Ages*. Garden City, N.Y.: Doubleday & Co., 1954.

Humma, John. "Language and Disguise: The Imagery of Nature and Sex in Tess." *South Atlantic Review* 54 (November 1989): 63–83.

Hyland, Peter. "The Little Woman in *Heart of Darkness*. *Conradiana* 20 (Spring 1988): 3–11.

Iser, Wolfgang. *The Fictive and the Imaginary: Charting Literary Anthropology*. Baltimore, Md.: The Johns Hopkins University Press, 1993.

Johnson, Bruce. "'The Perfection of Species' and Hardy's Tess." In *Thomas Hardy's "Tess of the D'Urbervilles": Modern Critical Interpretations*, edited by Harold Bloom, 25–43. New York: Chelsea House, 1987.

Kartiganer, Donald M. "The Divided Protagonist: Reading as Repetition and Discovery." *Texas Studies in Literature and Language* 30 (Summer 1988): 151–78.

Kellner, Hans. "A Bedrock of Order: Hayden White's Linguistic Humanism." *History and Theory: Studies in the Philosophy of History Beiheft* 19 (1980): 1–29.

Kincaid, James R. *Dickens and the Rhetoric of Laughter*. Oxford: Oxford University Press, 1971.

Kristeva, Julia. *Desire in Language: A Semiotic Approach to Literature and Art*. Translated by Thomas Cora et al. New York: Columbia University Press, 1980.

Kuchich, John. *Excess and Restraint in the Novels of Charles Dickens*. Athens: University of Georgia Press, 1981.

Larson, Janet L. *Dickens and the Broken Scripture*. Athens: University of Georgia Press, 1985.

Leavis, F. R. *The Great Tradition*. Harmondsworth: Penguin, 1974.

Leavis, F. R. and Q. D. Leavis. *Dickens the Novelist*. New Brunswick, N.J.: Rutgers University Press, 1979.

Leavis, Q. D. Introduction to *Jane Eyre* by Charlotte Brontë. Harmondsworth: Penguin, 1986.

———. Introduction to *Silas Marner* by George Eliot. Harmondsworth: Penguin, 1975.

Levine, George. *The Realistic Imagination*. Chicago: University of Chicago Press, 1981.

Litvak, Joseph. "Reading Characters: Self, Society, and Text in *Emma*." *PMLA* 100 (October 1985): 763–73.

Lloyd, Tom. "Language, Love, and Identity: *A Tale of Two Cities*." *The Dickensian* 88 (Fall 1992): 154–70.

London, Bette. "Mary Shelley, *Frankenstein*, and the Spectacle of Masculinity." *PMLA* 108 (March 1993): 253–67.

———. "Reading Race and Gender in Conrad's Dark Continent." *Criticism* 31 (Summer 1989): 235–52.

McConkey, James. *The Novels of E. M. Forster*. Ithaca: Cornell University Press, 1957.

McDowell, Frederick P. W. *E. M. Forster*. New York: Twayne, 1967.

McLaverty, James. "Comtean Fetishism and *Silas Marner*." *Nineteenth Century Fiction* 36 (December 1981): 318–36.

Mansell, Darrell. *The Novels of Jane Austen: An Interpretation*. New York: Macmillan, 1973.

Marcus, Steven. "Who Is Fagin?" In *Oliver Twist*, edited by Fred Kaplan, 478–95. New York: W. W. Norton, 1993.

Marie, Beatrice. "Emma and the Democracy of Desire." *Studies in the Novel* 17 (Spring 1985): 1–13.

Mellor, Anne K. *Mary Shelley: Her Life, Her Fiction, Her Monsters*. New York: Methuen, 1988.

———. *Romanticism and Gender*. New York: Routledge, 1993.

Miller, D. A. *The Novel and the Police*. Berkeley: University of California Press, 1988.

Miller, J. Hillis. *Charles Dickens: The World of His Novels*. Bloomington: Indiana University Press, 1958.

———. *The Ethics of Reading*. New York: Columbia University Press, 1987.

———. *Fiction and Repetition: Seven English Novels*. Cambridge: Harvard University Press, 1982.

———. "*Heart of Darkness* Revisited." In *Joseph Conrad, Heart of Darkness: A Case Study in Contemporary Criticism*, edited by Ross C. Murfin, 209–25. New York: St. Martin's Press, 1989.

———. *Thomas Hardy: Distance and Desire*. Cambridge: Harvard University Press, 1970.

Moglen, Helene. *Charlotte Brontë: The Self Conceived*. Madison: University of Wisconsin Press, 1984.

Mooneyham, Laura G. *Romance, Language and Education in Jane Austen's Novels*. New York: St. Martin's Press, 1988.

Morgan, Rosemary. *Women and Sexuality in the Novels of Thomas Hardy*. New York: Routledge, 1988.

Morgan, Susan. "*Emma* and the Charms of Imagination." In *Modern Critical Views: Jane Austen's "Emma"*, edited by Harold Bloom. New York: Chelsea House, 1987.

Mosse, George L. *Toward the Final Solution: A History of European Racism*. New York: Howard Fertig, 1978.

Mudrick, Marvin. *Jane Austen: Irony as Defense and Discovery*. Berkeley: University of California Press, 1968.

Nassaar, Christopher S. *Into the Demon Universe: A Literary Exploration of Oscar Wilde*. New Haven: Yale University Press, 1974.

Nelson, John S. "Tropal History and the Social Sciences." *History and Theory: Studies in the Philosophy of History Beiheft* 19 (1980): 80–101.

Nelson, Loury. "Night Thoughts on the Gothic Novel." In *Modern Critical Views: Frankenstein*, edited by Harold Bloom, 31–56. New York: Chelsea House, 1985.

Newsom, Robert. "*Bleak House*, I: Suspended Animation." In *Critical Essays on Charles Dickens's Bleak House*, edited by Elliot L. Gilbert, 122–43. Boston: G. K. Hall & Co., 1989.

Newton, K. M. *George Eliot: Romantic Humanist*. Towota, N.J.: Barnes and Noble, 1981.

O'Brien, Conor Cruise. Introduction to *Reflections on the Revolution in France*, by Edmund Burke. Harmondsworth: Penguin, 1986.

Oddie, William. *Dickens and Carlyle: The Question of Influence*. London: Centenary, 1972.

Olson, Jeane N. "E. M. Forster's Prophetic Vision of the Modern Family in *Howards End*." *Texas Studies in Literature and Language* 35 (Fall 1993): 347–62.

Peckham, Morse. *Beyond the Tragic Vision: The Quest for Identity in the Nineteenth Century*. New York: George Braziller, 1962.

Poole, Adrian. "'Men's Words' and Hardy's Women." *Essays in Criticism* 31 (October 1981): 328–45.

Preus, Nicholas E. "Sexuality in Emma: A Case History." *Studies in the Novel* 23 (Summer 1991): 196–216.

Punter, David. "1789: The Sex of Revolution." *Criticism* 24 (Summer 1982): 201–17.

Rader, Ralph. "The Comparative Anatomy of Three Baggy Monsters: *Bleak House*, *Vanity Fair*, *Middlemarch*." *The Journal of Narrative Technique* 19 (1989): 49–69.

———. "Literary Permanence and Critical Change." *Works-And-Days* 4 (Spring 1986): 9–15.

Ragussis, Michael. "The Ghostly Signs of *Bleak House*." In *Critical Essays on Charles Dickens's Bleak House*, edited by Elliot L. Gilbert, 143–63. Boston: G. K. Hall & Co., 1989.

Reid, Christopher. "Burke's Tragic Muse: Sarah Siddons and the 'Feminization' of Politics." In *Burke and the French Revolution: Bicentennial Essays*, edited by Steven Blakemore, 28–68. Athens: University of Georgia Press, 1992.

Rosmarin, Adena. "'Misreading' *Emma*: The Powers and Perfidies of Interpretive History." In *Jane Austen: Emma, a Casebook*, edited by David Lodge. London: Macmillan, 1991.

Ross, Michael J. "Forster's Arnoldian Comedy: Hebraism, Hellenism, and *A Room With a View*." *English Literature in Transition, 1880-1920* 23 (1980): 155–67.

Schlicke, Paul. *Dickens and Popular Entertainment*. New York: Allen and Unwin, 1985.

Sherwin. Paul. "*Frankenstein*: Creation as Catastrophe." *PMLA* 96 (October 1981): 883–903.

Shewan, Rodney. *Oscar Wilde: Art and Egoism*. New York: Harper and Row, 1977.

Smith, Johanna M. "'Too Beautiful Altogether': Patriarchal Ideology in *Heart of Darkness*." In *Joseph Conrad, Heart of Darkness: A Case Study in Contemporary Criticism,* edited by Ross C. Murfin, 179–98. New York: St. Martin's Press, 1989.

Spector, Stephen J. "Monsters of Metonymy: *Hard Times* and Knowing the Working Class." *ELH* 51 (Summer 1984): 365–84.

Stanliş, Peter. "Burke, Rousseau, and the French Revolution." In *Burke and the French Revolution: Bicentennial Essays*, edited by Stephen Blakemore, 97–119. Athens: University of Georgia Press, 1992.

Stone, Wilfrid. *The Cave and the Mountain*. Stanford: Stanford, Calif. University Press, 1966.

Tanner, Tony. "Colour and Movement in Hardy's '*Tess of the D'Urbervilles*.'" In *Thomas Hardy's Tess of the D'Urbervilles: Modern Critical Interpretations*, edited by Harold Bloom, 9–23. New York: Chelsea House, 1987.

Thomas, Brook. "Preserving and Keeping Order by Killing Time in *Heart of Darkness*. In *Joseph Conrad, Heart of Darkness: A Case Study in Contemporary Criticism*, edited by Ross C. Murfin, 237–55. New York: St. Martin's Press, 1989.

Thompson, Charlotte. "Language and the Shape of Reality in *Tess of the D'Urbervilles*. *ELH* 50 (Winter 1983): 729–62.

Thomson, Douglass. "The Passing of Another Shadow: A Third Ending to *Great Expectations*. *Dickens Quarterly* 1 (September 1984): 94–96.

Thurin, Susan Schoenbauer. "The Seven Deadly Sins in *Great Expectations*. *Dickens Studies Annual* 15 (1986): 201–20.

Tracy, Robert. "'The Old Story' and Inside Stories: Modish Fiction and Fictional Modes in *Oliver Twist*." *Dickens Studies Annual* 17 (1988): 1–33.

Trilling, Lionel. Introduction to *Emma*, by Jane Austen. Boston: Houghton Mifflin, 1957.

Vargish, Thomas. *The Providential Aesthetic in Victorian Fiction*. Charlottesville: University of Virginia Press, 1985.

Veeder, William. "The Negative Oedipus: Father, *Frankenstein*, and the Shelleys." *Critical Inquiry* 12 (Winter 1986): 365–90.

Watson, Nicola. *Revolution and the Form of the British Novel 1790-1825*. Oxford: Clarendon Press, 1994.

White, Hayden. *Metahistory: The Historical Imagination in Nineteenth-Century Europe*. Baltimore, Md.: Johns Hopkins University Press, 1973.

Wiesenfarth, Joseph. "Demythologizing *Silas Marner*." *ELH* 37 (June 1970): 226–44.

———. "*Middlemarch*: The Language of Art." *PMLA* 97 (May 1982): 363–77.

Winnifrith, Tom. *The Brontës and Their Background*. London: The Macmillan Press, 1973.

Worth, George L. "Mr. Wopsle's Hamlet: 'Something Too Much of This.'" *Dickens Studies Annual* 17 (1988): 35–46.

Youngquist, Paul. "*Frankenstein*: The Mother, the Daughter, and the Monster." *Philological Quarterly* 70 (Summer 1991): 339–59.

Index